THE GLORY OF THE PAGE

MEDIEVAL & RENAISSANCE ILLUMINATED MANUSCRIPTS
FROM GLASGOW UNIVERSITY LIBRARY

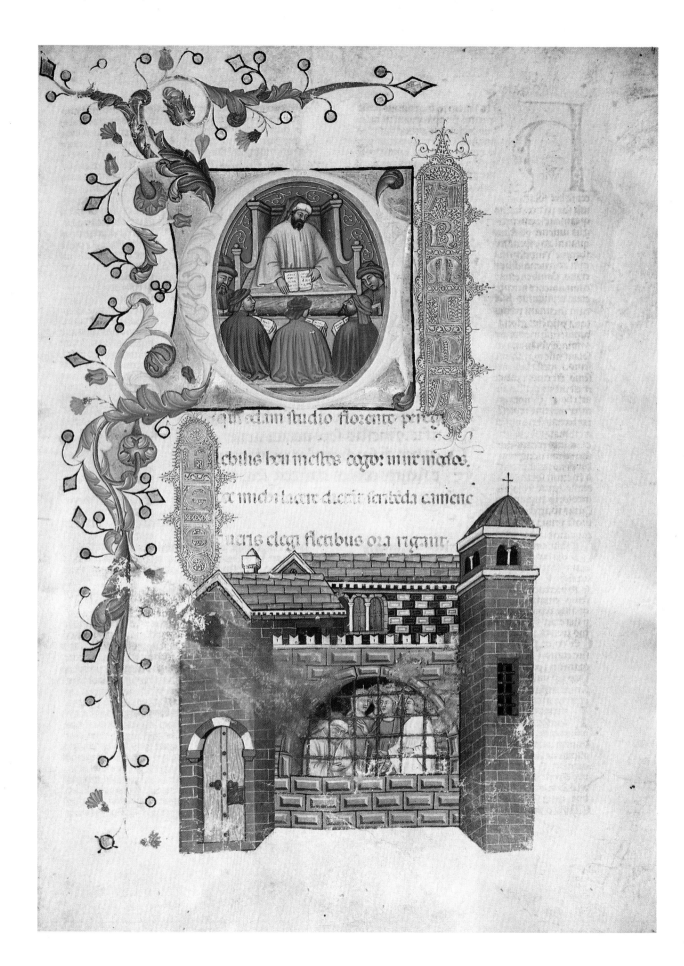

...qu ectu studio florente perer...

...chilis hru mestes cogo: unir mcates...

...x midi lucnr dicrir sentecia camine...

...ucris elegi flentibus ora rigant...

THE GLORY OF THE PAGE

MEDIEVAL & RENAISSANCE
ILLUMINATED MANUSCRIPTS
FROM GLASGOW UNIVERSITY LIBRARY

INTRODUCTION & CATALOGUE
BY NIGEL THORP
Deputy Keeper of Special Collections, Glasgow University Library

Published for GLASGOW UNIVERSITY LIBRARY
and the ART GALLERY OF ONTARIO
by HARVEY MILLER PUBLISHERS

Originating Publisher HARVEY MILLER LTD
20 Marryat Road · London SW19 5BD · England

© 1987 Glasgow University Library

Distributed in Canada by OXFORD UNIVERSITY PRESS · Don Mills, Ontario
and in the United States by OXFORD UNIVERSITY PRESS · New York

Catalogue of an Exhibition
organized for the Art Gallery of Ontario
and shown at
The Art Gallery of Ontario, Toronto,
16 October 1987 – 3 January 1988
The Museum of Fine Arts, Houston,
6 February – 24 April 1988
Virginia Museum of Fine Arts, Richmond,
14 June – 14 August 1988
Also shown at The Burrell Collection, Glasgow
7 November 1988 – 15 January 1989

British Library Cataloguing in Publication Data

University of Glasgow, *Library*
    The glory of the page: medieval and
    renaissance illuminated manuscripts
    from Glasgow University Library.
    1. Illumination of books and
    manuscripts – Catalogs
    I. Title II. Thorp, Nigel III. Art
    Gallery of Ontario
    016.7456'7 ND2897. G5U5

ISBN 0-905203-83-6
ISBN 0-905203-87-9

Colour Origination by Schwitter AG · Basle · Switzerland
Printed by Cheney & Sons Ltd · Banbury · Oxon

CONTENTS

FOREWORD

THE ART of the illuminated manuscript is not easily accessible to the public at large. Long neglected as a supposedly minor art in favour of more traditionally visible forms such as wall or panel painting, it has in recent decades gained increasing acceptance amongst scholars as an independent branch of the visual arts; but to those who cannot visit the manuscript reading rooms of national, university and other public libraries and museums, it is quite literally a closed book.

The fact that the volumes themselves are kept tightly shut on their shelves has, however, helped to ensure that the paintings and other decorations which they contain have been preserved with such freshness. This exhibition displays a brilliant range of achievement in painting and design from the Middle Ages and the Renaissance. The Principal of the University of Glasgow and the University Court generously gave permission for these major examples from collections in the University Library to be made available for display at three galleries in North America and, on their return, to be seen in their home city by the many visitors to the Burrell Collection.

The great majority of the manuscripts on display came to the University Library as donations from former students and other well-wishers during two hundred years. They represent only a small part of the extensive Special Collections which make the University Library one of the very finest in this country and on some subjects without rival in the world. This exhibition is evidence of the pride which the University and the City can take in those benefactors and their treasured inheritance as we approach a new century.

Henry Heaney
University Librarian and Keeper
of the Hunterian Books and MSS

PREFACE

ALTHOUGH the University of Glasgow is a medieval foundation, having been established in 1451, there is no evidence that illuminated manuscripts were among its early possessions. The manuscripts included here, and the early examples of decorated printed books that accompany them, have come to the Library over later centuries, both singly and in complete libraries. Seventeenth-century acquisitions, for instance, include a Bible from Cambuskenneth Abbey (no. 15) and a copy of Nicholas Love's *Mirrour* or devotional life of Christ (no. 33). Manuscripts donated individually in the eighteenth century are a Bible from the Netherlands (no. 115) and an early volume of Statutes (no. 26). The major donations, however, have been the complete libraries of private collectors, each assembled with enlightened persistence over a whole lifetime. These bibliophiles were able to select masterpieces from monastic and princely libraries as changing personal, political and social circumstances brought them onto the market.

The most notable of these collections was made by the University's greatest private benefactor, Dr William Hunter, and is the source of three-quarters of the volumes in the exhibition. William Hunter (1718 – 1783), was a student at the University and, after moving to London, became one of the leading medical authorities of his day. His yearly course of lectures on medicine and anatomy provided basic training for a whole generation of medical students and his great work on *The Anatomy of the Human Gravid Uterus*, published in Birmingham in 1774, remained a standard text for over a century. The foundation of his fortune was laid when, as consultant obstetrician to Queen Caroline, Consort of King George III, he built up a considerable practice among the aristocracy. Subsequent success in commercial speculations consolidated his wealth, enabling him to add widely to his research and teaching collections of medical and anatomical material. His library of manuscripts, printed books and drawings was primarily that of a working anatomist and scholar, but he had wide-ranging interests beyond his professional field. Fossils, shells, antiquities, coins, paintings, artefacts from the South Seas brought back by Captain James Cook, all filled the museum which he established at his house in Great Windmill Street, London. All his collections, together with funds for building a new museum, were left in his will to his old University, where they have provided material for study and research for almost two centuries. His library alone contains some 10,000 volumes and includes 650 manuscripts and over a thousand printed books from the fifteenth century.

During the first half of the nineteenth century, when Glasgow was one of the largest ports for trade with North America and Russia, the Hunterian Museum was the major British collection outside London. It was visited by travellers from all over the world, as is testified by the volumes of visitors' books which still survive in the Museum Records. In the 1870s the University moved from its medieval site in the centre of the city to what were then green fields of Gilmorehill, two miles to the west, and built a new Museum to house the Hunterian collections.

In neither of these nineteenth-century museums, however, was there space to display at any time the full extent of the illuminated manuscripts. The construction of a new University Library and the formation of the Department of Special Collections in the 1960s united Hunter's volumes with the other major benefactions and historical collections of the Library. Display space, however, remained very limited and only few examples could be viewed and occasional single volumes lent outside the University for display. This exhibition provides the very first opportunity for seeing the full range of Hunter's collection of medieval and Renaissance manuscripts.

Hunter's princely library contains many manuscripts of the first importance, from the Hunterian Psalter (no. 14), a landmark in book illumination, to the unique copies of Chaucer's *Romaunt of the Rose* (no. 36) and of the spirited collection of French stories known as *Les Cent Nouvelles Nouvelles* (no. 58). His fifteenth-century French and Italian volumes, both manuscript and printed, illustrate the work of the leading miniaturists of the time, from Jean Colombe (no. 57) and Jacques de Besançon (no. 60) to Francesco Antonio del Cherico (no. 83), Felice Feliciano (no. 82) and the Master of the Vitae Imperatorum (no. 76).

With the notable exceptions of the Bruges *Miroir de l'humaine salvation* of 1455 (no. 116) and the splendid Breviary illuminated by the Master of the First Prayer Book of Maximilian in Ghent in 1494, work from the Netherlands is less well represented in Hunter's collection. This deficiency was evidently noted by the Glasgow bibliophile William Euing (1788 – 1874), whose collection of medieval manuscripts was made almost exclusively of examples from this region: these were included in his library of some 17,500 volumes which was bequeathed to the University in his will. Two additional manuscripts from the Netherlands were presented in 1918 by the Earl of Rosebery, then Chancellor of the University: an early fifteenth-century masterpiece of Flemish art, a copy of Voragine's *Golden Legend* with over a hundred minatures (no. 114) and a beautifully executed Book of Hours and Psalter produced in Bruges in the middle years of the century (no. 117).

The libraries of other Glasgow scholars and bibliophiles, donated more recently to the University, have also contributed to the wealth of its holdings of manuscripts and early printed books. These have included the alchemical and other collections of Professor John Ferguson (1837 – 1916), represented in the exhibition by an English alchemical manuscript (no. 46); a small group of fine volumes from Dr Charles Hepburn (1891 – 1971), amongst them a beautifully preserved miniature Bible of the thirteenth century (no. 17); and the outstanding collection of emblem literature made by Sir William Stirling Maxwell (1818 – 1878) and bequeathed to the Library by his son Sir John Stirling Maxwell (1866 – 1956; see nos. 70, 129, 130 and 143).

The first section of the catalogue, nos 1 – 25, gives examples of books decorated and illuminated in Western Europe and Byzantium from the eighth century to the thirteenth, with a fifteenth-century fragment (no. 25) for comparison. This group has been selected to show major aspects of the historical development of book illumination in the period; the books are described in chronological order without being specifically grouped together by their place of origin, though it is not by historical accident that most of the twelfth-century volumes were produced in England and most of the thirteenth-century volumes in France.

The following four sections, on the other hand, are geographical groupings from England, France, Italy and the Netherlands respectively, and date from the fourteenth century to the mid sixteenth century. The selection includes several printed books illuminated or decorated in the manuscript tradition, particularly from Italy.

The last section, nos 133-143, contains comparative examples of printed books produced in the fifteenth and sixteenth centuries. These volumes have not been decorated by hand; their woodcuts and layout, however, are largely derived from the manuscript tradition. In the exhibition they are displayed alongside related manuscripts.

Acknowledgements

The proposal that Glasgow University Library should mount an exhibition of illuminated manuscripts was made by Dr Katharine Lochnan, Curator of Prints and Drawings at the Art Gallery of Ontario, Toronto. Her initial suggestion was warmly supported by William Withrow, Director of the Gallery, and by Henry Heaney, Librarian of Glasgow University Library, and has resulted in this extensive selection of paintings, drawings and other decorative work in books produced in Europe over a period of eight centuries being seen together in public for the first time.

Much information on the Library's manuscripts and early printed books was assembled by the former Librarian, R.O. MacKenna, to supplement the published catalogues of William Hunter's manuscripts (1908) and of his printed books (1930). This has been added to by successive Keepers of the Department of Special Collections, especially by Jack Baldwin, whose knowledge of the collections, and in particular of their earlier ownership, has been invaluable.

The present catalogue has been written with generous further assistance given by scholars and curators of manuscript collections both in Europe and in North America. I am particularly grateful to Jonathan Alexander, who guided the initial stages of my enquiries; to François Avril, who devoted much time during the annual closure of the Bibliothèque Nationale to identifying comparative examples; and to Albinia de la Mare, who read the catalogue in draft and made many improvements. For their contributions to individual entries, my warmest thanks are due also to: Lilian Armstrong, Wellesley; Janet Backhouse, London; Bernhard Bischoff, Munich; Hugo Buchtal, London; Donal Byrne, Aberdeen; Bert Cardon, Louvain; James Dickson, Glasgow; Michael Evans, London; Anna de Floriani, Genoa; Robert Gibbs, Glasgow; Marie-Thérèse Gousset, Paris; David Weston, Glasgow: Michael Gullick, Hitchin; Eberhard König, Berlin; Sigrid Krämer, Munich; Stephen Rawles, Glasgow; Nicole Reynaud, Paris; Nicholas Rogers, Cambridge; Lucy Freeman Sandler, New York; Kathleen Scott, Lansing; M. Smeyers, Louvain; Patricia Danz Stirnemann, Paris; David Weston, Glasgow; and Roger S. Wieck, Baltimore. I owe a particular debt to my wife, Monica Thorp, for making improvements to my typescript while turning it into electronic format, and to Arabella and Magnus Thorp for their own contributions to the word-processing.

My editors at Harvey Miller Publishers have overseen the preparation of the text with much kindly tact and patience. The responsibility for any remaining infelicities and inaccuracies, however, is mine.

It is a pleasure also to express my gratitude to my colleagues in the Department of Special Collections for allowing me to give so much time to preparing the catalogue: to Trevor Graham, University Photographer, for meeting apparently unending demands against intractable timescale, and Christine Leitch for controlling the supply of photographs; to James Brockman, Conservator, Oxford, Ian Maver, Conservator at the Royal Greenwich Observatory, Herstmonceux, and Nicholas Pickwoad, Adviser to the National Trust on book conservation, for their careful restoration of numbers of volumes described in the catalogue; and to John Ashman, the Library's Conservation Officer, and his temporary assistant Sarah Horrell, for infinite care in preparing for the well-being of the books at all stages of the exhibition.

Nigel Thorp, Glasgow 1987

INTRODUCTION

BEFORE the invention of printing in the mid fifteenth century, the production of a book of any kind was a laborious and expensive process. Its decoration generally involved a substantial addition of time and resources. From classical times, however, there had been a tradition of illustrating notable texts, and it is the development of this tradition from the late eighth century to the mid sixteenth century that forms the subject of this exhibition.

From the collections of Glasgow University Library it has been possible to make a selection illustrating many of the most important aspects of book decoration in the later Middle Ages and the early Renaissance, dwelling in particular on the English achievement of the twelfth century and the Continental flowering of the fifteenth century. There are examples from most parts of Western Europe, from Northern England to the South of Italy and Byzantium, which display not only a number of regional styles and tastes but also the influence of one period or place upon another. The Eastern art of Byzantium stimulated the development of the formal designs of the Romanesque period in the West, as may be seen here from a comparison of the eleventh-century Greek Gospels (no. 12) with the twelfth-century English Psalter (no. 14). The Romanesque was in its turn replaced in the thirteenth century by the exuberant experimentation of the International Gothic style, which included in its later stages in the fourteenth century an increasing interest in naturalistic representation. This movement was accentuated in the virtuoso skills of the miniaturists of the fifteenth century who, while strongly influenced by the traditions which their patrons and customers expected to be observed in book illustration, developed distinctive national schools of illumination which reflect the artistic and intellectual excitement of the age.

Books have always served a variety of purposes, and some of their functions are indicated by the different sizes and shapes of the books in the exhibition. The impressive twelfth-century copy of Josephus's *Jewish War* (no. 10) has three hundred leaves measuring some forty-five by thirty-two centimetres; weighing around ten kilograms, it was not meant to be easily transportable from its monastic setting, where it would have been amongst the volumes read aloud to monks in the refectory. The fifteenth-century Gradual (no. 25) was an even larger volume, with leaves of over fifty-five by forty centimetres, although only a few of them now survive: it would have been used to accompany the Mass and needed to be of a size for the words and chants to be visible to all the members of a choir. Most of the other volumes were intended for private reading, whether they were religious or classical texts, works of vernacular literature or reference copies of medical treatises, and they are accordingly easier to hold and consult. At the other end of the scale from the Josephus, the delicate copy of Clément Marot's translation from Petrarch (no. 70) is only twelve centimetres square, contains no more than thirty-six pages and is likely to have been a love token.

Most early decoration in manuscripts was connected with initial letters. This invention, recorded from the fifth century onwards, was a means of increasing the legibility of texts. Before the convention of marking divisions by spaces had been developed, words and sentences were traditionally run into each other in an unbroken succession across a written surface. In time books came to contain several sizes of decorated initial to indicate the status of different sections of text – the beginning of a new work, or book, or chapter, or paragraph. In its most spectacular development the decorated initial could fill a whole page, as in the magnificent 'carpet' pages of the Book of Kells, produced in the British Isles in the early ninth century.

Decorative motifs included the classical acanthus leaf, and a population of birds, fishes and animals which could indeed be substituted for letters by reproducing the letter form (no. 6). These foliate and zoomorphic elements, either singly or in combination, were to remain in constant use throughout the historical development of the decorated initial. Two examples from the eleventh century (nos. 3 and 4) have lion figures grappling with schematized leaf scrolls. In the late fifteenth century the foliage is far more luxuriant and colourful, and initials often contain realistic studies of natural life, such as an owl (no. 61, colour ill. 22) or an iris (no. 124, colour ill. 6).

When an initial contains figures, which may or may not be connected with the subject matter of the book, it is described as an 'inhabited initial' or 'figure initial'. This is very often an author portrait (e.g. nos. 9, colour ill. 7, and 22). When the body of the letter acts as a frame for a pictorial filling, often in the form of a narrative scene, it is termed an 'historiated initial' (e.g. no. 78, colour ill. 32).

Strictly speaking, an illuminated manuscript is one in which there is decoration using gold or another metal as a reflective surface to 'light up' the page. Although a gold pigment had been used in some instances from the Early Christian period onwards both for decoration and for script, it was not until the twelfth century that the technique was established in the West of applying gold-leaf directly to the page and burnishing it into a highly reflective surface. The process was introduced in imitation of Byzantine mosaics, miniatures and icons, in which a gold ground was a symbol of spiritual light. In the West, gold was also used as the ground for religious subjects (no. 14, colour ills. 5 and 6, and cover ill.; no. 27, colour ill. 9); this remained an essential element of miniatures and panel painting until the introduction of naturalistic background detail in the more worldly atmosphere of the fourteenth century.

Gold-leaf continued to be a general decorative feature of well-produced books, whatever the subject matter of the text. It was used for initial letters, for the bars framing a page and for highlights given by an endlessly inventive series of discs, wheat-ears, trefoils, lozenges and other shapes. The Italians in particular developed the decorative possibilities of gold frameworks, in combination with their distinctive leaf-scroll design, the 'white-vine' pattern (nos. 81, 85, 93, colour ills. 34 and 35; no. 82, colour ill. 33).

Although illumination may therefore be purely formal and does not necessarily contain any figurative element, Dante's famous reference in the *Divine Comedy* to 'that art which in Paris they call illumination' (*Purgatory,* Canto XI, 80), indicates that miniature painting in books was described by this term at an early stage. The term 'minature' itself denotes a painting which is generally separate from an initial, most frequently within a rectangular panel. The word is derived from the Latin *miniare,* meaning to colour with *minium,* a red mineral substance. Miniatures in manuscripts, therefore, while being generally on a smaller scale than contemporary panel painting, can occupy any proportion of a page, from a small space to mark a chapter heading (as in nos. 55 and 58), through half-page panels (nos. 59 and 73) to full-page pictures (nos. 14, 27, 122 and colour ill. 40, 125 and colour ill. 39).

The books themselves are stoutly made from highly durable animal skin, chiefly of cattle, goats, or sheep. The skin was prepared in a manner first developed as early as the second century B.C., supposedly in the ancient Greek city of Pergamum (now Bergama, in Turkey), from which the term 'parchment' is derived. The skin is soaked in running water for several days and then immersed in a solution of lime and water until the hair can be scraped off. It is then put back into the solution of lime for another week or two before being stretched on a frame, cleaned repeatedly with pumice and water and dried in the sun. Variations in this general method, and also in the species, age and health of the animals used, produced skins of different quality. Until the increase of commercial production methods in the thirteenth century allowed a more uniform sheet to be produced, it was not uncommon to find flay-holes – the result of disease or inflammation – and splits or other irregularities in the leaves. The holes could be avoided, the splits could be stitched together, and scribes would expect to fit their text around these imperfections. The finest skin, used for example in the miniature Bibles of the thirteenth century (nos. 16-18), has long been assumed to have been made from still-born or new-born animals, whether calf, kid or lamb, but there may also have been techniques for splitting skin, just as there are for splitting leather. Although the term 'vellum' was originally applied to fine calf-skin of this kind prepared for writing, it is difficult to tell what animal a particular skin is from and 'vellum' or 'parchment' have become the general terms for any skin used in manuscripts.

In most cases it is possible to distinguish between the hair-side of the skin and the flesh-side. The hair-side is generally darker in tone and is likely still to show the hair follicles; the flesh-side is lighter in colour and has a more even appearance. When individual sheets were made up into gatherings, or quires, for the scribe, hair-sides and flesh-sides of adjoining skins were placed together, so that when the book was opened the facing pages would have the same overall appearance.

The capacity of skin as a natural product to 'breathe', adjusting to varying conditions of temperature and humidity, has enabled it to withstand southern heat, continental cold and maritime moisture, as well as the micro-climate of a monastic cell or a scholar's or collector's book-cupboard. In addition to the material from which they were made, the structure of books has itself contributed to the preservation of their contents: books were normally kept shut, in chests or cupboards, or horizontally on shelves, and the harmful effects of light, air, dirt and atmospheric pollution over the centuries have been minimized. The inks and pigments themselves, being chiefly mineral preparations, are resistant to change, and the paintings and decorations are in general excellently preserved. The gold leaf is bedded on a ground of gesso and will only have suffered if the gesso has been disturbed by the page being flexed too much, or if the gold has been rubbed by contact with another page. The early use of verdigris or copper in the preparation of the colour green, however, can have an adverse effect on the page, eating into the prepared skin, as in the eleventh-century copy of Boethius (no. 4); and when silver has been used instead of or in addition to gold, as was sometimes the case in the fourteenth and fifteenth centuries, it has generally not escaped oxidization through contact with the air and has become black. In other respects the paintings can be seen just as they were when the loose bundles of sheets were given to the binder. This has kept the colours used in their decoration virtually as fresh as the day on which they were completed, when other extensive medieval uses of colour, such as on the surfaces of buildings, have been lost. Indeed, of all the artefacts of the period, except works in metal and stone, books are those which have lasted best, and the durability of the vellum is a highly important factor in their preservation.

The survival of these early books has also been assisted by the fact that the written word has always had a particular mystique attached to it. This was especially so when the majority of the population, including the rulers, were unlettered. Until the thirteenth century learning was almost exclusively the province of the religious orders: the Christian religion was based on the Word of God preserved in the Holy Book of the Bible, and large numbers of other books were the work of the Fathers of the Church interpreting Christian teaching. Gospel Books themselves were decorated as objects of veneration from at least the sixth century, both as holy relics for religious orders and as icons with which missionaries could impress and instruct pagans: the survival of this tradition into the eleventh and twelfth centuries can be seen in the full-page pictures of the Evangelists in a copy of the Greek Gospels (no. 12). Books, whether religious or secular, were generally of a size that meant they could be looked after easily, and they have tended to be handed down with care from one generation to the next. They are of course subject to some forms of decay and dismemberment. Their binding structures will break with lengthy use and will need to be replaced if the volume is to survive intact, and if the content of a volume is perceived as being out of date (and the skin is not scraped clean to be written on again), it can be broken up for other uses, most commonly in binding a new generation of books. Miniatures can also be cut out of the volume for which they were designed, whether for keepsakes, for the high purpose of making the art of the Middle Ages and Renaissance more accessible to modern man (which was John Ruskin's explanation of why he took scissors to manuscripts), or for the more pragmatic purpose, ever increasingly pursued, of making more money when a manuscript is sold. Nonetheless, when compared with other personal possessions of the period, such as fine clothes, furnishing, plates, furniture, decorations and ornaments, which were worn out through use or discarded because of changing fashions, books were far more likely to survive.

With the disappearance of so many other works of art and decorative objects of the Middle Ages, illuminated manuscripts are a rich testimony to the outlook of their times, both in their own right and because of the information about contemporary life contained in their illustrations. Of the hundreds of thousands of manuscripts which survive from these centuries, many contain decorative work of some kind and even richly painted manuscripts are to be numbered in thousands. A single book can contain a hundred or more paintings, as for example in the splendid early Flemish copy of the *Golden Legend* (no. 114, colour ill. 37), or the majestic volumes of Ludolf of Saxony's *Life of Christ* written for Charles VIII of France (no. 60). The large, formal compositions tend to to concentrate on grand scenes of religious and court life, but the backgrounds of these paintings often contain revealing views of ordinary life and manners. It was conventional for figures from the past to be dressed in contemporary costume, so that Julius Caesar appears in late fourteenth-century dress in a volume of Roman history written in France at that time (no. 49), and the eleventh-century physician Avicenna is depicted wearing academic dress of the late fifteenth century (no. 61). A history of Italy written in the 1450s has an illustration containing a fool making an impudently dismissive gesture (no. 79), and a collection of French tales is illustrated with pictures of contemporary domestic life including people in bed or in the bath (no. 58). In addition, blank space in the margins could be populated with all manner of illustrations that had nothing to do with the text but gave the artist an opportunity to exercise his skills with a free hand.

In a period that extends from the time of Charlemagne in the late eighth century to the sack of Rome in the sixteenth, and in which the Norman Conquest of England, the Black Death and the Spanish subjugation of the Netherlands are almost incidental, there are massive changes in social, cultural and economic conditions that are mirrored both in the content of the illuminations and in their means of production. The sobriety of the formal penwork foliage designs in English Romanesque manuscripts is a reflection of the desired simplicity of monastic life at this period: a Cistercian statute of 1131 decrees that initials should be made in one colour only and should not be illustrated with figures – a clear indication that historiated initials which had many colours and included figures were in use elsewhere. At this time the initial is likely to have been the work of the scribe who wrote out the text of the book. He would be able to organize the distribution of lines of the text round the shape of the initial, achieving a harmony in the design of the page as a whole (nos. 10, 11). However, examples from the same period are known, particularly in grander volumes, of initials that were designed by one artist and coloured by another, as in the great Winchester Bible (Winchester Cathedral Library) or in a glossed Epistles of Paul in Oxford (Bodleian Library MS Auct. D.I.13). In the Hunterian Psalter of about 1170 (no. 14), one of the most impressive manuscripts of the time, there is evidence of several artists working together, and the question of how they were organized is far from resolved. Lay artists and scribes were not unknown, but the production of books was centred in monastic scriptoria and books were made chiefly for corporate use.

With the foundation of the universities, the spread of learning and the emergence of the merchant class in the thirteenth century, the demand for books was greatly increased. Different means of production were found, particularly in Paris, where there were workshops specializing in the different processes of writing, providing ornamental decoration, and painting historiated initials or miniatures. Accounts survive which give rates for different sizes of illuminated initials, and a prospective purchaser could order a book to be decorated in accordance with his purse. The appearance of a market in book production, coupled with a refined appreciation of the arts in French court circles, meant that fashion played a greater part in determining the appearance of the page: workshops would seek to be ahead of their rivals in having the most up-to-date designs, so that it is possible to date many examples to within a small span of years. Monastic scriptoria still had their part to play, but in an increasingly secular world an illuminator would be a man – or woman, for some women artists are also known – pursuing a professional career and therefore in need of patrons.

From the fourteenth century onwards, the chief patrons were amongst the royal and princely families, for whom the possession of a library of fine books was a sign of status, as much so as a large retinue, splendid clothes, imposing surroundings and extensive stables. Some of these families would even employ their own illuminators as part of their household. One of the most notable examples is Charles V's brother, Jean de France, Duc de Berry, for whom the celebrated *Très Riches Heures* (Chantilly, Musée Condé) was painted by the Limbourg brothers in the early years of the fifteenth century. The Limbourgs' untimely death in 1416, when the Duc de Berry also died, left the illustration of this manuscript unfinished: the changed conditions of the later part of the century can be seen in the fact that the leading illuminator of his generation, the renowned Jean Colombe, was engaged by another ducal owner of the manuscript, Charles I of Savoy, to complete the volume some seventy years later as a commission. Colombe was then towards the end of his career, but an earlier example of his work can be seen in the Glasgow copy of Suso's *Miroir* (no. 37).

It is not surprising to find less original illuminators making use of secondary sources for their illustrations. From the thirteenth century the Parisian ateliers had developed a repertory of motifs for their work, essential for any system of mass production. Sometimes the pictures in one manuscript could serve directly as the models for a copy, as can be seen in an illustration of Boccaccio and Fortune in one of the two copies in Glasgow of the French translation of Boccaccio's *Fall of Princes,* which is the same as that in another copy of the work in the British Library (see no. 55). Pattern books containing illustrations, however, have seldom survived, and those for decorative alphabets are also very rare, so the presence of two such volumes in this exhibition is singularly fortunate. One is from France (no. 69), the other from the Netherlands (no. 129, colour ill. on back cover), and although they both date from the 1520s, they offer interesting examples of the process of designing initials which would have been followed at a much earlier period. Just as fascinating is the presence in the Boccaccio manuscript referred to above of a late seventeenth- or early eighteenth-century copy of an elaborate fifteenth-century painting of Adam and Eve in the Garden of Eden: comparison with the original miniature of this scene in Paris allows a detailed study of the way in which the artist viewed the painting style of his predecessor two centuries earlier.

The introduction of printing from movable type in the mid fifteenth century did not at first have an effect upon the design or decoration of manuscripts. Books were expected to be handwritten, and if they were not, their printers made them resemble traditional forms as closely as possible. The pages of a printed book were much the same size as those of manuscripts and their layout was the same, with the design of letters imitating the writing of a scribe; spaces were left for decorated initials or larger illuminations to be inserted by hand. The chief difference was that printers used paper for their books, and the paper of the time, although excellently strong and durable, was less suited for painting and gold decoration than vellum. Paper had been in increasingly common use for a variety of documents from the thirteenth century onwards, and even substantial paper volumes can be found considerably before the invention of printing, like the copy of Bartolo di Sassoferrato written in Bologna around 1400 (no. 73). This manuscript begins with a half-page miniature and has illuminated initials throughout the text in the conventional manner. When printers fifty years and more later made special copies of their works to be decorated with particular richness, they printed on vellum, the traditional material for manuscripts. The greater cost of vellum added to the value of the book and ensured the best surface for expensive illumination, as for example in the magnificent copy of the Roman Breviary printed by Nicolaus Jenson in Venice in 1478 (no. 101, colour ill. 29). The use of vellum for illuminated presentation copies of printed books can still be found in the sixteenth century, as in a copy of *Argonauticon* of 1519 made for Gilles de Maizières, Rector of the University of Paris (no. 67), and a copy of the 1527 edition of Thucydides with the arms of François 1 of France (no. 68). Even in these early years of the sixteenth century, however, the art of miniature painting in manuscripts had not been lost and was still responsive to new fashions: this can be seen, for example, in the Glasgow copy of Jean Lemaire de Belges's *L'Epistre du Roy* of c. 1515 (no. 66, colour ill. 1): here, the artist's creation of a chivalric pseudo-classical scene incorporates architectural motifs adopted from late fifteenth-century Italian designs, as well as the ultimate in *trompe-l'oeil* for a book illustration, a scene in which the text is presented as an integral part of the picture space. It was not long, however, before this impetus was exhausted, and the dominant technology of printing, with printed illustration, replaced the great traditional art of the illuminator and miniaturist.

1.   Louis de Clèves on horseback. Lemaire, France, c. 1515. MS Hunter 12 (S.2.2.), fol. 1. *Cat. no. 66*

19

2.   St Mark. Gospels, Byzantine, 11th century and later.
MS Hunter 475 (V.7.2.), fol. 110v *(slightly enlarged). Cat. no. 12*

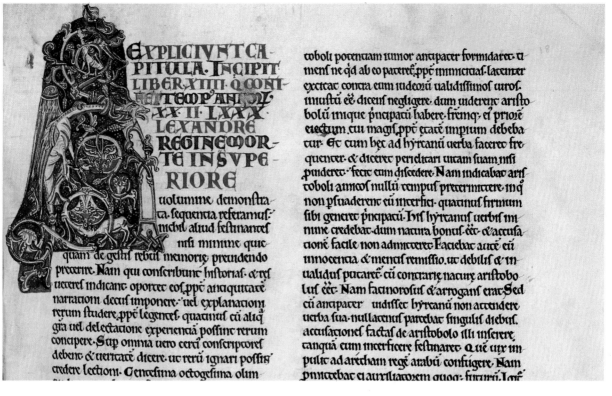

3. Initial A. Josephus, England, 1125-1150. MS Hunter 4 (S.1.4), fol. 136. *Cat. no. 10*

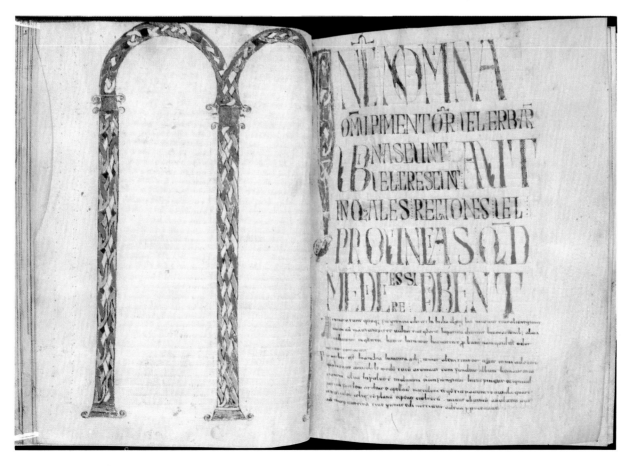

4. Opening from book of medical writings. Southern France, late 8th or early 9th century.
MS Hunter 96 (T.4.13), fols. 23v-24. *Cat. no. 1*

5.   Pentecost. Psalter, England, c. 1170. MS Hunter 229 (U.3.2), fol. 15v. *Cat. no. 14*

6.   Christ in Glory. Psalter, England, c. 1170. MS Hunter 229 (U.3.2), fol. 16. *Cat. no. 14*

7. Initial 'd'. Writings on the Calendar, Durham, 1125-1150. MS Hunter 85 (T.4.2), fol. 35. *Cat. no. 9*

8. Tree of Vices and Tree of Remedies. Raymond of Peñafort, ?France, mid 13th century.
MS General 339, fols. 41v-42. *Cat. no. 23*

9.   Coronation of the Virgin. Devotional and philosophical writings, London, c. 1325-1335.
MS Hunter 231 (U.3.4), p. 83. *Cat. no. 27*

And serue wel wthoute feyntise
Thou shalt be quyte of thyne empryse
Wt more guerdoun if that thou lyue
But all this tyme this y thee yeue
The god of loue whilome al the day
Had taughte me as ye haue herd say
And enfourmed compendrously
The vanysshide awey all sodeynly
And y alloone lefte all soole
So full of compleynt and of doole
ffor y sawe no man there me by
My woundes me greued wonderly
Ne ferto curen no thyng y knewe
Save the bothom taught of hewe
Wheron was sett hoolly my thought
Of other comfort knewe y nought
But it were thorugh the god of loue
Y knewe not ell to my bihoue
That myght me ease or comfort gete
But if he wolde hym entremete
The Roser was wthoute doute
Closed wth an hegge wthoute
As ye toforn haue herd me seyne
And fast y bisiede and wolde fayne

10.   Decorated page. Chaucer, England, c. 1440-1450. MS Hunter 409 (V.3.7.), fol. 57v. *Cat. no. 36*

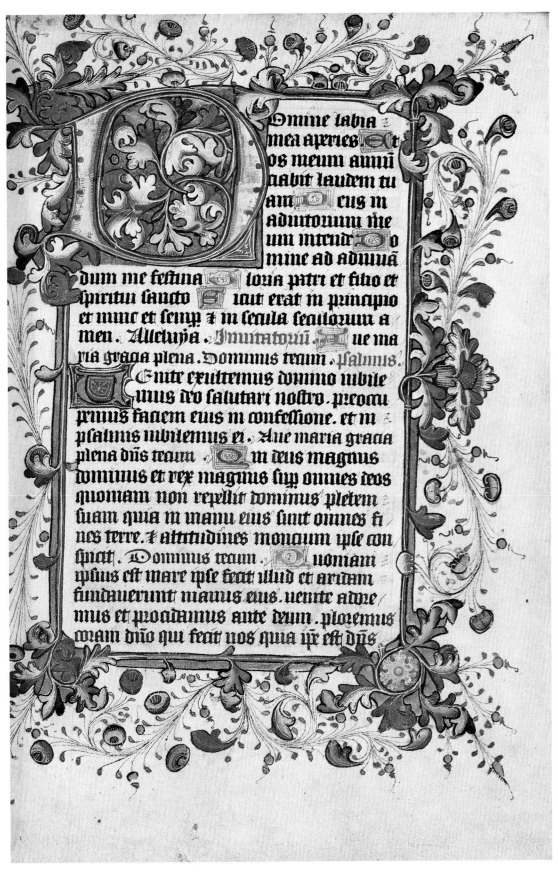

11. Decorated page. Book of Hours, England, mid 15th century. MS Hunter 268 (U.5.8), fol. 7. *Cat. no. 37*

12. Wheel of Fortune. Boccaccio, Paris, 1467. MS Hunter 371 (V.1.8), fol. 1. *Cat. no. 54*

13. Edward III paying homage to Philip IV. Chronicles of Saint-Denis, France, 1450-1475.
MS Hunter 203 (U.1.7), fol. 15. *Cat. no. 56*

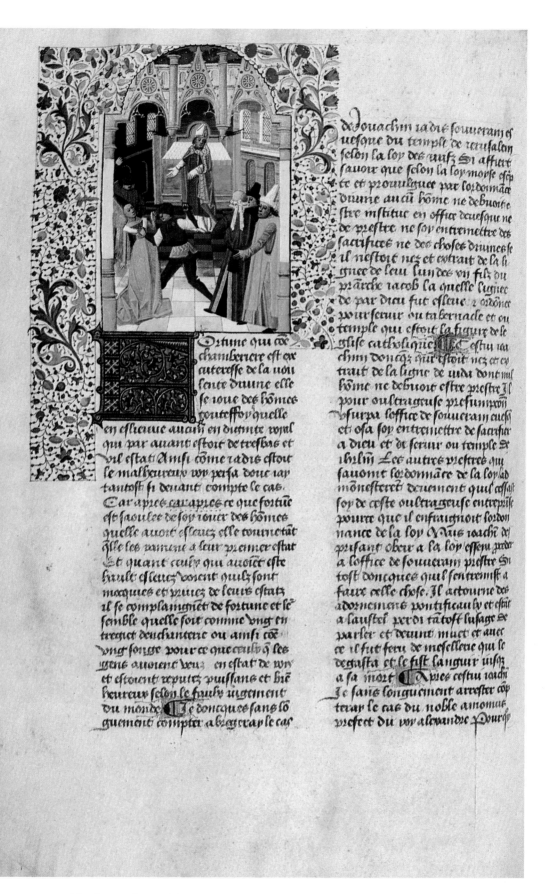

14. Lunette Scene of Joachim the High Priest. Boccaccio, Paris, 1475-1500.
MS Hunter 208 (U.1.12), fol. 206v. *Cat. no. 55*

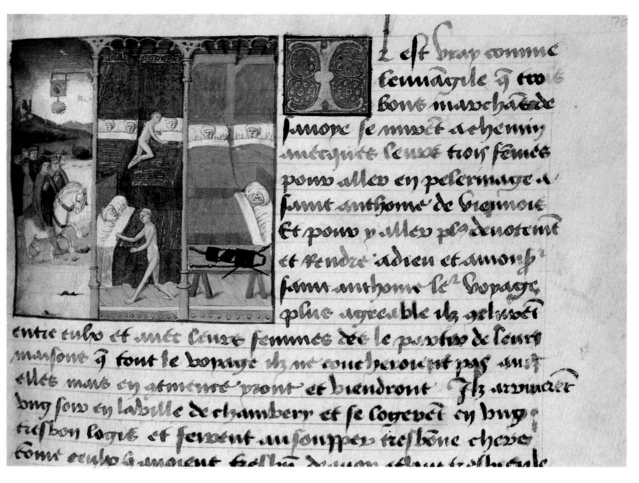

z est vray comme
lennagle q̃ two
bone marchãde
lmore se mnet achemin
mbergiez lenae trois femes
pono aller en pelermage a
fant anthome de bregnoie
Et pono y Aller plo denotent
et rendre adien et amons
fans anthome le hopage
plue agreable ilz aelnrez
entre culx et mbt leure femmes dee le partie de leure
mafone q̃ tout le hopage ilz ne concheroient pas aur
elles mais en gmene vront et biendront Ilz arvincer
vng sou en labille de chamberr et se logerer en vng
tresbon logie et servent aufoupper tresbône cheve
comt eulx q̃ amoient bellm de non clan trotheule

15. Scenes at an Inn. Cent Nouvelles Nouvelles, France, 1475-1500.
MS Hunter 252 (U.4.10), fol. 70. *Cat. no. 58*

sur terre et sur riuiere. pour vo
ler pice perdue fuisant lieure
cance z autre oiseaux et bestes
du sacre. de ses differentes
especes z naissance des noms di
uers dicelle especes. quant il doit
estre pris. de sa forme con
dicion et proie.
On trouue troie especes

16. Falcon and Prey. Tardif, France, c. 1494. MS Hunter 269 (U.5.9), fol. 12. *Cat. no. 62*

17.   Last Supper. Seuse, Bourges, 1470. MS Hunter 420 (V.4.4),
fol. 94. *Cat. no. 57*

18.   St John on Patmos. Apocalypse, Southern France, ?1480s. MS Hunter 398 (V.2.18), fol. 1v. *Cat. no. 59*

19.   Vision of Christ appearing to Charles VIII. Ludolph, Paris, 1490s.
MS Hunter 39 (T.1.7), fol. 97. *Cat. no. 60*

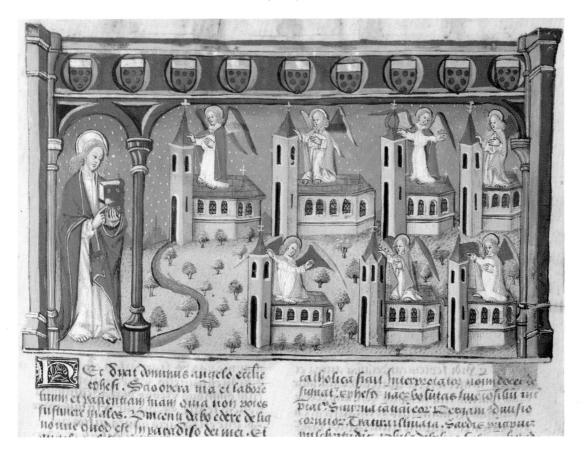

20.   St John and the Seven Churches. Apocalypse, Southern France, ?1480s. MS Hunter 398 (V.2.18), fol. 2. *Cat. no. 59*

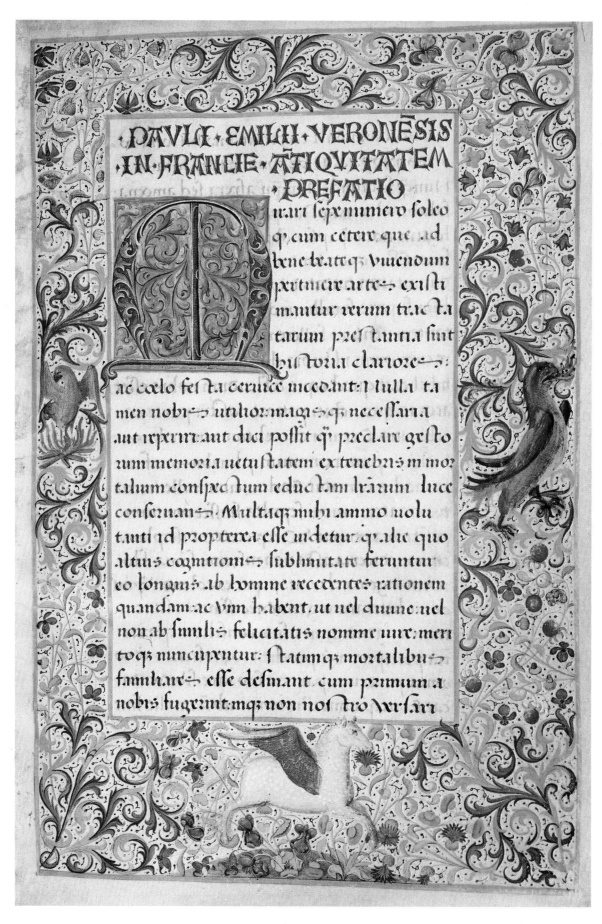

21.   Decorated page. Emili, France, 1490s. MS Hunter 98 (T.4.15), fol. 1. *Cat. no. 64*

22.   Avicenna lecturing. Avicenna, France, 1475-1500. MS Hunter 9 (S.1.9), fol. 1. *Cat. no. 61*

Prohemiale capitulu mapit in quo ¬
¬ dicendox et ad hab¬
¬ putauerunt non tra
benefica fit tantum
na/nec cuiq̃ nocere p
¬is̃ optime congruat potestati uel ¬
ret omnino. ut neq̃ ex bñficentia et
bom puenitat ad nos/neq̃ ex malis
mali. Quox error q̃ maximus est
¬ute humane statũ spectat ¬oarguer
¬bis ne et ipẽ fallaris impulsus au¬
niiq̃ui se putant esse sapientes. Nec
arrogantes sumus. ut comphensam
¬ucritatem gloriemi ⸗ q̃ doctrinam eius se¬
fare solus potest et reuelare secreta.

23. Initial A. Lactantius, England, mid 15th century.
MS Hunter 274 (U.5.14), fol. 1. *Cat. no. 38*

VRIMAM DICIT PREMISSA
COMMENDATIONE SALVTĒ,

ACIT, OPTI
MA CONCI
LIATRIX A
MICITIE VIR
IVS QVA
TE PRISTA
RI IAM

dudum clarissima fama cognoui ut nunc eruditissimis opib̃
uelur in presentis pectore perspecta tu ignotus cupiam fieri particep̃
⸗ amori ⸗ discipline tuc. Legi libellum sensu non corpore ma¬
gnum atc nuperrime transmissum ad illustrem militem Iacobũ
Antonium Marcellum ⸗ romane uenustatis ⸗ uenere nobilita
tis decus ⸗ iam sepe lectum tam optabile tuit tamq̃ iocundum
multa doctissime disceptata si non ingenio ut certe memorie/
mandare tacitus etiam sine uolumine mecum aliquando rele¬
go ⸗ phi acumen ⸗ theologi lumen ⸗ oratois ellegantiam.

24. Initial F. Sagundino, North-east Italy, c. 1463 and 1480s.
MS Hunter 201 (U.1.5), p. 269. *Cat. no. 107*

Jeronimi ad Eustochiuȝ de

FILIA, audi
obliuiscere p¬
cocupiscet re
quarto psalm¬
ut ƥm exemp
de cognatione
dæmonia inter
tiu: quā alibi
uidere bona
sufficit tibi e¬

populi & domus patris tui: ut car¬
bus: Ne respexeris in quit retro: n
sed in monte saluũ te fac: ne forte co¬
hēso aratro respicere post tergũ: ne
Xp̄i tunicã ad tollendũ aliud uestim¬
culũ. Pater filiã cohortat: ne memine

25. Initial O with Nativity. North-east Italy, c. 1400-1410.
MS Hunter 202 (U.1.6), fol. 8. *Cat. no. 72*

Commen
Conuiui¬
LATO ph¬
tuaginta
ortus fuer
pibus exp¬
natalica
tur. Pri¬
phiui ten
porphuu
¬dapes pretermisse fuerunt. Tand¬
¬rentius medicis platonicum ¬
¬nium architracliuium restituit. C
¬lare bandinus instituisset. regio¬
¬meos accipit munas. Anthonui¬
dicunt Cristophorum landinu

26. Initial P with Iris. Plato, Southern Netherlands, 1483.
MS Hunter 206 (U.1.10), fol. 33. *Cat. no. 124*

27. Decorated page with death-bed scene. Bartolo, Bologna, c. 1400. MS Hunter 6 (S.1.6), fol. 1. *Cat. no. 73*

28.   Decorated page. Quintus Curtius, Italy, c. 1480. MS Hunter 47 (T.2.5), fol. 1. *Cat. no. 102*

sic contriuit omnia ossa mea. O e mane
usqz ad uespaz finies me: sicut pullus hy
rudinis sic clamabo meditabor ut colum
ba. Attenuati sunt oculi mei: suspicietes
in excelso. O ne uim patior responde, p
me: qd dicā aut qd rñdebit mihi cū ipse
fecerim. Recogitabo tibi oēs ānos me
os: i amaritudine aie mee. O ne si sic ui
uit z i talib⁹ uita spūs mei corripies me
z uiuificabis me: ecce i pace amaritudo
mea amarissima. T u aūt eruisti animā
meā ut nō piret: proiecisti post tergū tuuz
oia peccata mea. Q uia nō infernus cō
fitebit tibi: neqz mors laudabit te: nō ex
pectabūt q descendūt in lacu ueritate tu
am. Q iues uiues ipse cōfitebit tibi: sicut
z ego hodie pat filiis notaz faciet ueritæ
tem tuā. O ne saluū me fac: z psalmos
nros cātabimus cūctis diebus uite nre i
domo dñi. ant. Cūctis diebus uite nostre:
saluos nos fac dñe. Ait. Omnes angeli eius:
laudate dūm de celis. ps. ipm. Capituluz.
O x precessit dies aut appropiqua
uit: abijciamus ergo opa tenebra
rum: z induamur arma lucis: sicut i die
honeste ābulemus. hymnus.
V Les diei nūcius: luce propinquaz
precinit: nos excitator mentiū: iam
christus ad uitā uocat. Auferte clamat
lectulos: egros sopore desides: casteqz
recte ac sobrie: uigilate iaz suz, primus.
I esum ciem⁹ uocibus: flentes pecātes
sobrie: intenta supplicatio: dormire cor
mundū uetat. T u christe somnū discu
te: tu rūpe noctis uincula: tu solue pec
cati uetus: nouūqz lumen ingere. O eo
patri. x. Repleti sumus mane: misericordia
tua. R. Exultauimus: z delectati sumus. Ad
bñdictus ant. Erexit dñs nobis cornu salu
tis: in domo dauid pueri sui. psal. Benedic
tus. Feria quarta inuitatoriuz. In manu
tua dñe: omnes fines terre. ps. Venite. Ad
nocturnum hymnus.
R Erum creator optime: rectorqz no
ster aspice: nos a quiete noxia: mer
sos sopore libera. T e sancte christe po
scimus: ignosce tu criminibus: ad confi
tendum surgimus: morasqz noctis rum

pimus. Q entem manusqz tollimus: p
phetam sicut nouimus: nobis gerendū
precipit: paulus qp gestis censuit. T ides
malum qd gessimus: occulta nostra pā
dimus: preces gementes fundimus: di
mitte qd peccauimus. P resta pater pi
issime. ant. Auertit dñs. antiphona tepo
re paschali. Alla. psalmus dauid.
D Jxit insipiens in corde suo: non e
deus. C orrupti sunt z abbomina
biles facti sunt in iniqtatibus: non est q
faciat bonuz. D eus de celo prspexit su
per filios hominum: ut uideat si est intel
ligens aut requirens deum. O mnes de
clinauerunt simul inutiles facti sunt: nō
est qui faciat bonū: non est usqz ad unū.
N ōne scient omnes qui operantur ini
quitatem: qui deuorant plebem meam:
ut cibum panis. D eum non inuocaue
runt: illic trepidauerunt timore ubi non
fuit timor. Q uoniam deus dissipauit os
sa eorum qui hominibus placent: cōfu
si sunt quoniaz deus spreuit eos. Q uis
dabit ex sion salutare israel: cū auerterit
dominus captiuitatem plebis sue: exul
tabit iacob z letabitur israel. psal. dauid.
E Xaudi deus orationem meam: et
ne despexeris deprecationez meā:
intende mihi z exaudi me. C ontristat⁹
suz in exercitatione mea: z conturbatus
sum a uoce inimici: z tribulatione pecca
toris. Q uoniaz declinauerunt i me ini
quitates: z i ira molesti erāt mihi. C or
meum conturbatū est in me: z formido
mortis cecidit sup me. T imor z tremor
uenerunt super me: z contexerunt me te
nebre. E t dixi quis dabit mihi pennas
sicut columbe: z uolabo z requiescam.
E cce elongaui fugiens: z mansi in soli
tudine. E xpectabam eum qui saluum
me fecit: a pusillanimitate spiritus z tem
pestate. P recipita domine z diuide lin
guas eorum: quoniam uidi iniquitatem
z contradictionem in ciuitate. D ie ac
nocte circūdabit eam super muros eius
iniquitas: z labor in medio eius z in iu
sticia. E t non defecit de plateis eius:
usura z dolus. Q uoniam si inimicus

b 4

29. Decorated page. Breviary, Venice, 1478. Hunterian Collection, Bf 1. 18, fol. 14. *Cat. no. 101*

30.   Decorated page. Avicenna, Venice, 1486. Hunterian Collection, Bw 3. 24, Bk. II, fol. 1. *Cat. no. 105*

31.   *(right)* Augustus entering Rome in Triumph. Niccolò da Ferrara,
Ferrara, 1450s. MS Hunter 41 (T.1.9), fol. 149. *Cat. no. 79*

Qui comincia la quarta parte ouero el quarto libro de polistoro. ¶Capitolo primo. Come Octauiano entrato in Roma triumphando fo chiamato emperadore da tutto el Senato e da tutto il popolo de Roma. Et de molte incidencie de citade e de phylosophi. ¶Rubrica Rubrica.

Oncie sia cosa ch... horamai da qui de... comincia nuouo regin... to in roma e an... ono imperio in tutto il mundo. Et comincia nu... oua fede per lo auenimento de Jhesu christo figliolo de dio eterno al modo pero a me pare da comenciare el q... to libro ouero la quarta parte de q... sto libro polistoro. La quale parte se... ne tanto piu nobele piu alta e piu autentica che laltre parte precedete. quanto piu alto piu nobele e piu au... tentico e Jhesu christo figliolo de dio onnipotente. Et bene che questa qu... ta parte non comprenda tante batta glie ciuile nauale campestre e inimich... uole quante comprendeno le precede... te parte non dimeno questa ultima parte tanto serae piu nobele quanto che oltra le bataglie ociose e immi... cheuole descritte in questa parte es... sa e fiorita e ornata di miracoli del le uertude del sangue de Jhesu xpo e della sua sanctissima fede. Et ecia...

dio e ornata di miracoli e del sangue di suoi sanctissimi martyri. E pero continuando ile cose contade ulti mamente nella precedente parte e da sapere che lanno septingentesimo uigesimo secundo della hedificacione de roma. Il quale anno era octuagesimo septimo de olympiade essendo Octauiano Ce saro la quinta fiata consolo e Lucio apuleio essendo la octaua ydo de ce naro cioe il sexto di de genaro Nel quale di e La pasqua epiphania. Il detto Octauiano per la incerita de tutto il senato per lo suffragio de tu tto il popolo de Roma fue chiamato e constituito augusto e principe de roma e de tutta la signoria Romana. Et es sendo offerta a lui tutta La monarchi a e tutta la signoria de roma. Lui con grande instancia la refutaua. Ma ti to fuogono li prieghi de Senatori e de tutto il popolo che egli laceptoe. Et co si quello giorno la summa de tutte le cose e tutto il regimento de roma co mincioe essere appresso de uno solo se gnore cioe octauiano. Con cio fos se che auanti per forca fosse stato u surpato il principato de Roma p julio cesare e per molti altri. In questo me desimo giorno nel quale octa... uiano se chiamato e constituito au gusto e principe de Roma egli co grandissima gloria triumphando en troe in roma. Et tra le altre pompe... mo... pe fatta dal suo charro triumphale

41

32. Initial S with Scipio crossing into Africa. Livy, Milan,
c. 1450. MS Hunter 370 (V.1.7), fol. 253. *Cat. no. 78*

33. Initial A. Cipolla, Verona, late 1450s.
MS Hunter 275 (U.5.15), fol. 3. *Cat. no. 82*

34. Decorated page. Cicero, Florence, 1450-1460.
MS Hunter 441 (V.5.11), fol. 1. *Cat. no. 81*

35. Decorated page. Justinus, Milan, 1450-1475.
MS Hunter 282 (U.5.22), fol. 1. *Cat. no. 85*

36. Genesis page. Bible, Genoa, c. 1490. MS General 1060, fol. 4. *Cat. no. 106*

37. St Antoninus of Piacenza. Voragine, Flanders, c. 1405-1410. MS General 1111, fol. 368. *Cat. no. 114*

38. Presentation of Book to Patron. Mirror, Bruges, 1455. MS Hunter 60 (T.2.18), fol. 1. *Cat. no. 116*

39. Opening with Annunciation and text-page. Breviary, Ghent,
1494. MS Hunter 25 (S.2.15), fols. 7v-8. *Cat. no. 125*

40. The Trinity. Missal, Northern Netherlands, c. 1460.
MS Euing 7, fol. 20. *Cat. no. 122*

41. Flight into Egypt. Book of Hours, French Flanders, c. 1460. MS Euing 4, fol. 55. *Cat. no. 120*

42.   St Mark. Book of Hours, Bruges, c. 1450-1460. MS General 288,
fol. 275v. *Cat. no. 117*

CATALOGUE

50

I · Early Manuscripts

1. Medical Writings

Varia Medica (Hippocrates, Galenus, etc.)
Southern France, late 8th or early 9th century.

MS Hunter 96 (T.4.13)

Vellum, 270 × 212 mm.; [iii], 186, [iii] leaves; written space 240 × 155 mm., 35-45 long lines, except fols. 1-23 which are in double columns of 32-39 lines.

Except for a fragmentary palimpsest in the National Library of Scotland (Adv. MS 18. 7. 8), this is the earliest western manuscript in Scotland. Beginning with a list of some thousand drugs and plants, it contains a working handbook of medical conditions, both acute and non-acute, with remedies.

The script is a pre-Caroline mixed minuscule. It has been assigned to Southern France or Northern Italy by E. A. Lowe; Bernhard Bischoff favours Southern France. The decoration consists chiefly in capital letters of varying sizes:

larger letters are generally coloured in green or red, while smaller ones are left plain but covered in a yellow wash. Large initials marking different sections of the text are given greater prominence with plaited strapwork and occasional bird motifs (fols. 33v, 35, 36v, 102). A list of contents in double columns over five pages (fols. 21v-23v) is embellished with an architectural frame constructed of columns and arches resembling that used in Canon Tables (tables of concordance for the Gospels). Large flayholes and other imperfections in the skin are not uncommon in books of this early date, particularly those intended for vernacular rather than religious use.

PROVENANCE: Bought for Hunter at the Pieter Burmann sale, Leyden, 27 September 1779, lot 1221.

BIBLIOGRAPHY: Young & Aitken, pp. 103-105; E. A. Lowe, *Codices Latini antiquiores*, II, Oxford, 1922, p. 12, no. 156; *Treasures*, p. 1, no.2; Ker, *William Hunter*, p. 17, Appendix A, XIX; W. T. Menke, *Western European Medicine in the Dark Ages* (unpublished studies, 1984-1986, deposited in Glasgow University Library).

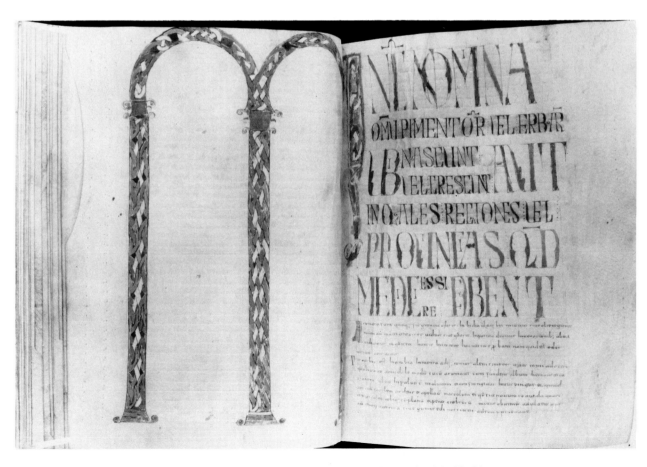

Opening from book of medical writings. MS Hunter 96, fols. 23v-24
(See also Colour Ill. 4)

2. Medical Writings

Varia medica (Hippocrates, etc.)
Southern Italy, ?Naples, early 10th century.

MS Hunter 404 (V.3.2)

Vellum, 282 × 180 mm.; [iii], 147, [ii] leaves; written space 215-235 × 180 mm., 24-29 long lines.

This compilation of medical works, notably the Commentary on the Aphorisms of Hippocrates, is written in the characteristic Beneventan script of Southern Italy. Current from the middle of the 8th to the end of the 13th century, the script formalized the cursive elements which had been eliminated in Caroline miniscule and turned them to calligraphic use.

Major penwork initials in the manuscript are ornamented in intricate knot patterns; they have vestigial leaf motifs, and some are coloured. The text is further enlivened by initials in the form of male heads and busts, generally for the letter Q, and by other figurative elements such as birds, fishes and even a representation of the sun with a face (fol. 55). These drawings are heightened with the red ink used for headings, numbers and the text of the Aphorisms and are likely to be the work of the scribe.

PROVENANCE: Bought by Hunter from the London bookseller Thomas Osborne between 1752 and 1768.

BIBLIOGRAPHY: Young & Aitken, pp. 322-324; E.A. Loew, *The Beneventan Script*, Oxford, 1914, pp. 19, 193, 224, 339, 2nd ed. updated by V. Brown, 1980, I, p. 19, II, p. 46; A. Beccaria, *I codici di medicina del periodo presalernitano*, Rome, 1956, pp. 243-246; B. Lawn, *The Salernitan Question*, Oxford, 1963, p. 7; *Treasures*, p. 2, no. 5; *Manuscripts at Oxford*, ed. A. C. de la Mare and B.C. Barker-Benfield, Oxford, 1980, p. 49; Ker, *William Hunter*, p. 18.

Penwork initial Q, MS Hunter 404, fol. 1

3. Sedulius, Easter Song, and other texts

Sedulius, Carmen paschale, Epistola ad Macedonium, Hymnus abecedarius; Turcius Rufus Asterius, Carmen; Bellisarius Scholasticus, Carmen acrostichum.
Netherlands, 11th century.

MS Hunter 57 (T.2.15)

Vellum, 287 × 197 mm.; 26 leaves; written space 204 × 110 mm., 27 long lines.

The chief work in this manuscript is the *Easter Song* by the early 5th-century Christian poet Sedulius, written probably in Greece before 431. Its five books of hexameters, based stylistically on Virgil, give an account of Biblical miracles, frequently treated from an allegorical point of view, which served as a model for other writers in the Middle Ages and, later, for Milton. This copy is now incomplete, lacking two central gatherings. It is accompanied by other works by and about Sedulius.

The initials beginning the prefatory letter of Sedulius to Macedonius and the Song itself are characteristic of a tradition of stylized leaf scroll found with variations across much of Western Europe in this period. The grotesque lion figure in the initial P of the Song may be compared with the similar figure in Hunter's early Boethius (no. 4), a North Italian design of about the same date. The tradition of emphasizing the first letter of each line of a work in verse goes back to classical times: the first letters were written in red ink outside the ruled frame for the text and were originally heightened with silver, which has since oxidized.

PROVENANCE: Abbey of St Adalbert, Egmont, Netherlands (mark on fol. 1 identified by M.R. James); bought for Hunter at the Pieter Burmann sale, Leyden, 27 September 1779, lot 1232.

BIBLIOGRAPHY: Young & Aitken, pp. 62-63; Ker, *William Hunter*, p. 17; cf. Sedulius, *The Easter Song. Being the First Epic of Christendom*, trans. G. Sigerson, Dublin, 1922; Sedulius, *Paschale carmen*, ed. N. Scheps, Delft, 1938.

Portrait initial Q, MS Hunter 404, fol. 146v

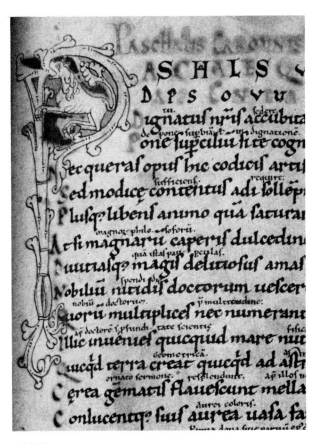

Initial P,
MS Hunter 57, fol. 5

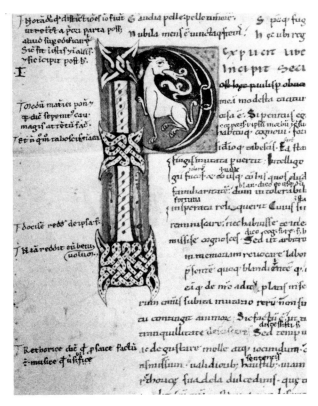

Initial P. MS Hunter 272, fol. 7v

4. Boethius, The Consolation of Philosophy

Anicius Manlius Torquatus Severinus Boethius,
De consolatione philosophiae.
Italy, 11th century.

MS Hunter 272 (U.5.12)

Vellum, 232 × 142 mm.; [iv], 40, [iv] leaves;
written space 168 × 85 mm., 33-36 long lines.

The son of a statesman and consul, Boethius
(c.480-524) became a friend and adviser of the
Ostrogoth king Theodoric and, like his father,
held the office of consul in 510, when his close
contemporary and former pupil, Cassiodorus
(see no. 5), was quaestor. In 522, his two sons
became joint consuls in their turn. Devoted in his
scholarly pursuits to preserving and translating
the learning of Greece and Rome, his most
famous work is *The Consolation of Philosophy*,
written while he was imprisoned on a charge of
treason at Ticinum (Pavia). He was later executed there in 524, aged about 45.

This copy has a remarkable title-page written
in red, green and brown capitals. Large initials of
foliate or knot pattern mark the beginning of each
of the five books. The same colours of red, green,
blue and yellow are used for each without any
figurative element, except in the initial P to Book
II (fol. 7v) where the lion motif seen in the
Sedulius (no. 3) is also present. Here the blue is
of unusual intensity, and the central shaft of the
upright column of the P was embellished with
silver, which has since oxidized. The manuscript, beautifully written in a very clear hand,
has been heavily annotated.

PROVENANCE: Bought by Hunter from Archibald Dodd, 27
July 1775.

BIBLIOGRAPHY: Young & Aitken, pp. 220-221; W. Wein-
berger, 'Anicii Manlii Severini Boethii Philosophiae conso-
lationis libri quinque', *Corpus Scriptorum Ecclesiasticorum*,
67, 1934, p. xvii, no. 27; Ker, *William Hunter*, p. 21.

5. Cassiodorus, Tripartite History of the Church

Magnus Aurelius Cassiodorus,
Historia ecclesiastica tripartita.
Southern Germany, third quarter
of the 12th century.

MS Hunter 217 (U.2.8)

Vellum, 340 × 235 mm.; [iii], 172, 2, [vii] leaves; written space 264 × 175 mm., 37 long lines.

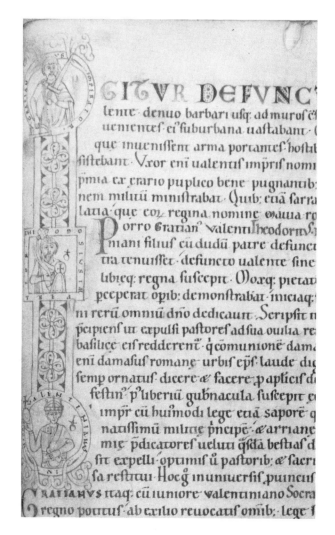

Initial I with Emperors Gratian, Theodosius I, Valentinian II. MS Hunter 217, fol. 127

The chief legacy of Cassiodorus's long life as statesman and scholar (c.485-c.580) was to have helped preserve the classic culture of Europe during the Dark Ages. He founded two monasteries on his family estate of Vivarium, at Syllacium in Calabria, and there established a monastic tradition of scholarship. From 503 onwards, he held a succession of important political offices under four Ostrogothic rulers beginning with Theodoric the Great (474-526), and sought to build a harmonious Italian state based on the co-operation of Gothic and Roman elements. However, his hopes were shattered by the victories in Northern Italy of the Byzantine general Belisarius. After the fall of Ravenna in 540, when he retired from public life, Cassiodorus devoted his considerable energies to assembling an important collection of theological and classical works, commenting on the Scriptures and teaching the monks of his monasteries precise rules for the copying and preservation of his precious manuscripts.

Although Cassiodorus is cited in many texts as the author of the *Tripartite History*, the work was written, at his instigation, by one of his assistants, Epiphanius. It fuses into a single narrative the three histories of Socrates, Sozomenus and Theodoretus, covering the years 306-439. This copy includes, in the initial to Book IX (fol. 127), portraits of the three emperors whose powers overlapped in the late 4th century – Gratian (emperor, 375-383), Theodosius I (emperor, 379-395), and Valentinian II (emperor, 375-392), who established the orthodox Christian state. The initial to Book II (fol. 166v) includes a portrait of Theodosius II (emperor, 408-450), who endorsed the Theodosian code in 438.

One of 138 manuscripts of the *Tripartite History* listed by W. Jacob, this copy is grouped textually with others centred on Paris and Reims. The script, however, shows that it was written in Southern Germany (cf. B. Bischoff, *Kalligraphie in Bayern. Achtes bis zwölftes Jahrhundert*, Wiesbaden, 1981, pp. 38, 99, pl.28, for Munich, Bayerische Staatsbibliothek, Clm 17177); this location is emphasized by the imperial flavour of

the portrait initials. The initials introducing other books are of leafscroll and interlace designs, highlighted with silver; those for Books IV and V (fols. 42 and 54v) include a devil's head, and the initial for Book XI (fol. 160) has an eagle and a dragon. Lesser initials, also silvered, are often outlined with red dots in a manner that recalls earlier Insular styles.

PROVENANCE: 15th-century ex-libris of the Monastery of St Paul, Utrecht (fols. 2 and 172); bought for Hunter at the Pieter Burmann sale, Leyden, 27 September 1779, lot 1224.

BIBLIOGRAPHY: Young & Aitken, pp. 161-162; W. Jacob, 'Die handschriftliche Überlieferung der sogenannten Historia Tripartita des Epiphanius-Cassiodor'. *Texte and Untersuchungen äzur Geschichte der altchristlichen Literatur*, 59, Reihe V, Band 4, Berlin 1954, no. 93, pp. 40, 135-140; Ker, *William Hunter*, p. 17; for a comparison of the script cf. Oxford, Bodleian Library, MS Canon. Bibl. Lat. 60, described in S. Krämer, 'Die Bibliothek von Ranshofen im frühen und hohen Mittelalter', in *The Role of the Book in Medieval Culture, Proceedings of the Oxford International Symposium, 26 September – 1 October 1982*, ed. P. Ganz, Brepols-Turnhout, 1986, p. 63.

6. Anselm, Treatises

Anselmus, Cur deus homo, De trinitate,
De spiritu sancto, De azymo; Petrus Damianus,
De processione spiritus, De simonia; Honorius,
Elucidarium; Marbodus Pellicarius,
Liber de gemmis.
? Flanders, mid 12th century.

MS Hunter 244 (U.4.2)

Vellum, 271 × 198 mm.; 111 leaves; written
space 213 × 140 mm., fols. 1-104 with 28 long
lines, fols. 105-111 in double columns of 28 lines.

Anselm, first Prior then Abbot of Bec in Normandy, later became Archbishop of Canterbury
(1093-1109), at a stormy period in the relationship between Church and Crown. His study
on Atonement, the dialogue *Cur deus homo* (Why
God became Man), was written in Rome in 1097
during a prolonged absence from his see. It was
the most important contribution in the Middle
Ages to the theology of Redemption: Anselm
countered the theory that Satan had a claim on
man, and demonstrated the necessity of the
Incarnation.

In addition to strapwork initials in red, and
secondary initials with rudimentary foliate decoration, this manuscript contains three large
initials composed of animal forms – an S in the
shape of a lion (fol. 2v), a G in the shape of two
interlocked dragons (fol. 71v) and an A composed of five remarkably acrobatic dogs (fol.
82v). The dogs and dragons are drawn in red,
with a foliate motif issuing from one mouth in
each case, as in the initials of the Sedulius (no. 3)
and the Boethius (no. 4); the dragon initial is in
addition made more substantial by the figures
being set against a blue ground. Underdrawing,
which is visible in all three large initials, is
particularly evident in the lion figure, the outline
of which is emphasized by further drawing in
silverpoint. They are all early examples of the
Romanesque delight in making decorative initials
from form alone, without the support of the
outline of a letter.

PROVENANCE: Bought for Hunter at the Pieter Burmann sale,
Leyden, 27 September 1779, lot 2348.

BIBLIOGRAPHY: Young & Aitken, pp. 196-197; Ker, *William
Hunter*, p. 17.

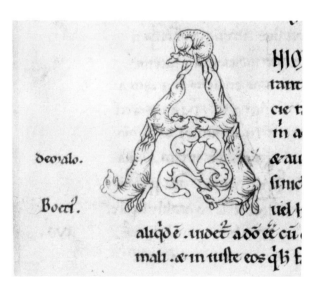

Initial S; initial G; initial A.
MS Hunter 244, fols. 2v, 71v, 82v

7. Raban Maurus, Treatise on the Universe

Rabanus Magnentius Maurus, De universo.
(De rerum naturis)
?Northern England, mid 12th century.

MS Hunter 366 (V.1.3)

Vellum, 341 × 233 mm.; [iv], 224, [iv] leaves;
written space 260 × 157 mm., in double columns
of 40-42 lines.

Raban Maurus (776 or 784 – 856), Benedictine
Abbot of Fulda and later Archbishop of Mainz
and one of the greatest theologians of his day,
wrote this work after leaving Fulda in 842,
probably as the result of political difficulties with
King Louis the German. The text, prefaced by a
letter to King Louis, is an encyclopedia consist-
ing of eighteen books based on Isidore of Seville's
Etymologiae which upheld a mystical interpretation of the world.

The decorated initials in this copy are simple
but firmly controlled patterns which, as C. R.
Dodwell says of the whole Romanesque style, are
'immobile without being lifeless' (*The Canterbury School of Illumination*, Cambridge, 1954,
p. 33). The play of lozenge, scroll and leaf forms
is a harmonious balance of red and green, and
echoes the minor decoration of the text. The
harmony is particularly evident in the list of
chapter headings and the facing large initial P
which begins Book I (fols. 3v-4). A feature of the
decorative design of this large initial is a split
petal motif associated by Sir Roger Mynors with
Durham and found also in work from Fountains
Abbey (e.g. Oxford, Bodleian Library, MS Laud
Misc. 310); the geometric loops in the bowl of
the P may be compared with those in other
northern manuscripts in Oxford (Bodleian Library, MSS Laud Misc. 241 and 308), both from
Roche Abbey, Yorkshire.

PROVENANCE: Bought by Hunter from Thomas Osborne,
probably between 1764 and 1768.

BIBLIOGRAPHY: Young & Aitken, pp. 292-293; Ker, *William
Hunter*, p. 18.

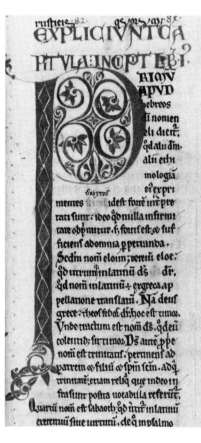

Initial P. MS Hunter 366, fol. 4

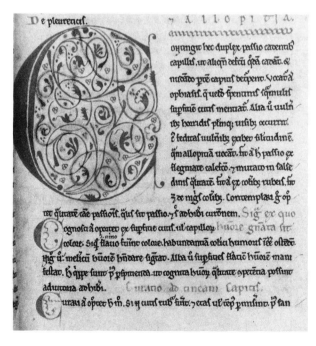

Initial C. MS Hunter 435, fol. 2

8. Alexander of Tralles, Practice of Medicine and other texts

Alexander Trallianus, Practica;
(Anon.), Pharmacopoeia, Nominum medicorum explicatio; Pseudo-Galenus, De passionibus mulierum.
England, mid 12th century.

MS Hunter 435 (V.5.5)

Vellum, 241 × 163 mm.; [iii], 136, [iii] leaves; written space 168 × 99 mm., 30 long lines.

The chief work in this medical compendium is the handbook of the Greek physician Alexander of Tralles in Lydia, who practised pharmacy in Rome in the mid 6th century, prescribing remedies like iron for anaemia and rhubarb for liver weakness and dysentery.

The major initials introducing books or a new work (fols. 2, 45, 111v) have swirling arabesque designs in red, blue and green, and in these individual elements such as the shape of the heads on the scrolled stems help to identify the place in which it was written. Different centres developed different details, retaining a liveliness of form within the regularity of the overall design. The trilobe leaf shape and the clusters of triple circles in red, blue or green suggest that this manuscript was produced in the West Country: they are found in three manuscripts datable to the third quarter of the 12th century from Cirencester Abbey, now in Oxford (Jesus College, MSS 52, 53 and 70, the last two written by the same scribe, Canon Fulco). There is similar work in manuscripts from Gloucester (e.g. Oxford, Jesus College, MS 65) and from Winchcomb Abbey, Gloucestershire (Oxford, Jesus College, MS B.102). In these examples, light guide-lines for the initials are still visible. The scribe left a rectangular space for all the large initials in the text, as in the Raban Maurus (no. 7); in other manuscripts of the same period, the lines of text are made to follow the shape of the initial (see nos. 9-11).

PROVENANCE: Hunter's source not traced.

BIBLIOGRAPHY: Young & Aitken, pp. 358-359.

9. Writings on the Calendar

Kalendarium; ?Beda, Decennovennales circuli, Dialogus de temporibus; Beda, De temporum ratione, De vernali equinoctio epistola; Dionysius Exiguus, Epistolae duae; Anon., De variis relationibus; Abbo Floriacensis, Computus, Sententia de ratione sphaerae; Hyginus, De sphaera.
England, Durham, second quarter of the 12th century.

MS Hunter 85 (T.4.2)

Vellum, 285 × 200 mm.; 149 leaves; written space 185/215 × 128 mm., 31-40 long lines.

Written by several scribes in Bede's homeland of Northumbria, this volume contains works concerning the use of the Calendar by the Venerable Bede (672/673 – 735), as well as others by Dionysius Exiguus (late 5th – early 6th century), Abbo of Fleury (c. 945/950 – 1004) and Hyginus. A few elaborate initials with foliate interlace and penwork designs supplement the regular appearance of secondary initials in green, red and purple. The major work in the collection is Bede's *Treatise on the Reckoning of Times*; it is introduced by an initial 'd' in red, green, purple, blue and yellow, containing a seated representation of the author (fol. 35). He is identified by the inscription 'S. BEDA. P[resbiter]' and holds a quill pen in his right hand. The opening words of the preface, 'De natura rerum et ratione temporum...', appear on the scroll he is holding in his left hand. The codex form had replaced the scroll some centuries before Bede was writing, but here the scroll has been used to confer an authoritative sense of antiquity and to provide a larger space for the words than an open book would have done. The scroll form may also have been selected for aesthetic reasons, as its curving shape is wholly in accord with the subtle contours of the design.

PROVENANCE: Durham Cathedral Priory; bought for the Hunterian Library in 1810 (Hunterian Museum Records, MR 51/85).

BIBLIOGRAPHY: Young & Aitken, pp. 91-94; R. A. B. Mynors, *Durham Cathedral Manuscripts*, Oxford, 1939, pp. 55-56; *Bedae opera de temporibus*, ed. C.W. Jones, Cambridge, Mass., 1943, pp. 168, 170, 174; M. L. W. Laistner and H. H. King, *A Hand-List of Bede Manuscripts*, Ithaca, N.Y., 1943, pp. 121, 149; H. S. Offler, *Medieval Historians of Durham*, Durham, 1958, p. 11 and n. 21; W. Levison, 'Die Annales Lindisfarnenses et Dunelmenses', *Deutsches Archiv für Erforschung des Mittelalters*, 17, 1961, pp. 447-506; *Treasures*, pp. 4-5, no. 11; Ker, *Medieval Libraries*, p. 72; G. Viré, 'La transmission du De astronomia d'Hygin jusqu'au XIIIe siècle', *Revue d'Histoire des Textes*, 11, 1981, p. 167, no. 26, and pp. 257-261; Ker, *William Hunter*, p. 11, n. 1.

Initial 'd'. MS Hunter 85, fol. 35
(See also Colour Ill. 7)

57

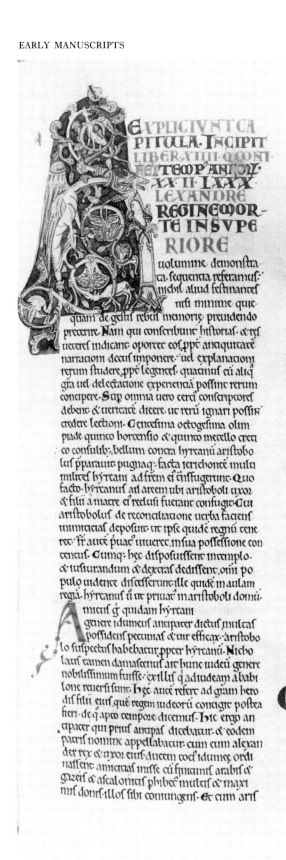

Initial A. MS Hunter 4, fol. 136
(See also Colour Ill. 3)

10. Josephus, Jewish Antiquities, and Jewish War

Flavius Josephus, Historiae antiquitatis Judaicae, Historia belli Judaici.
England, second quarter of the 12th century.

MS Hunter 4 (S.1.4)

Vellum, 456 × 324 mm.; [iii], 299, [iv] leaves; written space 345 × 230 mm., in double columns of 50-51 lines.

During the 12th century in England, book production reached the highest standards of design and execution. This beautifully written copy of Josephus, possibly meant for reading aloud in a monastic refectory, is prefaced by Jerome's appreciation of the first-century historian, extracted from his *Lives of Famous Men*.

The outlines of most of the large initials are embellished with delicate penwork interlace patterns based on leaf motifs, in red, green and brown, with occasional use of animal shapes and human faces. The initial introducing the main text (fol. 2) includes roundels set in a column which contain drawings of a nimbed Christ and of a classical scribe writing on a scroll (cf. the representation of Bede in no. 9). There are in addition three splendid coloured initials: a capital I in the shape of a spiritedly drawn standing figure on a purple ground blowing an uplifted horn (fol. 156v), and two capital A's, also on purple grounds, made of elaborate interlace designs incorporating grotesque creatures and human figures. In the first capital A (fol. 136), the shafts and cross-piece of the letter are made from the body and neck of a dragon combined with a section of a panel or column; they may be compared with the same initial in another Josephus manuscript contemporary with this one (Cambridge University Library, MS Dd. 1. 4, fol. 220; cf. *English Romanesque Art*, Manuscripts no. 43, p. 108, repr. p. 52, dated c. 1130). The delineation of the second capital A (fol. 165) relies more strongly on the shape of the purple ground; it is particularly interesting for the elongated human figure with a dragon's head which forms the right-hand shaft. The arrangement of the text to fit the shape of these letters suggests that the initials were drawn before the accompanying lines were written, and may indicate that both text and decoration were the work of the same hand.

PROVENANCE: Reading Abbey, effaced inscription on fol. 1; Hertford Priory; St Albans Abbey; bought by Hunter at the sale of George Parker, 2nd Earl of Macclesfield, London, 14 January 1765, lot 369.

BIBLIOGRAPHY: Young & Aitken, pp. 6-7; *Trésors*, p. 3, no. 5; Ker, *Medieval Libraries*, p. 101; Ker, *William Hunter*, p. 13; Baldwin, *William Hunter*, p. 4, no. 6.

11. Bede, Commentary on Acts, and Retraction

Beda, Expositio super Actus apostolorum,
Liber retractionis in Actus apostolorum;
?Beda, Expositio de nominibus locorum.
England, mid 12th century.

MS Hunter 438 (V.5.8)

Vellum, 247 × 169 mm.; [iv], 119, [v] leaves;
written space 175 × 106 mm., 26 long lines.

In the field of theology Bede was ranked in the Middle Ages only after the Four Doctors of the Latin Church – Gregory the Great, Ambrose, Augustine and Jerome – and it was only later that his historical writings came to be regarded as more significant than his interpretation of the Scriptures. *The Commentary on the Acts of the Apostles*, completed soon after 709, is one of his numerous Biblical studies; it is accompanied here by his *Retraction* (written in all probability between 725 and 731), and a glossary of geographical names attributed to Jerome but probably written by Bede.

The Caroline minuscule here is a more angular script than that of the Josephus (no. 10), and the decorative initials in red, green, blue and purple are rather less skilful. The large penwork initials, however, are firmly executed: their motifs of men and dragons fighting in the coils of entangling foliage are carried over from earlier Anglo-Norman manuscripts. They demonstrate the controlled draughtsmanship of Romanesque art in which the parts, however rich in detail, are subordinated to the overall design.

It is interesting to note that the decoration of the volume is in two distinct sections. Coloured initials are used only as far as the end of the *Commentary*, to fol. 73v; thereafter, with a single exception, the marginal initials are in the same ink as the text, providing an undifferentiated setting for the elaborate penwork design.

PROVENANCE: Bought by Hunter at the John Ratcliffe sale, London, 27 March 1776, lot 1592.

BIBLIOGRAPHY: Young & Aitken, pp. 360-361; M.L.W. Laistner and H.H. King, *A Hand-List of Bede Manuscripts*, Ithaca, N.Y., 1943, pp. 21, 23; *Trésors*, pp. 2-3, no. 4; *Treasures*, pp. 5-6, no. 15; Ker, *William Hunter*, p. 15.

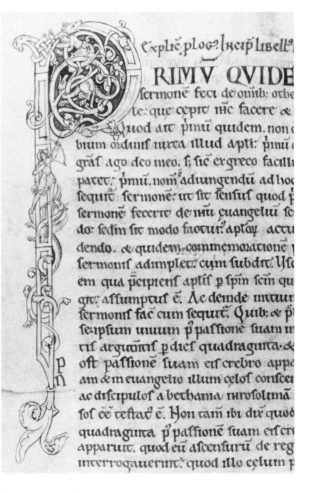

Initial A; initial P.
MS Hunter 438, fols. 74 and 82v

St John. MS Hunter 475, fol. 274v
(St Mark, fol. 110v, reproduced in Colour Ill. 2)

12. Greek Gospels

Quattuor Evangelia Graece [το τετραεγαγγελιον]
Provincial Byzantium, in three sections:
11th century, late 12th or early 13th century,
and 15th century.

MS Hunter 475 (V.7.2)

Vellum, 185 × 140 mm.; [v], 1-109, [ii], 110-
367, [v] leaves; written space 137 × 100 mm.,
fols. 1-16 with 17 long lines (15th century), fols.
17-108 with 17-24 long lines (12th/13th century),
fols. 110-367 with 18 long lines (11th century).

The major part of this volume contains an 11th-
century copy of the Gospels of St Mark, St Luke
and St John, with portraits of the Evangelists
(fols. 110v, 173v, 274v). It is completed by a late
12th- or early 13th-century copy of St Matthew's
Gospel, which includes a full-page picture
(fol. 28v), together with the Canon Tables of
Eusebius. In the 15th century, a further section
was added containing the order of the marriage
service.

Although the picture of St Luke has flaked
badly, the three 11th-century pictures are good
examples of provincial Byzantine art. The forms
of the bodies are clearly articulated through the
fall of the draperies and the flesh is modelled with
a multiplicity of hues. In the schematic treatment
of the architecture and furniture, by contrast, the
concern is with the decorative surface of a flat
plane. Both this decorative element and the
'damp-fold' style of depicting clothing exercised a
profound influence on the art of the Romanesque
period, as a comparison of these pictures with
those in the Hunterian Psalter (no. 14) will show.
The Greek tradition is seen also in the content of
the pictures: whereas St Mark and St Luke are
both depicted at work writing, St John is shown
dictating his Gospel to his disciple Prochoros, the
reputed author of the *Acta Joannis*, which contains a detailed account of the writing of the
fourth Gospel. The later picture of St Matthew,
which has also suffered from flaking, is a less
forceful composition than its predecessors,
though in the same tradition.

PROVENANCE: Bought by Hunter at the César de Missy sale,
London, 18 March 1776, lot 1638.

BIBLIOGRAPHY: Young & Aitken, pp. 394-395; I.C. Cunningham, *Greek Manuscripts in Scotland*, Edinburgh, 1982, no.
59; Ker, *William Hunter*, p. 15, Appendix A, XVII;
Baldwin, *William Hunter*, p. 7, no. 12.

13. Boethius, The Consolation of Philosophy

Anicius Manlius Torquatus Severinus Boethius,
De consolatione philosophiae.
England, c. 1120-1140.

MS Hunter 279 (U.5.19)

Vellum, 245 × 176 mm.; [ii], 66, [ii] leaves;
written space 171 × 130 mm., 32 long lines, with
marginal and interlinear gloss.

This volume, though sadly mutilated, preserves a
drawing unique amongst Boethius manuscripts
(fol. 45v). It shows Ulysses reaching the safety of
his ship just as his crew are being changed by
Circe's enchantment, not into swine (cf. Homer,
Ovid and Boethius himself), but into a variety of
animals, as had been the fate of her earlier
visitors. The scene illustrates the observation by
Philosophy that a man who abandons goodness
sinks to the level of an animal, which is amplified
with a poem based on the Odyssey recounting
how Ulysses is saved by Hermes from Circe's
curse. The accompanying anonymous commentary looks at the Circe myth from a 'scientific'
point of view, seeing it as an illustration of the
principle of the relationship between all physical
bodies, which enables one to be turned into
another. The draughtsmanship of the composition is remarkably clear, flowing and dramatic;
the animal shapes show the artist's easy familiarity with the fantastic creatures which inhabited
the initials of contemporary manuscripts.

A fragment of another drawing (fol. 31), shows
that the manuscript also contained the common
illustration of Boethius in prison (cf. no. 71).
The only initial to survive, at the beginning of
Book V (fol. 54v), is a penwork 'd' composed of
grotesque animals and birds locked in combat,
surmounted by a stag blowing a horn. Such
mundus inversus images became a repeated subject in manuscript decoration at this period.
Another example in the collection is the picture
of a donkey playing a harp in the Hunterian
Psalter (no. 14), a literary motif quoted by
Philosophy from Greek sources in Book I of the
Consolation.

PROVENANCE: Apparently in Scotland not long after it was
written, to judge from an inscription referring to King
David I (1123-1153) on fol. 20; bought by Hunter at the
Gregory Sharpe sale, London, 8 April 1771, lot 1467.

BIBLIOGRAPHY: Young & Aitken, p. 225; J. Beaumont, 'The
Latin Tradition of De consolatione', in *Boethius*, ed. M.
Gibson, Oxford, 1981, pp. 296-297; D. Bolton, 'Illustra-
tions in Manuscripts of Boethius' Works', ibid., p. 429;
English Romanesque Art, p. 102, Manuscripts no. 32; Ker,
William Hunter, p. 15, Appendix A, XIII.

Ulysses escaping from Circe. MS Hunter, 279, fol. 45v

Initial 'd'. MS Hunter 279, fol. 54v

Pentecost. MS Hunter 229, fol. 15v

14. Psalter

Psalterium.
England, c. 1170.

MS Hunter 229 (U.3.2)

Vellum, 292 × 191 mm.; [iv], 210, [iv] leaves; written space 216 × 95 mm., 21 long lines; miniatures, fols. 1-6, of 12 Labours of the Month and 12 Signs of the Zodiac; full-page pictures, fols. 7v-21v: Creation and Temptation of Adam (fol. 7v); the Expulsion from Eden, Adam delving and Eve spinning (fol. 8); Abraham's Sacrifice of Isaac (fol. 9v); Temptation of Jesus, Raising of Lazarus (fol. 11v); Jesus breaking bread at Emmaus, Jesus appearing to the disciples (fol. 12); Thomas resolving his doubt, Jesus saving Peter on the Sea of Tiberias (fol. 13v); the Ascension (fol. 14); Pentecost (fol. 15v); Christ in Glory, with symbols of the Evangelists (fol. 16); an angel presenting a palm to the Virgin, the Virgin showing the palm to the Apostles (fol. 17v); Death and Funeral of the Virgin (fol. 18); Entombment and Assumption of the Virgin (fol. 19v); King David tuning his Harp (fol. 21v); a full-page Beatus initial, fol. 22; illuminated initials for all psalms and canticles, including 97 historiated initials; gold initial letters to second and subsequent verses of each psalm.

One of a small group of elaborately illuminated 12th-century English psalters, this book is among the most splendid examples of Romanesque art. The volume opens with a Calendar containing a beautifully conceived series of Labours of the Month within each illuminated initial H of the Habet dies, and Signs of the Zodiac in roundels. Between the Calendar and the Psalms are the thirteen full-page pictures which are the chief glory of the work. They illustrate scenes from the Old and New Testaments and give in addition a particularly interesting series illustrating the Assumption of the Virgin. After more than eight centuries these illuminated pages retain their original brilliance and their vivid colours.

The style is a mixture of Byzantine modelling and English linear pattern: thin, flat figures are set against grounds of burnished gold. Less attention is paid to spatial relationship than to surface design, and this extends to the patterns incised in the gold surface, each page having a different design. The 'damp-fold' drapery style (cf. no. 12), which had been popular in England from the 1130s, appears here in a more rigid and stylized version. In harmony with the long faces and staring eyes of the figures, this stylization results in pictures which, with their striking colour schemes, are among the most expressive in English Romanesque art.

(See also Cover Illustration and Colour Ills. 5 and 6)

The appearance in the Calendar of three commemorations of St Augustine, taken with the absence of the translation of St Benedict, suggests that the Psalter was commissioned for use in a house of Augustinian canons, or by an individual connected with that Order. The date of 1170 is likely because of the lack of the commemoration on 29 December of Thomas of Canterbury, who was murdered in 1170 and canonized in 1173. The appearance of several northern saints in the Calendar, while not definitely attributing the Psalter's place of use to a northern or eastern diocese, indicates that it is not specifically southern; the title of 'York Psalter' by which it has previously been known does not exclude the possibility that it was intended for use in, for example, the diocese of Lincoln.

The Psalms themselves are richly decorated with gilt initial letters for every verse. Each Psalm begins with a decorated initial, and Psalms 1, 26, 38, 51, 52, 80, 97, 101 and 109 are particularly large and elaborate. Although the initial for Psalm 68 is lacking, it would certainly have been accorded similar treatment. Thus the Psalter is divided into ten parts, the result of combining a formal division into three parts at Psalms 1, 51 and 101, with the eight-part liturgical division of Psalms 1, 26, 38, 52, 68, 80, 97 and 109. Some of the subjects of the figured initials relate to the Psalms they illustrate, such as the antlered hart for Psalm 41 which begins 'Like as the hart desireth the water-brooks'; others give scenes from the life of David. Less specific illustrations include animals and birds, such as the lion and stork for Psalm 22, a centaur spearing a man armed with a battle-axe for Psalm 77, a monkey peering into a mirror for Psalm 42, and even a donkey accompanying a singing goat on the harp (cf. the stag blowing a horn in the initial in no. 13). Such a combination of types of psalm illustration is not seen in English psalters before this and may reflect the influence of a continental model. The illuminations themselves have close stylistic associations with a contemporary English Psalter that is now in Copenhagen (Kongelige Bibliotek, MS Thott. 143), and it has been suggested that the same artists were responsible for both.

Christ in Glory. MS Hunter 229, fol. 16

BIBLIOGRAPHY: Young & Aitken, pp. 169-174; De Bure, I, p. 16, no. 50; Burlington Fine Arts Club, *Exhibition of Illuminated Manuscripts*, London, 1908, no. 31; New Palaeographical Society, *Facsimiles of Ancient Manuscripts*, First Series, London, 1903-1912, pls. 189-191; E.G. Millar, *English Illuminated Manuscripts from the Xth to the XIIIth Century*, Paris and Brussels, 1926, pp. 41-42; J. Wardrop, 'Early English Illuminated Manuscripts at South Kensington', *Apollo*, 12, 1930, pp. 99-107; F. Wormald, 'The Development of English Illumination in the Twelfth Century', *Journal of the British Archaeological Association*, Third Series, viii, 1943, p. 44; T.S.R. Boase, *English Art, 1100-1216*, Oxford, 1953, pp. 241-243; M. Rickert, *Painting in Britain: the Middle Ages*, London, 1954, p. 98; T.S.R. Boase, *The York Psalter*, London, 1962; *Trésors*, pp. 3-4, no. 6; C.M. Kauffmann, *Romanesque Manuscripts 1066-1190* (A Survey of Manuscripts Illuminated in the British Isles, III), London, 1975, pp. 117-118; P.D. Stirnemann, *The Copenhagen Psalter*, unpublished doctoral thesis, Columbia University, 1976, pp. 160-180; *Treasures*, p. 6, no. 16; *The Hunterian Psalter*, ed. N.R. Thorp, with introductory essays by J.H. Brown and N. Pickwoad, Oxford Microform Publications, 1983; Baldwin, *William Hunter*, p. 1, no. 1; Ker, *William Hunter*, p. 14, Appendix A, VIII; *English Romanesque Art*, p. 127, Manuscripts no. 75

PROVENANCE: Change of ownership in the 13th century marked by the addition of devotional texts and prayers in the final leaves, originally written for a female supplicant, with endings subsequently altered to the masculine plural; apparently in France in the late 16th or early 17th century, when inscriptions in French were added to some of the full-page pictures; bought for Hunter at the Louis-Jean Gaignat sale, Paris, 10 April 1769, lot 50.

Thomas resolving his doubt; Jesus saving Peter on the Sea of Tiberias. MS Hunter 229, fol. 13v

The Ascension. MS Hunter 229, fol. 14

Decorated page with initial for St Mark's Gospel
MS General 1126, fol. 258v

Initial M in original size

15. Bible

Biblia.
France, Paris, workshop of Gautier Lebaube,
second quarter of the 13th century.

MS General 1126

Vellum, 309 × 209 mm.; [i], 323, [i] leaves;
written space 190 × 122/131 mm., in double
columns of 58-63 lines.

The growth of Paris in the 13th century as the
centre of commerce, learning and the court
brought with it the development of the most
extensive book trade in Europe. Increasing pro-
fessionalism led to different crafts being responsible for writing, flourishing and illumination.
Much of the demand, often from the laity, was
for Bibles, particularly following the introduction
of the Vulgate in its one-volume Paris revision,
which was issued about 1220 to standardize this
basic work for the schools.

Of the multiplicity of workshops engaged in
this trade, only a handful have so far been
identified by name. Among them is that of
Gautier Lebaube, active in the late 1230s and
1240s, who is known most exceptionally through
a signed self-portrait in a full-page miniature now
in the Glazier Collection in the Pierpont Morgan
Library, New York. Thirteen of the fifteen
manuscripts so far traced to his workshop are
Bibles; this manuscript adds to their number.

The manuscript has been sadly mutilated –
perhaps in Scotland during the iconoclasm of the
Reformation, for it was in Cambuskenneth
Abbey in the 15th century. Ten whole leaves and
initials on twenty-six others are lost; nonetheless
some eighty remaining initials allow an attribution to Lebaube. The distinctive feature of their
decoration is a novel use of light, bright colours,
including pink, bright red, blue, green, yellow
and white, rather than the red and blue combination of most contemporary work. Animal-headed
birds with body and wings parallel to the initial
and a long tail ending in a tightly-wound coil,
such as that surviving on fol. 1, are another
feature of the Lebaube style; a particular type of
foliate motif with pairs of facing and downturned
leaves is also characteristic.

PROVENANCE: Augustinian Abbey of Cambuskenneth, near
Stirling, in the 15th century, ex-libris on fols. 1 and 3; in
Glasgow University Library by 1691.

BIBLIOGRAPHY: Ker, *MMBL*, II, p. 924; Ker, *Medieval
Libraries*, p. 28; cf. Branner, pp. 72-75 and Appendix VF.

16. Bible

Biblia.

France, Paris, ?Mathurin workshop, 1240-1250.

MS Hunter 338 (U.8.6)

Vellum, 154 × 109 mm.; [ii], 605, [ii] leaves; written area 107 × 71 mm., in double columns of 43 lines; 81 historiated and decorated initials, occasionally heightened with gold or silver, including fol. 1, Jerome; fol. 5, Creation; fol. 259, David; fol. 287, Solomon and Rehoboam; fol. 457, St Matthew; fol. 505, St Paul.

This copy of the Vulgate Bible is written on the finest vellum, allowing the whole of the text to be given in a volume approximately one quarter of the size of the Lebaube Bible (no. 15). Its eighty-one initials are very close in style to those produced by the Mathurin workshop which, like Lebaube's, seems to have specialized in the production of Bibles. Bibles comprise twenty-one of the twenty-five volumes attributed by Branner to the Mathurin workshop, and the majority are of a similar size to this manuscript.

The initials are small and rather cramped, like most of those painted by this workshop. Pink and blue are the dominant colours, the figures simply drawn with flat drapery and firmly outlined in black. With only six initials containing figures, this Bible is similar to the more modestly decorated productions of the Mathurin group, which can otherwise have up to fifty-four historiated initials in the Old Testament alone. Particular features that link this manuscript with the Mathurin workshop are the long necks or tails of grotesques twining around the shaft of the letters (fols. 1, 447, 457, 486, 519v), the shape of their rear legs, the terminal extensions to the initials, and the appearance of pointed swellings at the heads of the letter decorations. A repeated motif in the manuscript, found in many parts of France and England, is a stork holding a grain or a circular object in its upraised beak (fols. 216v, 241, 326v, 471, 549). The faces also, such as that of David (fol. 259), while schematized, have more strength of outline than in much of the ordinary work of the group.

PROVENANCE: Bought by Hunter at the Joseph Smith sale, London, 25th January 1773, lot 188.

BIBLIOGRAPHY: Young & Aitken, pp. 273-274; Ker, *William Hunter*, p. 15, Appendix A, XIV; cf. Branner, pp. 75-77, 184-191, 214-215.

Decorated page with initial L showing St Matthew. MS Hunter 338, fol. 457

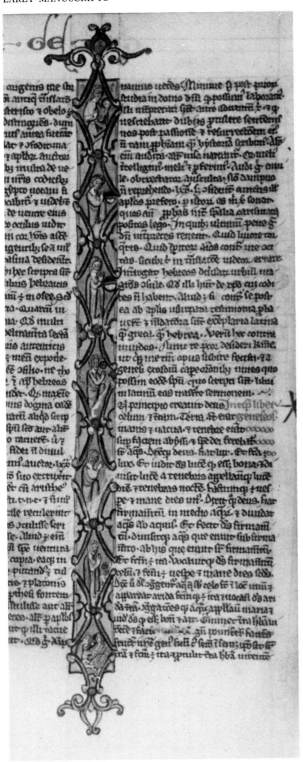

Initial I showing Creation. MS Hepburn 1, fol. 3v *(enlarged)*

17. Bible

Biblia.
France, mid 13th century.

MS Hepburn 1

Vellum, 126 × 91 mm.; [ii], 448, [ii] leaves;
written space 96 × 66 mm., in double columns of
48 lines; 140 historiated and decorated initials.

Even smaller than the previous volume (no. 16),
this is a truly pocket-sized Bible, intended for
private use. It is written on the finest vellum and
weighs only 400 grams. Not all the stages in the
production of a manuscript were necessarily carried out at one time or even in the same place.
Although the text of this copy was written in
France, the historiated and decorated initials
cannot be assigned to any of the identified Parisian workshops, and the unusual decoration of
the Creation page (fol. 3v) may even point to a
German influence. The small size of the historiated and figure initials (mostly about 15mm.
square) makes their treatment inevitably schematic, but their profusion shows a considerable
concern for the harmonious appearance not only
of individual pages but also of the whole volume.

PROVENANCE: Ex-libris inscription of 'Foyraci' of Charente,
1539, fol. 449v; ex-libris of François d'Escoubleau de
Sourdis, Archbishop of Bordeaux 1599-1628, fol. 1; bookplate of James Stewart Geikie, M.D., 19th/20th century;
bequeathed to the Library by Dr C. A. Hepburn in 1971.

BIBLIOGRAPHY: Ker, *MMBL*, II, p. 932.

18. Bible

Biblia.
North-east Italy, third quarter
of the 13th century.

MS Euing 1

Vellum, 200 × 145 mm.; [ii], 365, [ii] leaves;
written space 137 × 87 mm., in double columns
of 57 lines.

The 13th century has been the least studied of all
the periods of Italian illumination, and much
work remains to be done on the currents from
East and West which affected its development –
the influence of Byzantine models, particularly in
the late 12th century, and the contribution of the
new style of French and English work during the
13th century.

The historiated and other decorated initials of
this Bible cannot immediately be connected with
any particular centre, though the use of some
elements, such as the eagle occupying the initial
which introduces St John's Gospel (fol. 313v),
points to the Veneto-Paduan area. In the design
of his portrait initials, the miniaturist has responded to the small space available to him –
generally a square of only 11 or 12 mm. – by
painting chiefly busts or waist-length figures.
The full-length representations of God in the
seven Creation panels (fol. 3) are an exception;
and in one other instance the initial accommo-
dates a whole figure, that of Isaiah (fol. 192v), by
the device of depicting him sleeping with his
knees drawn up to his chin. Faces are characterized by the use of orange dots to colour cheeks
and lips; drapery folds may be either drawn in
ink or painted. The initials are uniformly painted
in a variety of reddish brown colours against a
deep blue background, with decorative white and
orange dots in lines or clusters, and dragons are a
repeated motif.

PROVENANCE: Bequeathed to the Library by William Euing in
1874.

BIBLIOGRAPHY: Ker, *MMBL*, II, pp. 871-872.

Initial I with Creation panels.
MS Euing 1, fol. 3

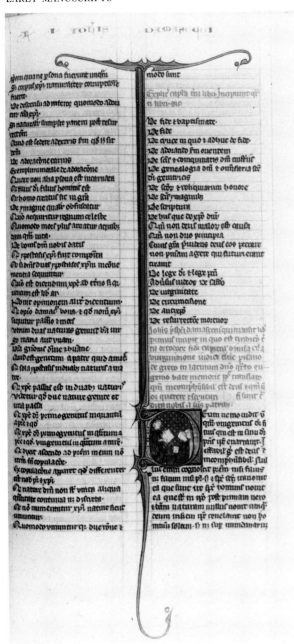

Decorated page with initial D. MS Hunter 369, fol. 69

BIBLIOGRAPHY: Young & Aitken, pp. 295-296; Ker, *William Hunter*, p. 18, Appendix A, XX; cf. Branner, pp. 102-107, 229, 230.

19. Augustine, Treatises, and other works

Aurelius Augustinus, De libero arbitrio, De natura boni, Enchiridion, De spiritu et anima; Johannes Damascenus, Expositio fidei orthodoxae; Gregorius Magnus, Dialogorum libri IV.
France, Paris, Bari workshop, 1255-1265.

MS Hunter 369 (V.1.6)

Vellum, 343 × 226 mm.; [ii], 172, [iv] leaves; written space 238 × 143 mm., in double columns of 49 lines. Works by Lactantius, fols. 165-172, did not form part of the original volume.

Augustine of Hippo (354-430), a Doctor of the Church, was among the most significant figures in the foundation of the Christian tradition of the West. His *Treatise on Free Will*, which begins this compendium, was written in 388, soon after his conversion to Christianity under the influence of Bishop Ambrose of Milan.

There was much demand for such texts in the university circles of Paris in the 13th century, and they were well served by professional scribes and workshops. The essentially linear style of illuminations from the Bari workshop is known from a score of manuscripts identified by Branner, which are for the most part Bibles, Missals and Graduals. The figures have slim shoulders and large heads and are outlined in broad ink lines which are also used to mark the major folds of the drapery, given otherwise in continuous colour. The long nose with its round tip echoes the long face with a rounded chin, and the wide arch of the upper eyelid gives the expression a pronounced stare. The Bari workshop produced initials both with painted and with gold backgrounds. Here, in the first inhabited initial showing Augustine reading to a student (fol. 1), the background is gold; other initials show two angels supporting a representation of the soul (fol. 50), the author and students (fol. 69), and the author dictating to a student or scribe (fol. 114v) and have backgrounds of a finely painted diaper pattern.

Compared with the rather archaic figure forms, the marginal decoration is more progressive and up to date. At important divisions in the text it extends the full height of the written columns and beyond, in alternating sections of red and blue with a variety of white line decorations and gold roundels. The spikes growing out of these uprights, particularly at the terminals, developed over the following decades into the elaborate traceries of the Gothic style.

20. Writings on the Calendar

?Johannes de Saxonia, Kalendarium novum; Johannes de Garlandia, Tabula principalis, Contratabula; Petrus de Dacia, Tabula de loco lunae; Johannes de Saxonia, Computus novus; Anon., De diebus criticis; Gulielmus de Conchis, Dialogus de mundo.
France, Paris, third quarter of the 13th century.

MS Hunter 444 (V.5.14)

Vellum, 250 × 176 mm.; [vii], 48, [vii] leaves; written space 177 × 130 mm., in double columns of 39 lines.

This manuscript contains a collection of works by John of Saxony, John Garland, Peter of Dacia and William of Conches, chiefly on chronology, astronomy and astrology and written in a variety of hands.

The beginning of William of Conches's *Dialogue on the Constitution of the Universe* is marked by a small illuminated initial and an extended framework, with terminals that have sprouted into both leaf shapes and a conventional grotesque (p. 51). The motif of a dog chasing a rabbit or other quarry, again in combination with a grotesque, is found in a psalter produced by the Bari atelier in the late 1250s (London, B.L., Add. MS 17868, fol. 82v) and in a manuscript of Adso's gloss on Justinian of about 1260 (Paris, Bibl. Nat., fr. 22969, fol. 5) from the Johannes Grusch workshop. Terminals with different leaves can be seen in a work from the Cholet group of about the same date (Vienna, National-bibliothek, MS 2315, fol. 100v). While the workshop which produced this manuscript has not yet been identified, its awareness of the new fashions in decoration is indicated by the appearance of old and new motifs side by side.

PROVENANCE: Bought by Hunter at the Joseph Letherland sale, London, 14 March 1765, lot 3539.

BIBLIOGRAPHY: Young & Aitken, pp. 367-368; Ker, *William Hunter*, p. 13, Appendix A, IV; cf. Branner, p. 83, 105, 131.

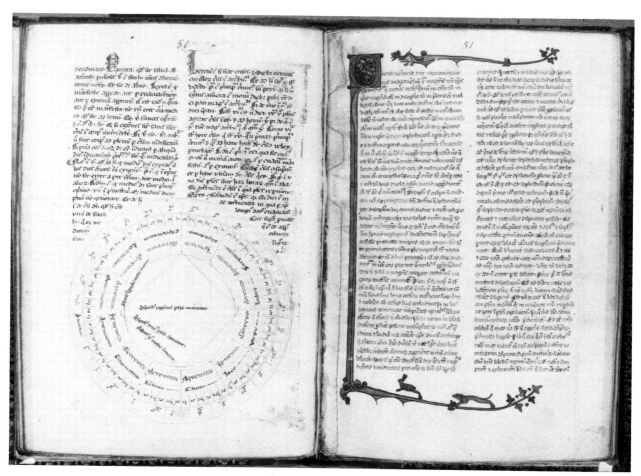

Opening with diagram and decorated page. MS Hunter 444, pp. 50-51

Decorated page. MS Hunter 205, fol. 1
(below): Detail of lower border

21. Seneca, Works

Lucius Annaeus Seneca, Opera.
France, Paris, 1280-1290.

MS Hunter 205 (U.1.9)

Vellum, 368 × 264 mm.; [ii], iii, 191, [iv] leaves; written space 252 × 159 mm., in double columns of 46-47 lines.

In the late 13th century, increasing attention was paid to the framework of historiated and decorated initials, which encouraged a variety of designs incorporating outcrops of foliage and a greater population of birds and animals. During the course of the 14th century, these scenes became larger and more naturalistic, but here the development has only recently begun: the extended stems embracing the text on fol. 1 have grown into a perch for a bird at the top of the page and a bushy space at the bottom where a hunting dog runs after its quarry. The figure initial itself, depicting Seneca instructing a group of students, seems of secondary importance. The illuminator's concern is with these newer motifs: the human face of the grotesque on the frame, for example, is much more finely observed than the faces in the initial, partly because there is not the same restriction on space in the margin as there is in the initial. The spiky boxes on the frame are details which François Avril has noted in other manuscripts of the period (e.g. Paris, Bibl. Nat., fr. 1457 and 1471). The whole page is close to the work of Maître Honoré, the foremost miniaturist in Paris at this period, and is characteristic of the elegance of the Parisian style of the later 13th century.

PROVENANCE: Bought by Hunter from Archibald Dodd, 27 July 1775.

BIBLIOGRAPHY: Young & Aitken, pp. 147-148; Ker, *William Hunter*, p. 21, Appendix A, XXIII; for Maître Honoré see Henry Martin, *Les miniaturistes français*, Paris, 1906, pp. 59-64; for Maître Honoré and Bibl. Nat. fr. 1457, *Roman de César*, see Georg Graf Vitzthum, *Die Pariser Miniaturmalerei von der Zeit des hl. Ludwig bis zu Philipp von Valois*, Leipzig, 1907, pp. 46-47.

22. Bartholomew the Englishman, Treatise on the Properties of Things

Bartholomaeus Anglicus, De proprietatibus rerum.
France, Paris, 1290s.

MS Hunter 391 (V.2.11)

Vellum, 309 × 220 mm.; [ii], 275, [ii] leaves; written space 218 × 139 mm., in double columns of 51 lines.

Though very close in style to the Seneca manuscript (no. 21), the decoration of the first page of this manuscript shows an evolution in terms of fashion. There is the same conservatism in the picture of the author instructing a group of students, which fits the Parisian University milieu. Many of the frame details are almost identical, from the overall design of the columns – thick elements of alternating blue and red alongside a slender stalk which develops into a spiral foliate pattern at the terminal, encased in a spiked and gussetted framework – to the spiky boxes and rose thorns with gold roundels. The terminal leaf forms have, however, become more luxuriant, and the chasing animals are drawn in a less perfunctory way. Particular attention is given to the figure with legs of a beast playing a pipe and drum at the head of the column in the inner margin. The presence of beasts' legs may qualify him for inclusion in the category of grotesque hybrid, but the modelling of form and the flow of his lined clothing and hat create a well-observed drawing that reveals a new sense of three-dimensionality.

Bartholomew the Englishman was a Franciscan friar from Oxford who became professor of theology at the University of Paris. In 1231, he was sent to teach at the Order's house at Magdeburg and, while he was there, he completed his encyclopedia, which he had probably begun in Oxford. This work, devoted to the natural sciences of his time, ranged from theology and medicine to geography and zoology, and was intended as a tool for Biblical and theological students and preachers.

Decorated page. MS Hunter 391, fol. 1
(below): Detail of lower border

PROVENANCE: 15th-century ex-libris of the Abbey of St Louis, Poissy; bought for Hunter at the Count Lauragais sale, Paris, 11 June 1770, lot 187.

BIBLIOGRAPHY: Young & Aitken, pp. 312-313; Meyer, p. 115; Ker, *William Hunter*, pp. 14-15, Appendix A, X.

23. Raymond of Peñafort, Treatise on Penance; Tancred, Treatise on Matrimony; and other works

Raymundus de Pennaforte,
Summa de casibus poenitentiae;
Tancredus, Summa de matrimonio; etc.
?France, mid 13th century.

MS General 339

Vellum, 106 × 74 mm.; i, 290 leaves; written space 79 × 45/50 mm., 30-33 long lines.

Raymond of Peñafort (1175/1180-1275) was confessor, chaplain and Grand Penitentiary to Pope Gregory IX and subsequently Master General of the Dominicans. He had taught at Barcelona and Bologna before he began the massive task of bringing order into the unwieldy collections of decretals (papal rulings on matters of canonical discipline) which had grown up over the centuries. There were a dozen or so of these compilations, which he condensed into a single series, completing the work in 1234. His *Treatise on Penance*, originally written between 1222 and 1229 to provide a handbook for confessors who administered the sacrament of penance, quickly became very popular; it was reissued in 1234 with the addition of Raymond's revision of a treatise on matrimony by his fellow Spaniard, the canonist Tancred (c. 1185-1234/1236). The two works are generally found together, as in this early copy. The volume also contains a number of shorter works added in the later 13th-century: amongst these additions, Sigrid Krämer has identified the *Planctus ante nescia* (fol. 41), as one of the *Carmina Burana*, a collection of love songs, drinking songs, religious poems, lyrics and satires attributed to the wandering scholars and students of Western Europe from the 10th to the 13th centuries.

The coloured drawings on fols. 41v-42 of this manuscript, between the treatise on penance and that on matrimony, are of the tree of vices and the tree of remedies against vices, and may be of German origin. The trunk of the tree of vices is entwined by a snake, labelled 'serpens antiquus', representing temptation, and the schematic leaves bearing the names of the vices hang downwards, except for a row at the top. All the leaves identifying the remedies, however, point upwards. Trees of virtues and vices had been popular for over a century, and were used to illustrate other texts such as the *Speculum virginum* (for an example from Salzburg dating from the second quarter of the 12th century see C. R. Dodwell, *The Canterbury School of Illumination*, Cambridge, 1954, p. 90, pl. 596) and the Apocalypse. A tree of remedies is far less common and tends not to have a fixed content: it was substantially influenced by personal taste.

PROVENANCE: Hunter's source not traced.

BIBLIOGRAPHY: Ker, *MMBL*, II, pp. 912-913.

Tree of Vices and Tree of Remedies. MS General 339, fols. 41v-42
(See also Colour Ill. 8)

24. Medical Writings

Hippocrates, Aphorismi, De ratione victus
in morbis acutis, Prognostica; Theophilus,
De urinis; Claudius Galenus, Ars medicinalis.
Southern France, second half
of the 13th century.

MS Hunter 32 (T.1.1)

Vellum, 395 × 267 mm.; [ii], i, 172, i leaves;
written space 252/277 × 165 mm., in double
columns of 29-73 lines.

This heavily annotated manuscript contains
several works by Hippocrates with extensive
commentaries by Galen, and Galen's own *Art of
Medicine*, again with a commentary. The original
text is written in large letters on alternating lines,
the commentaries in smaller letters on each line.

The decorated initials which begin each section contain similar motifs to those used in
Northern France, such as coiled stems, grotesques, heads, loops terminating in spiky lines, and
gold roundels. The overall effect, however, is in
this case less harmonious; the softer colouring
points to a different tradition and the flat drawing
of the two doctors examining a flask in the
historiated initial (fol. 10) – which is presumably an uroscopy – is unsophisticated. The

medical nature of the texts may point to an origin
connected with the great medical school of Montpellier: the designs and decorations are certainly
provincial and have a southern flavour.

The boards of the binding are covered with
decorated leatherwork cut from larger panels,
which François Avril has identified as the same as
those on a number of volumes in Paris (Bibl.
Nat., fr. 723, 738, 1608, 12444, 12781) which
were included in the sale of the library of the
Château d'Anet, the palace built by Henri II for
Diane de Poitiers. The panels, which may originally have been wall-coverings, have embossed
gilt patterns and large foliate motifs in black
brushwork; they may have been used for bindings by Tanguy du Chastel (who owned fr. 723,
738 and 12781) or Jacques d'Armagnac, duc de
Nemours, who owned the Hunterian volume as
well as one of those in Paris. Other manuscripts
from the Château d'Anet now at Glasgow are
Hunter 373 (no. 50) and General 334 (no. 53),
1125 and 1189.

PROVENANCE: 'Duc de Nemours, conte de la marche', probably Jacques d'Armagnac, 15th-century inscription, fol.
172v; Château d'Anet sale, 1724, mark fol. 1; Hunter's
source not traced.

BIBLIOGRAPHY: Young & Aitken, pp. 31-32; MacKinney, p.
128.

Decorated page. MS Hunter 32, fol. 1

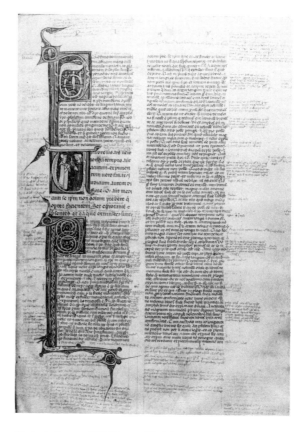

Decorated page. MS Hunter 32, fol. 10

Decorated page. MS General 999, fol. 1

25. Fragment of a Gradual

Graduale.
?Italy, 15th century.

MS General 999

Vellum, 535 × 395 mm.; [i], 10, [i] leaves.

The Gradual was the book containing the complete collection of chants for the Mass. They are amongst the largest books made in the Middle Ages, for they had to be capable of being read at a distance by members of a choir grouped round a single copy.

The fate of many medieval manuscripts, when they survived the circumstantial perils of fire and flood, was to be cut up for other purposes. Many were used in the bindings of newer manuscripts or of printed books, which appeared in growing numbers after the introduction of printing in the mid 15th century. Groups of leaves surviving from such practices are unlikely to have any major decoration intact but can, as here, preserve marginal drawings. Some of the bottom of the drawing was lost when the original volume was trimmed by a binder, which suggests that the drawing was added close to the time of the writing of the manuscript. The scene of Christ's Entry into Jerusalem is a familiar one. It illustrates a phrase in the text immediately above, and has been executed with a certain naive charm. James Dickson has noted that the cutting instrument wielded by the two men in what are doubtless meant to be olive trees is of interest because it was specifically designed for shredding newly sprouted shoots for animal fodder.

PROVENANCE: Not traced.

BIBLIOGRAPHY: Ker, *MMBL*, II, p. 915.

II · England

26. Statutes of the Realm

Statuta Angliae, in Latin and French.
England, ?London, first half of the 14th century.

MS General 336

Vellum, 105 × 70 mm.; [i], v, 214, ii, [ii] leaves; written space 74 × 40 mm., 20 long lines.

This pocket copy of the laws of England from Magna Carta (1215) to the reign of Edward III (1312-1377) was doubtless written for an itinerant lawyer. The last statute entered, as an addition, dates from the early 1350s, some ten years before Edward ordered that the use of French in the courts should be discontinued.

The collection is prefaced by two illuminated pages, a Crucifixion and a picture of an enthroned king: the conjunction of Church and State. The Crucifixion is close to a type found in a group of Fenland psalters of the early 14th century – the Peterborough Psalter in Brussels (Bibl. Royale, MS 9661-62, fol. 56v), the Ramsay Psalter (part in New York, Pierpont Morgan Library, MS M. 302, fol. 3) and the Gough Psalter (Oxford, Bodleian Library, MS Gough Liturg. 8, fol. 61).

Here the composition focuses on the central figures of Christ, the Virgin and St John, the chief identifying features being the posture of Christ, with straight fingers, the loin-cloth falling away from the rise of the abdomen and contorted legs, and the gesture of each of the bystanders holding one hand to a cheek. The wavy lines on the surface of the Cross are common to all these examples, as is the treatment of the drapery in, for instance, the folds at the waist; the decoration of the nimbus of Christ and that of Mary is also very close, as well as the more common edging of white dots and lines to the neck, sleeve and hem of a garment. Points tooled into the surface of the gold, more numerous in the other psalters, appear here in clusters of four. A curious feature of St John is the apparent substitution of a Roman hairstyle for the conventional curled and flowing locks of hair, but there is evidence of redrawing at this point.

The profile portrait of the king on the facing page has also been slightly redrawn. It may be compared with the more usual three-quarter view in, for example, contemporary volumes of statutes in Oxford (Bodleian Library, MS Rawl. C. 292 of c. 1320 and MS Rawl. C. 454; see O. Pächt and J.J.G. Alexander, *Illuminated Manuscripts in the Bodleian Library*, Oxford, III, Oxford, 1973, nos. 576 and 602).

PROVENANCE: Peter Bales, inscription fol. iii (perhaps the writing master, 1547-?1610); donated to the Library by Aeneas Macleod, 1786.

BIBLIOGRAPHY: Ker, *MMBL*, II, pp. 910-911; cf. L.F. Sandler, *The Peterborough Psalter in Brussels and other Fenland Manuscripts*, London, 1974, pp. 28, 41, 54, 57, 108-121; eadem, *Gothic Manuscripts*, II, pp. 45-49, nos. 40-42.

Crucifixion and Enthroned King. MS General 336, fols. 9v-10

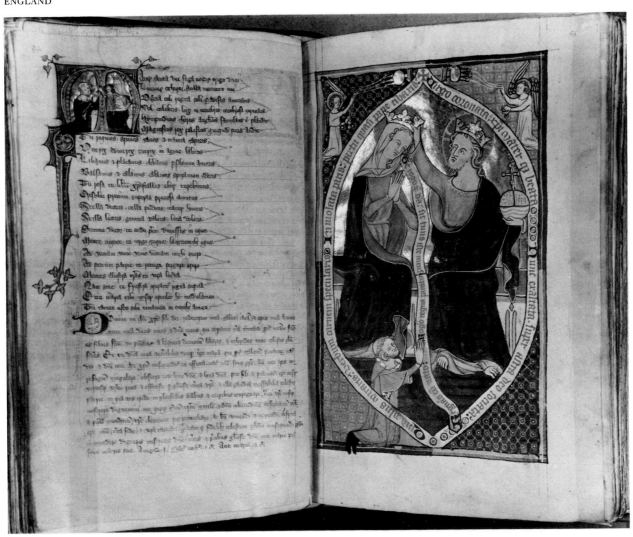

Opening with Coronation of the Virgin. MS Hunter 231, pp. 82-83
(See also Colour Ill. 9)

Plato, Seneca and Aristotle. Detail from MS Hunter 231, p. 276

27. Devotional and Philosophical Writings

Anselmus, Orationes; Aurelius Augustinus,
Invocatio Spiritus Sancti, De assumptione
Beatae Virginis Mariae; Lucius Annaeus Seneca,
De septem artibus liberalibus,
De quatuor virtutibus cardinalibus, etc.
England, London, c. 1325-1335, illuminated by
the chief artist of the Taymouth Hours.

MS Hunter 231 (U.3.4)

Vellum, 295 × 189 mm.; [ii], iv, 243 (paginated
as 486), [iii] leaves; written space
243 × 138 mm., 37 long lines.

In this very personal compilation of thirty-eight
texts, six texts are from St Augustine, fourteen
are by or attributed to Seneca and ten are anonymous. It was made for Roger of Waltham, Canon
of St Paul's, London, and possibly Keeper of the
Wardrobe of Edward II. Roger is named as the
supplicant not only in two of the thirteen historiated initials but also in two of the full-page
pictures. It was exceptional for such a collection
of philosophical texts to contain illustrations in
the 14th century, and the choice of their subject
matter can be assumed to have been agreed with
Roger, if not indeed actually selected by him. He
is known to have compiled another collection of
works on moral philosophy based mainly on
Seneca (e.g. London, B.L., Royal MS 8.G.VI).

The first of the three full-page pictures is of the
Coronation of the Virgin (p. 83), a scene found in
a number of psalters of the period. While the
grouping of the figures of Christ and the Virgin is
standard, there is some variety in the detail of
Christ's action: he may be seen holding the
Virgin's crown with both hands, or placing the
crown with one hand while holding a book in the
other, or (as here) holding an orb representing
the world. Among the closest to the Hunterian
manuscript, both in iconography and style, is the
Peterborough Psalter, or Psalter of Hugh of
Stukeley, of the early 14th-century (Cambridge,
Corpus Christi College, MS 53), where angels
with censers accompany the scene. In none,
however, is there any scroll bearing a text, as in

this case; a less lengthy scroll would have been
sufficient for the purpose of mentioning Roger by
name.

The two other remarkable full-page pictures
are very different. One is in three compartments
(p. 85), depicting (1) the face of God with angels
bearing the soul of Bishop Germanus; (2) St
Benedict and St Paul contemplating the Creator;
and (3) Roger and another figure praying on
either side of a diagram of the twelve spheres.
The other (p. 276) presents portraits of Plato and
Aristotle flanking Seneca, all of them seated and
holding open books. The style of painting and
decoration, from the incised patterns in the gold
ground to the presence of a simple pattern of
three leaves at the outer corners of the frame, is
very close to that of the Trinity picture in an
early 14th-century Book of Hours in Cambridge
(Grey-Fitzpayn Hours, Fitzwilliam Museum,
MS 242, fol. 28v). Particularly noticeable in both
manuscripts is the staring face of God, strongly
echoed in this volume in the figures of Seneca
and Aristotle. Despite the variations in the overall design between the three full-page pictures,
they are clearly the work of a single artist,
identified by Lucy Sandler as the chief hand in
the Taymouth Hours (London, B.L., Yates
Thompson MS 13). Because of Roger's association with the Court, it is likely that this artist
worked in London. The major pictures and the
minor initials offer a fascinating example of his
range of treatment, subject matter and decorative
design.

Exceptionally for its time, the writing on this
manuscript starts on each page above the top
line, a practice that was generally discontinued
from about 1230.

PROVENANCE: Made for Roger of Waltham, d. c.1336;
Andrew Bridge, 17th century; bought by Hunter from
Thomas Osborne, c.1768.

BIBLIOGRAPHY: Young & Aitken, pp. 176-183; Ker, *William
Hunter*, p. 18, Appendix A, XX; Sandler, *Gothic Manu-
scripts*, II, pp. 109-110, no. 99; for Cambridge, Corpus
Christi College, MS 53, and Cambridge, Fitzwilliam
Museum, MS 242, see ibid., pp. 73-75, no. 66 and pp. 36-
37, no. 31.

28. Writings on Alchemy

Anon., Synonima alchemiae; Mappae clavicula; Gulielmus de Furnivall, Opus de arsenico sublimato; Albertus Magnus, Semita recta; Anon., De salibus, De divinatione; Albertus Magnus, De secreto philosophorum.
England, late 14th century.

MS Hunter 110 (T.5.12)

Vellum, 226 × 257 mm.; [i], iv, 74, i, [i] leaves; written space 172/184 × 125 mm., fols. 1-9 and 70-74 in double columns of 50-52 lines, the remainder 42-48 long lines.

The medieval fascination with transmutation, whether of bodies – as seen in the Boethius commentary (no. 12) – or of the inanimate stuff of nature, produced many compilations dealing with the properties of matter and the means of changing them. A furnace was an essential piece of equipment in this search, and several models are illustrated in this copy of Albertus Magnus's *Straight Path in the Art of Alchemy*. These simple diagrams give an example of illustrative work in a technical sphere far removed from that of the grander illuminated volumes of the time.

PROVENANCE: Hunter's source not traced.

BIBLIOGRAPHY: Young & Aitken, pp. 111-112.

Illustrated page with furnaces. MS Hunter 110, fol. 28

29. John Gower, Vox Clamantis, etc.

John Gower, Vox clamantis, Chronica tripertita, Carmina minora, Traitié.
England, c. 1400.

MS Hunter 59 (T.2.17)

Vellum, 299 × 191 mm.; [ii], 132, [ii] leaves; written space 244 × 130 mm., 51-53 long lines.

'Moral Gower', as Chaucer calls him in *Troilus and Criseide*, used the Peasants' Revolt of 1381 in his *Vox clamantis* to describe the faults of the various classes of society. The earlier portion contains a vivid account of the uprising in the form of an allegory; the remainder is a version in Latin of the strictures that he had already made in a 30,000-line poem in French, the *Speculum meditantis*.

In this copy of the revised version of the *Vox clamantis* and *Chronica tripertita*, the text is preceded by a full-page representation of the author firing his shafts at the world (fol. 6v). This globe is composed of the elements of air, earth and water in three compartments – a highly stylized form of pink clouds against a blue sky for air, a segment of green with scattered blades of grass drawn in black, like the ground on which the archer is standing, for earth, and a segment with rippling waves for water (cf. the globe in the Coronation of the Virgin in no. 27). The picture has been identified by Kathleen Scott as the work of an artist who painted the same scene in another copy of Gower's *Chronicle* (London, B.L., Cotton Tiberius A.IV, fol. 9); other versions are present in a copy of the *Vox clamantis* in Oxford (Bodleian Library, MS Laud Misc. 719) and in another manuscript in San Marino (Huntington Library, HM 150; see Scott, *Later Gothic Manuscripts*, forthcoming).

A second illustration (fol. 129) includes a shield with the Gower arms supported by two flying angels, with a cloth-covered bier at the foot of the page; Gower did not die, however, until 1408, some years after this manuscript was written. There seems also to have been another illustration on fol. 131v but its details have been lost.

PROVENANCE: Bought for Hunter at a sale at Mechlen, 1770.

BIBLIOGRAPHY: Young & Aitken, pp. 64-68; G. C. Macaulay, *The Complete Works of John Gower*, IV, Oxford 1902, pp. lxii-lxiii; J.H. Fisher, *John Gower: Moral Philosopher and Friend of Chaucer*, London, 1965, p. 306, no. 51; *New CBEL*, I, col. 553; A. I. Doyle and M. B. Parkes, 'The Production of Copies of the Canterbury Tales and the Confessio amantis in the early fifteenth century', in *Medieval Scribes, Manuscripts and Libraries. Essays presented to N. R. Ker*, London, 1978, p. 164, n. 3; Ker, *William Hunter*, p. 15, Appendix A, XII.

The author firing his shafts at the world. MS Hunter 59, fol. 6v

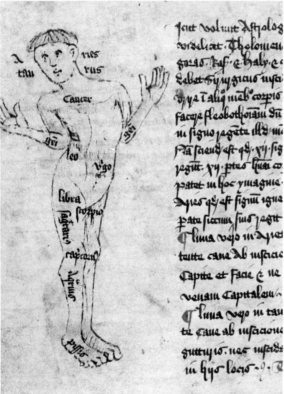

30. John of Arderne, Mirror of Phlebotomy, and Practice of Surgery

Johannes Arderne, Speculum phlebotomiae, Practica chirurgiae.
England, late 14th or early 15th century.

MS Hunter 112 (T.5.14)

Vellum, 233 × 154 mm.; [ii],1-92, [i], 93-101, [iii] leaves; written space 188 × 110 mm.

Arderne, of Newark in Nottinghamshire, was surgeon to the royal household and to the army for much of the middle years of the 14th century, and may have developed his skills on active service with the armies during the Hundred Years' War. He was born in 1307 and died some time after issuing, in 1376, this treatise on the cure of anal fistula, one of the deadliest operations in medieval surgery. Thought to have lost only half of his fistula patients, he was considered a remarkably successful surgeon; his great advance at the time was to avoid the corrosive after-care treatment used by other practitioners.

In other respects, Arderne was more traditional, practising astrology for the prevention of ailments, diagnosis, treatment and prognostication of the outcome. His treatise on surgery includes the best examples from the Middle Ages of diagrams of instruments and of treatments to be effected, closely coordinated with the text. The unusual frontispiece with which this copy begins (fol. 1v) shows a physician with a medicine box and ladle sitting within a fence enclosing a herb garden. The rather rudimentary drawing of this picture and of the illustrations throughout the volume probably points to a provincial origin.

PROVENANCE: Charles Bernard, 1650-1711; Hunter's source not traced.

BIBLIOGRAPHY: Young & Aitken, pp. 113-114; John Arderne, *Treatises of Fistula in Ano, Haemorrhoids, and Clysters*, ed. D'Arcy Power, London, 1910, (Early English Text Society O.S. 139) pp. xxxiv-xxxv; MacKinney, p. 128; P.M. Jones, '"Sicut hic depingitur...": John of Arderne and English Medical Illustration in the 14th and 15th centuries', *Die Kunst und das Studium der Natur vom 14. zum 16. Jahrhundert*, ed. W. Prinz and A. Beyer, Weinheim, 1987, pp. 103-126, 379-392; cf. P. M. Jones, *Medieval Medical Miniatures*, London, 1984, pp. 69-71.

Frontispiece; Zodiac man, MS Hunter 112, fols. 1v and 48v

31. John of Arderne, Mirror of Phlebotomy, and Practice of Surgery

Johannes Arderne, Speculum phlebotomiae, Practica chirurgiae.
England, second quarter of the 15th century.

MS Hunter 251 (U.4.9)

Vellum, 251 × 175 mm.; [iv], 103, ii, [iii] leaves; written space 174 × 109 mm., 38 long lines.

This is a later and more elaborately decorated copy of the works of the leading English surgeon of the 14th century (see no. 30). One of the chief drawings illustrates the twelve Signs of the Zodiac influencing the various areas of the body, from Aries for the head and face to Pisces for the feet; it was a caution to surgeons not to operate or let blood when the moon was in the house influencing the affected part. This system of celestial domination seems to have been inherited from Greek traditions, and was already standardized by the early years of the Christian era.

Drawings of Zodiac men are likely to date from at least the time of Roman Egypt and are found in hundreds of medical manuscripts. Many (cf. no. 30, fol. 48v) are rudimentary drawings in pen and wash, with the Zodiac signs merely written in; others, as here, show the artist at his most skilful.

PROVENANCE: Richard Nix or Nykke (?1447-1535), Bishop of Norwich from 1501, who also owned MS Hunter 117, a Middle English collection of medical receipts from the 14th century; ?Dr Richard Mead (d. 1754); Hunter's source not traced.

BIBLIOGRAPHY: Young & Aitken, pp. 201-202; John Arderne, *Treatises of Fistula in Ano, Haemorrhoids, and Clysters*, ed. D'Arcy Power, London, 1910 (Early English Text Society O.S. 139), p. xxiv; John Arderne, *De arte phisicale et de cirurgia*, trans. D'Arcy Power, Wellcome Historical Medical Museum, Research Studies in Medical History, no. 1, 1922; A.B. Emden, *A Bibliographical Register of the University of Oxford to A.D. 1500*, II, Oxford, 1958, p. 1382; *Trésors*, p. 15, no. 24; MacKinney, p. 128; Ker, *William Hunter*, p. 27, Appendix C; cf. H. Bober, 'The Zodiacal Miniature of the Très Riches Heures of the Duke of Berry: its sources and meaning', *Journal of the Warburg and Courtauld Institutes*, 11, 1948, pp. 1-34; P. M. Jones, *Medieval Medical Miniatures*, London, 1984, pp. 69-71.

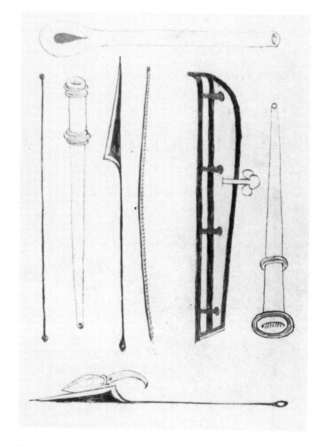

Zodiac man; surgical instruments. MS Hunter 251, fols. 47v and 43

Decorated page. MS Hunter 215, fol. 1

Decorated page (detail) with portrait of a bishop.
MS Hunter 215, fol. 150

BIBLIOGRAPHY: Young & Aitken, pp. 158-159; *The Cartulary of Holy Trinity, Aldgate*, ed. G.A.J. Hodgett, London, 1971 (London Record Society Publications, 7); Ker, *William Hunter*, p. 14, Appendix A, VII; Baldwin, *William Hunter*, pp. 4-5, no. 7.

32. Aldgate Cartulary

Cartularium Prioratus Sanctae Trinitatis
infra Aldgate.
England, London, written by
Thomas de Axbridge, 1425-1427.

MS Hunter 215 (U.2.6)

Vellum, 338 × 236 mm.; [vi], 208, [i] leaves; written space 236 × 162 mm., 39-42 long lines.

This volume of charters of the Priory of the Holy Trinity in Aldgate, London, was written by Brother Thomas de Axbridge. In the introduction he explains that one of the reasons he made it was in order to facilitate the collection of rents, for, he says, 'the world has progressed to such evil and contradicts ancient facts unless copies of charters are everywhere produced in evidence'. The Priory was founded in 1108 by Queen Matilda, Consort of Henry I: acting on the advice of Archbishop Anselm, she entrusted the control of the Priory to her confessor, Norman, said to have been the first Augustinian in England. With its detailed record of leases, agreements, rentals and the like, the cartulary provides a wealth of information, not only on the social and economic life of medieval London, but also on its topography and changing land use.

The certainty of its dating also makes this cartulary valuable for the history of English illumination. Two artists can be distinguished in the painted initials, both working in broadly the same style, but with some variation. The first artist, who was a little old-fashioned for the time, painted the elaborate decoration on the opening page (fol. 1): an initial with the Scutum Dei Triangulum provides a statement of the doctrine of the Trinity, and a crown recalling the Priory's royal foundation is decorated with leaves in tones of the same colours and with penwork sprays terminating in gold discs and other shapes. This hand also painted the initials on the following eight pages and on fol. 179. The colours of the second artist, who painted the border and initials on fols. 149-150, are less rich (or perhaps his preparation of pigments has not allowed them to survive so well), but his flower-forms are more inventive. In addition to hanging an anachronistic shield with the arms of Edward the Confessor on to the frame, he also includes a careful portrait of a young bishop (fol. 150).

PROVENANCE: Stephen Batman, 16th century; John Anstis, London, in 1713; bought at his sale, 12 December 1768, lot 511, by Thomas Astle; acquired by Hunter probably in the 1770s.

33. The Mirrour of the Blessed Lyf of Jesu Christ, and other works

Pseudo-Bonaventura, Meditationes vitae Christi, translated into English by Nicholas Love; A shorte tretice of the hiest and most worthi sacrament of Cristes blessed body and the merveyles ther of; Adam Cartusienses, Soliloquium de instruccio anime.

England, York, c. 1430-1440.

MS General 1130

Vellum, 294 × 202 mm.; [i], 145, [i] leaves; written space 200 × 125 mm., 30 long lines.

This manuscript contains conventional leaf and spraywork decoration in red, blue, green and yellow. The illuminated initial on fol. 142 reproduces the arms of Robert, Lord Willoughby of Eresby; it introduces a treatise on the sacrament, Adam the Carthusian's *Soliloquium*, and may suggest a connection with Axholme or Beauvale Charterhouse. Kathleen Scott has proposed that the illumination was done in the same York shop and possibly by the same illuminator who produced a Book of Hours of York Use (York Minster Library, MS XVI.K.6). The dialect features of the text are those of Nottinghamshire.

The main text is a devotional *Life of Christ* in a free translation of sections of the *Meditationes vitae Christi*, which has been attributed variously to St Bonaventura, the Augustinian Cardinal Bonaventura Baduarius, and to Joannes Gorus. The development of the Gospel harmony, or *Life of Christ*, had been encouraged in earlier centuries by orders forbidding the lay reading of the Bible itself, for example in 1229 at the Council of Toulouse. In 1408, Archbishop Arundel prohibited the reading of English Bibles without episcopal licence and two years later authorized this substitute, which became, according to Margaret Deanesley, 'probably more popular than any other single book in the 15th century'. Nicholas Love (d. 1424), who made the English version before 1410, was Prior of the Carthusian house of Mountgrace de Ingleby, Yorkshire.

PROVENANCE: Robert, Lord Willoughby of Eresby (1409-1452); in the Library before 1691.

BIBLIOGRAPHY: Ker, *MMBL*, II, p. 925; L. F. Powell, *The Mirrour of the Blessed Lyf of Jesu Christ*, Oxford, 1908 (Roxburghe Club); E. Salter, 'The Manuscripts of Nicholas Love's Myrrour of the Blessed Lyf of Jesu Christ and related texts', in *Middle English Prose: Essays on Bibliographical Problems*, ed. A. S. G. Edwards and D. Pearsall, London, 1981, p. 124; A.I. Doyle, 'Reflections on some Manuscripts of Nicholas Love's *Myrrour of the Blessed Lyf of Jesu Christ*', *Leeds Studies in English*, N.S. 14, 1983, pp. 82-93, at p. 87; cf. M. Deanesley, 'Vernacular Books in England in the Fourteenth and Fifteenth Centuries', *Modern Language Review*, 15, 1920, pp. 353-354.

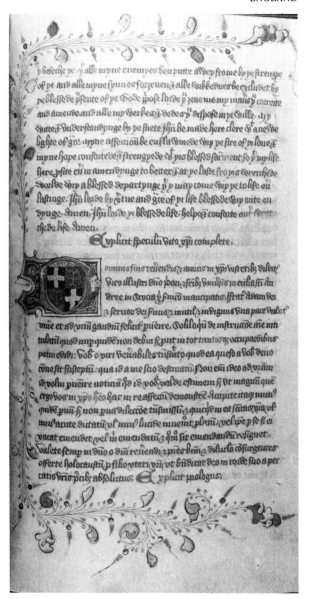

Decorated page. MS General 1130, fol. 142

34. Pietro de' Crescenzi, Treatise on the Advantages of Country Life

Petrus de Crescentiis, Libri ruralium commodorum XI.
England, mid 15th century, style of border probably London.

MS Hunter 75 (T.3.13)

Vellum, 285 × 192 mm.; [ii], 190, [ii] leaves; written space 214 × 140 mm., 35 long lines.

The elaborate illumination in this volume has much in common with the decorative work in the Aldgate cartulary (no. 32). A similar frame of red, blue and gold (fol. 1v) is festooned with heavily lobed leaves in the same tones. The pen spraywork has, however, taken on more precise botanical forms: in addition to green terminals, gold discs and coloured petal shapes, there are clover-leaves, barbed cinquefoils, daisy buds and a spray of bell-shaped flowers (perhaps inspired by the bellflower genus campanula), giving the text an appropriately rural setting. The emphasis on bells is explained by the name of Belton or Beltun which occurs in two of the corner-pieces of the frame and in many of the decorations preceeding each book of the work, where other motifs from the frame also reappear: the bell hanging from the frame, with a barrel, or tun, in its mouth, is itself an elaborate punning representation of the name. Such a rebus is not uncommon in ownership inscriptions but is very rarely encountered in a border, as here: Kathleen Scott notes the example of the Prayerbook of Abbot Islip, with borders containing eyes and slips (Manchester, John Rylands University Library, MS Lat. 1165). The coat of arms, which includes three sheep-bells pendent (or) on a bend dexter (sable), could indicate that the book was intended for a private owner named Belton; but corporate ownership, such as that of the Priory of Grace Dieu at Belton, Lincolnshire, may also be possible.

Pietro de' Crescenzi (c. 1233-c. 1320), a native of Bologna, wrote his agricultural encyclopedia between 1304 and 1309; it became the most important treatise on agronomy of the Middle Ages. While he refers frequently to classical and later writers, including Palladius, Pliny the Elder and Avicenna, his work is based on a lifetime of personal experience. The intended audience was not so much landed aristocrats as the newly-emergent *borghesi* investing their wealth in farms and country estates, who could refer to this practical guide for information on matters from arboriculture to falconry and from fishing to veterinary science. The work is dedicated to Aimerico Giliani da Piacenza, Master General of the Dominicans, and to Charles II of Sicily; it continued in use until the 16th century.

PROVENANCE: 'Belton' or 'Beltun' (?family of this name); E. Mompesson, 1560; bought by Hunter at the Joseph Ames sale, London, 5 May 1760, lot 839.

BIBLIOGRAPHY: Young & Aitken, pp. 82-83; Ker, *William Hunter*, p. 13, Appendix A, II.

Decorated opening. MS Hunter 75, fols. 1v-2

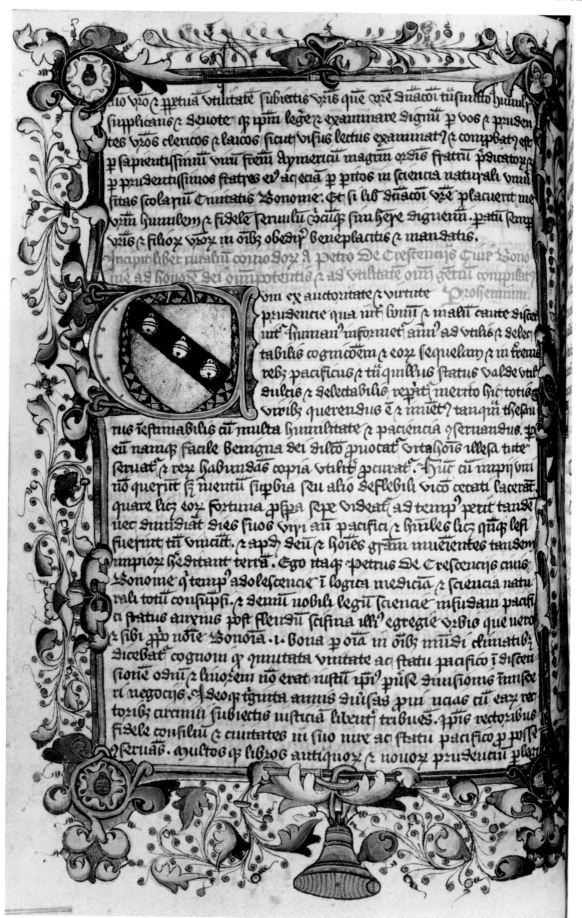

Decorated page. MS Hunter 75, fol. 1v

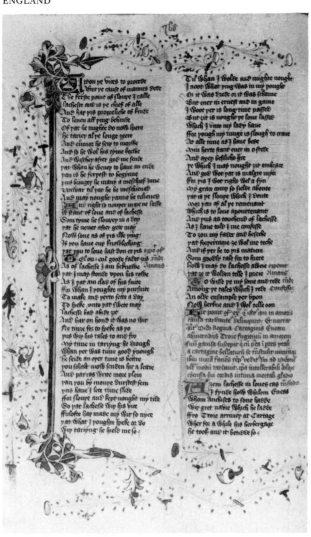

Decorated page. MS Hunter 7, fol. 65v

35. John Gower, Confessio amantis

England, second quarter of the 15th century.

MS Hunter 7 (S.1.7)

Vellum, 417 × 284 mm.; [ii], ii, 181, [i] leaves; written space 282 × 186 mm., in double columns of 46 lines.

Although he wrote extensively in French and Latin (see no. 29), Gower's chief claim to fame as a poet rests on this work in English, in which he displays his gifts as a storyteller. Completed in its first version in 1390, when Gower was around 60, it is a lover's account of his confession to Genius, the priest of Venus, under headings supplied by the seven deadly sins: these are illustrated by tales in which the general nature of the sin is described together with the particular forms it may take in a lover. The poet ultimately receives absolution and is dismissed from the service of Venus, for which his age makes him unfit. If a 17th-century inscription in the book indicating that it was owned by the Benedictine Abbey of Bury St Edmunds is correct, this is likely to be the copy which was read by John Lydgate (cf. no. 41).

The decorative scheme in the volume was for the beginning of each book to be marked by an illuminated and decorated page. The fact that some of these pages are lost may mean that they included miniatures as well. The floral and leaf motifs of the surviving decorated pages, more stylized than those in the contemporary Chaucer manuscript (no. 36), are in the same style as the spraywork of many of the borders in a Book of Hours and Psalter in New York (Pierpont Morgan Library, M. 893, datable before 1446), and Kathleen Scott has suggested that it may be from the same shop.

PROVENANCE: ?Abbey of Bury St Edmunds (17th-century inscription, fol. iv: '...This book as I was told by the Gent: who presented it to me did originally belong to the Abby of Bury in Suffolk.'); bought by Hunter at an anonymous sale, London, 2 April 1770.

BIBLIOGRAPHY: Young & Aitken, pp. 10-11; G. C. Macaulay, *The Complete Works of John Gower*, II, Oxford, 1901, pp. cxliv-cxlv; Ker, *Medieval Libraries*, p. 350 (index entry only); J.H. Fisher, *John Gower: Moral Philosopher and Friend of Chaucer*, London, 1965, p. 304, no. 11; *New CBEL*, I, col. 553; R. M. Thomson, 'The Library of Bury St Edmunds in the eleventh and twelfth centuries', *Speculum*, 47, 1972, p. 618 n. 3; Ker, *William Hunter*, p. 14, Appendix A, IX; for copies of the *Confessio Çäamantis* containing miniatures see K.L. Scott, 'Lydgate's Lives of Saints Edmund and Fremund: a newly-located manuscript in Arundel Castle', *Viator*, 13, 1982, pp. 337-338, n. 8.

36. Geoffrey Chaucer, The Romaunt of the Rose

England, c. 1440-1450.

MS Hunter 409 (V.3.7)

Vellum, 273 × 201 mm.; [v], 150, i, [iii] leaves; written space 145 × 90 mm., 24 long lines.

Guillaume de Lorris's poem on the Art of Love was one of the most popular of all poems in the Middle Ages. Probably written in the first half of the 13th century, it is an allegory of courtly love designed for the amusement of an aristocratic audience; the long continuation by Jean de Meung, written about 1275-1280, includes numerous digressions covering virtually the whole field of medieval thought, from satires on women to discussions on the physical sciences and the relationship between nature and art.

Less than a third of the Middle English translation of the poem has survived. The Hunterian manuscript is the only extant copy and is itself incomplete. A version of the text printed by W. Thynne in 1532 was used by Max Kalusa in his edition to complete passages lacking in the manuscript. Although the question of the authorship of the translation has caused considerable argument, it has become generally accepted that Chaucer wrote the first section of what remains, to line 1705, and that this was completed before he left for Italy in 1372.

The Glasgow manuscript was copied some decades after Chaucer's death in 1400. Elegantly decorated with gilt letters and floral sprays throughout, it contains one particularly ornate page with an abundance of floral designs, chiefly of Lords-and-Ladies or Cuckoo Pint (fol. 57v). This flower is an appropriate accompaniment to a poem on love, and the artist has made exuberant play with its suggestive appearance, which is depicted with even greater bravura than the blooms in the Crescenzi (no. 34).

PROVENANCE: Bought by Hunter at the Thomas Martin sale, 18 May 1774, lot 240.

BIBLIOGRAPHY: Young & Aitken, pp. 329-331; M. Kaluza, *Chaucer und der Rosenroman*, Berlin, 1893; *The Romaunt of the Rose*, ed. M. Kaluza, London, 1891; J.E. Wells, *A Manual of the Writings in Middle English 1050-1400*, New Haven, 1916, pp. 648-650; R. Sutherland, *The Romaunt of the Rose and Le roman de la rose*, Oxford, 1967; *New CBEL*, I, cols. 557-559; Ker, *William Hunter*, p. 15, Appendix A, XVI; Baldwin, *William Hunter*, p. 2, no. 2; for the powers attributed to Lords-and-Ladies see C.T. Prime, *Lords and Ladies*, London, 1960.

Decorated page. MS Hunter 409, fol. 57v
(See also Colour Ill. 10)

37. Book of Hours, and Psalter

Kalendarium, Horae, Psalterium.
England, mid 15th century.

MS Hunter 268 (U.5.8)

Vellum, 225 × 156 mm.; [ii], ii, 164, iv, [ii] leaves; written space 137 × 85 mm., 27 long lines.

The rich ornamentation of this book includes whole-page illuminated frames with fine leafwork and flower forms in pink, blue, orange and green, heightened with white and yellow. Gold is used extensively, with gilt letters and sprays on almost every page, in addition to the frame bars and the backgrounds of the large seven- and eight-line initials at the major divisions of the text. Although the repertory of motifs is conventional, the vigorously executed work is of a high standard.

The Book of Hours is of the Use of Sarum. Nicholas Rogers has noted that it contains the Hours of the Name of Jesus, a rare text, of which there is a copy also in another roughly contemporary English Book of Hours in Oxford (Bodleian Library, MS Dugdale 47).

PROVENANCE: Anthony Cope of Bedhampton, Hampshire, inscription dated 1553; Hunter's source not traced.

BIBLIOGRAPHY: Young & Aitken, pp. 214-216.

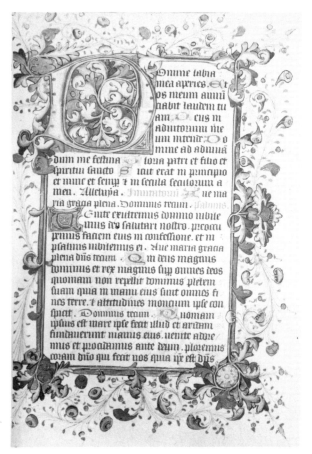

38. Lactantius, Treatises

Lucius Caecilius Firmianus Lactantius,
De ira Dei, De opificio Dei.
England, written by Thomas Candour, mid 15th century.

MS Hunter 274 (U.5.14)

Vellum, 240 × 180 mm.; [i], ii, 72, viii, [i] leaves; written space 153 × 101 mm., 24-25 long lines.

The illuminated initials in this manuscript are completely at variance with contemporary English tradition. The flower forms, the colouring of red, blue and green and the spray penwork terminating in coloured dots or wheat-ear and trefoil gold ornamentation betray its English ancestry, but the character has quite changed. The letters, rather than the background, are in gold; the background, coloured in compartments of red and blue and sometimes green, is enlivened with clusters of triple white dots. The rather heavy luxuriance of conventional English decoration of the period is replaced by a gay, disciplined elegance proclaiming the overriding influence of Renaissance Italy. The vine-scroll or white-vine design is directly copied from the Italian style of illumination, perhaps from a manuscript brought to England from Italy.

These initials are found especially in manuscripts written by the scribe Thomas Candour of Shrewsbury and may therefore have been executed for him. According to Kathleen Scott, the style of the spray surrounding the initials goes back to the early 1420s in English manuscripts, so that this manuscript and its fellows (e.g. a volume in Oxford of works by Poggio and other humanists, Bodleian Library, MS Bodley 915; cf. O. Pächt and J.J.G. Alexander, *Illuminated Manuscripts in the Bodleian Library, Oxford*, III, Oxford, 1973, p. 94, no. 1088) may indeed represent a second generation in the shop to which Candour perhaps repeatedly took his books for decoration. Together with Candour's humanistic script, the initials are evidence of the long periods that he spent in Italy: he was with the Papal Curia in Florence in 1442, became a Doctor of Canon Law at Padua in 1446 and seems to have spent most of the time between 1447 and 1452 in Rome. He later returned to England and died in 1476 or 1477.

PROVENANCE: Bought by Hunter at the David Mallet sale, London, 10 March 1766, lot 886.

Decorated page. MS Hunter 268, fol. 7
(See also Colour Ill. 11)

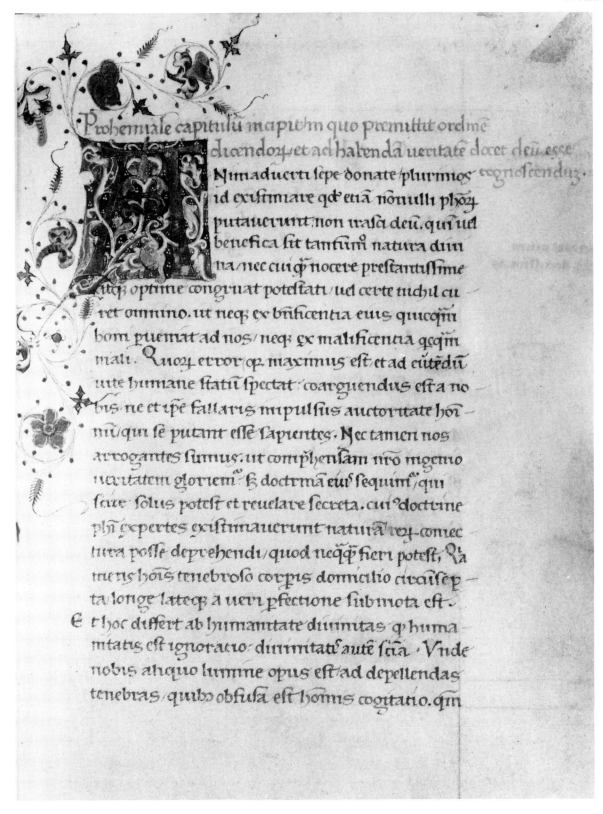

Decorated page. MS Hunter 274, fol. 1
(See also Colour Ill. 23)

BIBLIOGRAPHY: Young & Aitken, pp. 221-222; Oldham, *Notes on Bindings*, p. 15: '?Netherlands'; Bodleian Library, *Duke Humphrey and English Humanism*, Oxford, 1970, p. 32; *Manuscripts at Oxford*, ed. A. C. de la Mare and B. C. Barker-Benfield, Oxford, 1980, pp. 95-96, XXII, nos. 2-3; Ker, *William Hunter*, p. 14, Appendix A, V; for other manuscripts written by Thomas Candour see J.J.G. Alexander and E. Temple, *Illuminated Manuscripts in Oxford College Libraries, the University Archives and the Taylor Institution*, Oxford, 1985, p. 51, no. 516, and Index, p. 117.

39. Ranulf Higden, Polychronicon

John of Trevisa, Dialogue of the lord and the clerk; Ranulf Higden, Polychronicon, translated by John of Trevisa.
England, c. 1470.

MS Hunter 367 (V.1.4)

Vellum, 357 × 251 mm.; [iv], 209, [iv] leaves; written space 245 × 156 mm., in double columns of 46-51 lines.

Commissioned from his chaplain John of Trevisa (c. 1330-1412) by Thomas, Lord Berkeley, this translation of the Monk of Chester's chronicle was finished, as the colophon records, on Thursday 18 April 1387. It is written in seven books, in imitation of the seven days of Genesis, and was a standard work of general history, covering the period from the Creation until 1357. Although Higden did not himself write the final section, he did not die until c.1363 and was therefore to some extent a contemporary of his translator. Hunter's copy is one of some fourteen complete manuscripts surviving of the translation; he also owned two copies of the original Latin text (MSS Hunter 72 and 223).

Less ambitious in its design and execution than the Gower or the Chaucer (nos. 35 and 36), this volume is nonetheless skilfully decorated. Standard colours of blue, red and green are used, with heightening and details in white and yellow. There is a generous amount of gold in the background of the initial and in the shaft of the frame, with discs and trefoils of gold in the upper and lower borders. The large leaves are sharply serrated, smaller leaves being more schematic. The pen spraywork tends to be horizontal in the upper border and circular in the lower border and in both cases is worked more solidly than in the preceding volumes. Kathleen Scott has established that the decoration is related both by its design and by the execution of the motifs to a group centred on a copy of Alain Chartier's *Quadrilogue*, etc., in Oxford (University College, MS 85); the Hunter illuminator is likely to have been an assistant in the shop which produced this group rather than the master artist of the Chartier manuscript (see Scott, *Later Gothic Manuscripts*, forthcoming).

PROVENANCE: Bought by Hunter at the John Anstis sale, London, 12 December 1768, lot 464.

Decorated page. MS Hunter 367, fol. 56

BIBLIOGRAPHY: Young & Aitken, pp. 293-294; John Trevisa, *Dialogus inter militem et clericum, etc.*, ed. A.J. Perry, London, 1925 (Early English Text Society, 167), p. lxxvii; A.C. Cawley, 'Relationships of the Trevisa Manuscripts and Caxton's Polychronicon', *London Medieval Studies*, I, no. 3, 1939, pp. 463-482; J. Taylor, *The Universal Chronicle of Ranulph Higden*, Oxford, 1966, p. 138; *New CBEL*, I, col. 467; A.S.G. Edwards, 'The Influence and Audience of the *Polychronicon*: Some Observations', *Proceedings of the Leeds Philosophical and Literary Society (Literary and Historical Section)*, 17, 1978-1981, pp. 113-119; Ker, *William Hunter*, p. 14, Appendix A; cf. *Polychronicon Ranulphi Higden*, ed. C. Babington, London, 1865-86 (Rolls Series, 41).

40. Thomas Elmham, Metrical History of Henry V

Thomas Elmham, Liber metricus
de Henrico Quinto.
England, third quarter of the 15th century.

MS Hunter 379 (V.1.16)

Vellum, 333 × 235 mm.; [iv], 37, ii, [iv] leaves; written space 214 × 130 mm., 27 long lines.

From the middle years of the 15th century a new influence came to bear on the decoration of books in England. Flemish and Netherlandish artists offered an alternative to the traditional English designs and were patronized by the Court. The lattice work within the large initial T which begins this text (fol. 9) may be compared with Netherlandish examples from earlier in the century in no. 113 and no. 115; the surrounding penwork is more squarely in the English tradition, which had included flourish-work borders since at least the mid 14th century.

Written in 1418, Elmham's *Metrical History* covers the first years of Henry V's reign, from 1413 to 1416. It is based on the anonymous *Gesta Henrici Quinti*, completed the previous year by one of the King's chaplains in an attempt to justify Henry's renewed recourse to war in the quarrel with Charles VI of France. Henry, taking advantage of the internal troubles of France, had demanded the restoration to the English crown of all the land that Edward III had owned in 1360, together with Anjou and Normandy. In support of this extravagant claim, he invaded France in 1415 and again in 1417.

Elmham, formerly a monk at St Augustine's Abbey, Canterbury, had in 1414 been appointed under royal patronage Prior of the Cluniac monastery of Lenton in Nottinghamshire; the following year he became Vicar General (and Chamberlain) of the province of England and Scotland, and the *Metrical History* may have been written in connection with such preferment. Elmham discloses his authorship by spelling his name with the first letter of each of the first twelve lines ('Thomas Elmham', fol. 9) and of the last twenty lines ('Thomas Elmham Monachus', fol. 36v). His work also reveals numbers of details, not included in the *Gesta*, which must have come from personal knowledge: in, for instance, the account of the pageant celebrating Henry's return home after the battle of Agincourt in 1415 he describes, with disapproval, the horned head-dresses of the ladies watching from the windows.

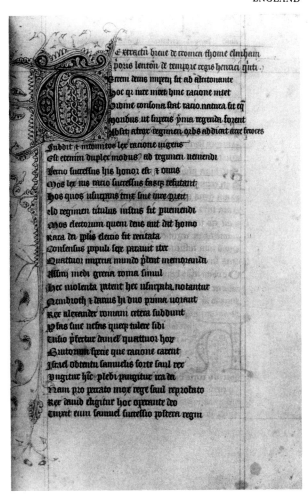

Decorated page with initial T. MS Hunter 379, fol. 9

Hunter owned another copy of Elmham's work written a little earlier by a versatile amateur scribe, Roger Wall (MS Hunter 263; see M.B. Parkes, *English Cursive Book Hands 1250-1500*, Oxford, 1969, p. 22).

PROVENANCE: St Augustine's Abbey, Canterbury; John Twyne, M.P.; John Twyne the younger, 1579; John Stow (the chronicler), 1586; Thomas Martin of Palgrave; bought by Hunter from Thomas Payne catalogue of 1770, no. 7393.

BIBLIOGRAPHY: Young & Aitken, p. 304; *Liber metricus de Henrico Quinto: Memorials of Henry the Fifth, King of England*, ed. C. A. Cole (Rolls Series 11), London, 1858, pp. 80-166; Ker, *Medieval Libraries*, p. 42; *New CBEL*, I, col. 803; J. S. Roskell and F. Taylor, 'The Authorship and Purpose of the Gesta Henrici Quinti', *Bulletin of the John Rylands Library*, 53, 1971, pp. 428-464 and 54, 1972, pp. 223-240; Ker, *William Hunter*, p. 20, Appendix A, XXI; A. G. Watson, 'John Twyne of Canterbury as a Collector of Medieval Manuscripts', *The Library*, 6th Ser., Vol. 8, no. 2, 1986, pp. 131-151, Appendix no. 14.

41. John Lydgate, Fall of Princes

England, c. 1470-1480.

MS Hunter 5 (S.1.5)

Vellum, 437 × 318 mm.; [ii], ii, 212, i, [ii] leaves; written space 320 × 204 mm., in double columns of 42 lines.

The major decoration of this volume is in six full-page borders, filled with delicate sprays of penwork in a foreign style, in which an elegant balance of colour is provided by leaves, flower patterns and gold highlights (fols. 41, 125v, 139, 161, 172, 191). The emphasis is on surface variety harmoniously controlled over a large area. Kathleen Scott has identified three other manuscripts with work by the artist of these borders, a copy of Bartholomew the Englishman's *De proprietatibus rerum* in Bristol (City Reference Library, MS 9), a Psalter in Oxford written by Stephen Dodesham, the scribe of no. 42 (Trinity College, MS 46; cf. J.J.G. Alexander and E. Temple, *Illuminated Manuscripts in Oxford College Libraries*, Oxford, 1985, p. 58, no. 589), and a Book of Hours in Cambridge (Fitzwilliam Museum, MS 56; see Scott, *Later Gothic Manuscripts*, forthcoming).

John Lydgate (c. 1370-1449) is credited with some 145,000 lines of verse, almost a quarter of which is contained in the *Fall of Princes*, his single longest work. The poem is based on Laurent de Premierfait's translation of Boccaccio's *De casibus virorum illustrium* (see nos. 54-55). Lydgate greatly amplifies the French text, however (itself a substantial increase on the original), with additions from a variety of sources including the Bible, Ovid and other works by Boccaccio. The original dramatic framework is of a succession of unfortunates – from Adam and Eve to King John of France, taken prisoner at Poitiers in 1356 – passing in a vision before the author. In Lydgate's hands, however, the action is sacrificed to the creation of a universal encyclopedia of history and mythology, exhaustively fleshed out with moral teaching. The ponderous didactic element and the continual invective against women may be explained by Lydgate's life as a monk at the great Benedictine Abbey of St Edmund at Bury (cf. no. 36). The translation was commissioned from Lydgate in 1431 by Humphrey, Duke of Gloucester, younger brother of Henry V and Protector of England during the minority of Henry VI, and it occupied the following eight years of his life.

PROVENANCE: Calthorpe family, c. 1555; Lumner family of Norfolk, c. 1579-1582; bought by Hunter at the sale of George Parker, 2nd Earl of Macclesfield, London, 14 January 1765, lot 743.

BIBLIOGRAPHY: Young & Aitken, pp. 7-8; John Lydgate, *Minor Poems*, ed. H.N. MacCracken, London, 1911 (Early English Text Society, Extra Series, 107), p. xvi, no. 37; John Lydgate, *Fall of Princes*, ed. H. Bergen, London, 1923-1927 (Early English Text Society, Extra Series, 121-124), Vol. IV, pp. 79-81; C. Brown and R.H. Robbins, *Index of Middle English Verse*, New York, 1943, 1168; *A Manual of the Writings in Middle English 1050-1500*, ed. A.E. Hartung, Vol. 6, New Haven, 1980, p. 2099, [47], no. 17; Ker, *William Hunter*, p. 13, Appendix A, IIIa; for a copy of the *Fall of Princes* with 157 miniatures (London, B.L., MS Harley 1766) see K.L. Scott, 'Lydgate's Lives of Saints Edmund and Fremund: a newly-located manuscript in Arundel Castle', *Viator*, 13, 1982, p. 336.

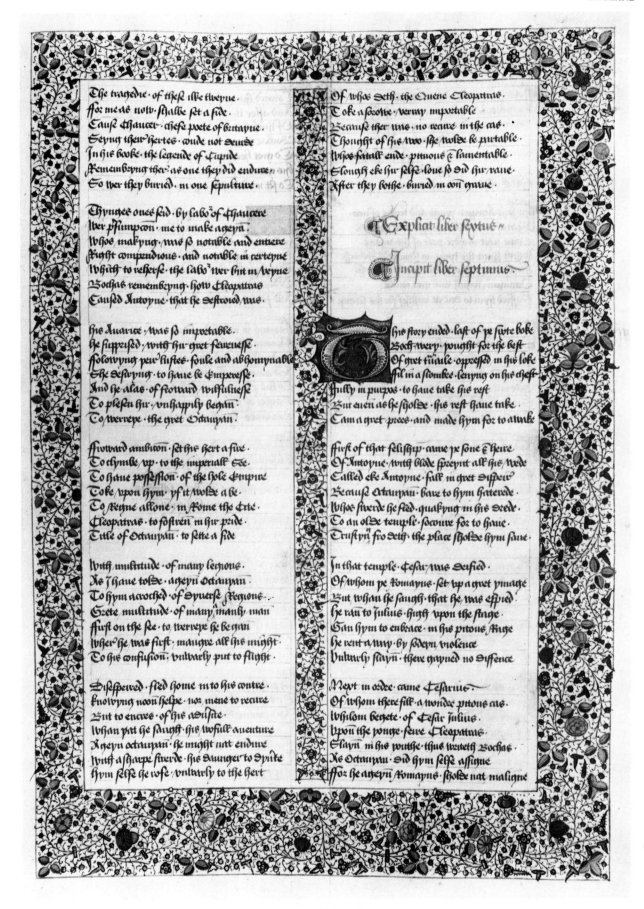

The tragedie · of these ilke tweyne ·
ffor me as nolv · schalle set a side
Cause Chaucer · chefe poete of Britayne
Seyng their hertes · wold not deuide
In his booke · the legende of Cupide
Remembryng ther · as one they did endure
So ther they buried · in one sepulture ·

Thynges ones seid · by labour of Chaucere
Iter presumpcon · me to make ageyn ·
Whos makyng · was so notable and entiere
ffirst compendious · and notable in certeyne
Which to reherse · the labour ther but in veyne
Bochas remembryng · how Cleopatras
Caused Antoyne · that he destroied was ·

His Auarice · was so importable ·
He supprised · with hur grete feruenesse ·
ffolowyng peur listes · foule and abhomynable
The desiryng · to haue be Emperesse ·
And he alas · of frolward wilfulnesse
To plesen hur · vnhappily begynn ·
To werreye · the grete Octauian ·

ffrolward ambition · set his hert a fire ·
To clymbe vp · to the imperiall See ·
To haue possession · of the hole empire
Toke vpon hym · yf it wolde a be ·
To reyne allone · in Rome the Citie ·
Cleopatras · to sostreyn in hur pride ·
Title of Octauian · to sette a side

With multitude · of many legions ·
As I haue tolde · ageyn Octauian ·
To hym accoched · of dyuerse Regions ·
Grete multitude · of many manly man
ffurst on the see · to werreye he began
Wher he was first · maugre all his might ·
To his confusion · vnwarly put to flight ·

Disspeired · fled home in to his contre ·
knowyng noon helpe · nor mene to recure
But to encres · of his adusite ·
Whan pat he saught · his woful auenture
Ageyn Octauian · he might nat endure
With a scharpe swerde · his daunger to spike
hym selfe he rose · vnwarly to the hert

Of whos deth · the Quene Cleopatras ·
Toke a sorolve · veruy importable
Because ther was · no recure in the cas ·
Thought of his two · she wolde be partable ·
Whos fatall ende · piteous & lamentable ·
Enough eke hur selfe · loue so did hur raue ·
After they bothe · buried in con graue ·

¶ Explicit liber sextus ·

¶ Incipit liber septimus ·

This story ended · last of pe syxte boke
Bochas wery · pought for the best
Of grete trauaile · oppressed in his loke
fil in a slombre · lenyng on his chest
ffully in purpos · to haue take his rest
But euen as he scholde · his rest haue take ·
Cam a grete prees · and made hym for to awake

ffirst of that felislyp · cam pe sone & heire
Of Antoyne · with blode spreynt all his wede
Called eke Antoyne · folk in grete dispeir
Because Octauian · bare to hym hattrede ·
Whos swerde he fled · quakyng in his drede ·
To an olde temple · socoure for to haue ·
Trust vpn fro deth · the place scholde hym saue ·

In that temple · Cesar was deified
Of whom pe Romayns · set vp a grete ymache
But whan he saught · that he was espied ·
he ran to Iulius · hiegh vpon the stage ·
Gan hym to enbrace · in his piteous Rage
he rent alvay · by sodeyn violence
Vnkursly slayn · there gayned no diffence ·

Next in ordre · came Cesarius ·
Of whom there fil · a wonder piteous cas ·
Whilom begete · of Cesar Iulius ·
Vpon the yonge feire · Cleopatras ·
Slayn in his youthe · thus writeth Bochas ·
As Octauian · did hym selfe assigne
ffor he ageyn Romayns · scholde nat maligne

Decorated page. MS Hunter 5, fol. 161

42. The Mirrour of the Blessed Lyf of Jesu Christ

Pseudo-Bonaventura, Meditationes vitae Christi, translated into English by Nicholas Love.
England, Sheen, written by Stephen Dodesham, 1475.

MS Hunter 77 (T.3.15)

Vellum, 287 × 213 mm.; [ii], i, [i], 165, [i] leaves; written space 178/201 × 128 mm., in double columns of 26-30 lines.

Another copy of this popular devotional text (see no. 33). The scribe, Stephen Dodesham, is identified in a contemporary inscription on a flyleaf (fol. iii verso). Dodesham (d. 1481/82) was a monk of Witham Charterhouse near Frome, Somerset, which had been founded c. 1178 by Henry II as part of his expiation for the death of Thomas Becket; he later moved to Sheen Charterhouse in Richmond, Surrey, founded by Henry V in 1414. A.I. Doyle has noted that Dodesham wrote other works subsequently acquired by Hunter: an English translation of Richard of St Victor's *De preparatione animi ad contemplationem*, and Dionysius Cato's *Disticha de moribus ad filium*, with an English version in seven-lined stanzas, both of which were originally part of the same volume (MSS Hunter 258 and 259). In addition to two further copies of Love's *Myrrour* (Cambridge, Trinity College, B.15.16, and Oxford, Bodleian Library, Rawlinson A.387B), he also wrote a Psalter now in Oxford (Trinity College, MS 46; cf. J.J.G. Alexander and E. Temple, *Illuminated Manuscripts in Oxford College Libraries*, Oxford, 1985, p. 58, no. 589) and many other manuscripts in a long career which began in the late 1420s.

The elaborate foliate frame and initial introducing the text (fol. 3v) are in the conventional colours of red, blue and green on a gold ground, with white and yellow heightening. The frame is characterized in addition by the elongated acanthus leaves which entwine its coloured bars, and by the appearance of two barbed quatrefoils with leaves amongst the pen spraywork of the lower border.

PROVENANCE: Charterhouse of Sheen, inscription fol. iii verso; possibly in the possession of Thomas Martin of Palgrave (1697-1771), who owned MSS Hunter 258 and 259; Hunter's immediate source not traced.

Decorated page. MS Hunter 77, fol. 3v

BIBLIOGRAPHY: Young & Aitken, p. 85; M.B. Parkes, *English Cursive Book Hands 1250-1500*, Oxford, 1969, p. 6, and revised ed., London, 1979, p. 25; A.I. Doyle, 'Reflections on some manuscripts of Nicholas Love's *Myrrour of the Blessed Lyf of Jesu Christ*', Leeds Studies in English, N.S. 14, 1983, p. 88; L. F. Powell, *The Mirrour of the Blessed Lyf of Jesu Christ*, Oxford, 1908 (Roxburghe Club); E. Salter, 'The Manuscripts of Nicholas Love's *Myrrour of the Blessed Lyf of Jesu Christ* and related texts', in *Middle English Prose: Essays on Bibliographical Problems*, ed. A. S. G. Edwards and D. Pearsall, London, 1981, p. 124.

43. Benvenuto Grassi, Treatise on the Use of the Eyes

Benvenutus Grapheus, De usu oculorum, translated into English.
England, fourth quarter of the 15th century.

MS Hunter 503 (V.8.6)

Vellum, 179 × 135 mm.; [ii], ii, 68, [ii] leaves; written space 105 × 86 mm., in single columns of 15-16 lines.

The leaf sprays in red, blue and green, with white and yellow heightening, and the initials on gold grounds are standard decorative work of the period. Smaller initials are alternately gilt and in penwork, and line-fillers are added in spaces at the end of sections. Both of these characteristics are seen mostly in Books of Hours: stems and leaves hooked round the shape of the initial, as they are here, are found for instance in a Book of Hours of Sarum Use in Oxford (Bodleian Library, MS Rawlinson Liturg. f. 3), which is likely to have been produced in London about 1454 (see A. G. Watson, *Catalogue of Dated and Datable manuscripts c. 435-1600 in Oxford Libraries*, Oxford, 1984, no. 687; O. Pächt and J.J.G. Alexander, *Illuminated Manuscripts in Çäthe Bodleian Library, Oxford*, III, Oxford, 1973, no. 912). Kathleen Scott notes that the larger size of the painted motifs, the smaller number of them and the regularity of their execution, combined with the rather obvious rectangular space, are all features which indicate a late date.

PROVENANCE: Bought by Hunter from Thomas Osborne after 1761.

BIBLIOGRAPHY: Young & Aitken, p. 411; Ker, *William Hunter*, p. 18, Appendix A, XX.

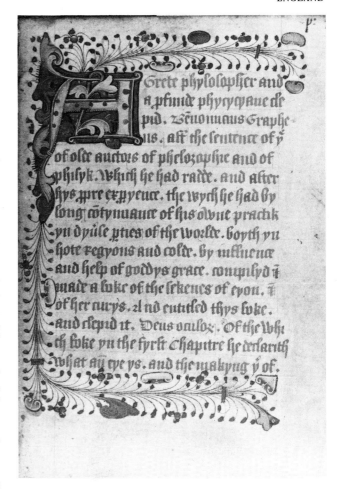

Decorated page. MS Hunter 503, p. 1

Decorated page. MS General 335, fol.1

44. Abstract and Commentary on Aristotle's Physics and On the Soul, with other texts

Abstraccio super octo libros phisicorum Aristotilis; Abstraccio super tres libros de anima; Richard Lavenham, De causis naturalibus. England, late 15th century.

MS General 335

Vellum, 172 × 122 mm.; ii, 102, iv leaves; written space 98 × 67 mm., 26 long lines.

The garland of leaves forming the letter Q on the first page of this manuscript is an example of Flemish influence at work on English book decoration. Though small in scale, it is a vivacious design, combining conventional white linework on a blue ground with an adventurous use of gold paint and colour for the initial itself. Both the letter-forms and the penwork ornamentation of the smaller gold initials in the text are very similar to those in the Flemish Bonaventura (no. 123).

Except for the clasps, the volume preserves its contemporary leather binding of blind-stamped panels on oak boards with small brass bosses.

PROVENANCE: Reading Abbey, early 16th century; John Palmer, late 16th century; presented to the Library in 1870.

BIBLIOGRAPHY: Ker, *MMBL*, II, pp. 909-910; Ker, *Medieval Libraries*, p. 155.

Initial V. MS Hunter 399, fol. 120v

45. Sir Thomas More, Dialogue of Comfort agaynst Tribulation

England, London, 1540s.

MS Hunter 399 (V.2.19)

Paper, 301 × 207 mm.; [ii], v, 339, viii, [ii] leaves; written space 188 × 107 mm., 19-24 long lines.

Written during the fifteen months of his final imprisonment in the Tower of London before he was executed on a charge of treason in 1535, More's *Dialogue of Comfort* is his spiritual testament. The dialogue is conducted between two Hungarians, Uncle Anthony and his nephew Vincent, who discuss the problems of human suffering, under the threat of the imminent invasion of their country by the Turks after the sack of Buda in 1526 and before Suleiman's second invasion of 1529. It portrays the resistance that must be made to attacks on Christian faith and can be read as an extended metaphor for Henry VIII's attack on the Church of England.

This explosive work can have circulated in only a small number of manuscripts before it was printed in 1553. Of the five which still survive, the Hunterian manuscript is the most elegantly produced and contains numerous skilfully drawn initials incorporating dragons, grotesques and people in contemporary dress, in an elaborate updating of medieval practice. Smaller initials are often drawn with a criblé background similar to that used in contemporary printing; the long cadels, or flourishes, offer additional scope for much decorative penwork. The watermarks in the paper (close to Briquet 11370, 11383, 11386 and 12662) indicate a date in the early 1540s for the manuscript; the Tudor coat of arms on the blind-stamped London binding may in addition suggest that someone close to the royal household either commissioned this copy or obtained it soon after More's death.

PROVENANCE: ?William Cecil, Lord Burghley (1520-1598), who is likely to have owned the manuscript included in a sale of 1687 (see Yale edition, pp. l-li, n. 3) which may be the Hunterian copy: Hunter's library contains a manuscript of Henry of Huntingdon's *History of the English*, MS Hunter 288, bearing Cecil's autograph, which was lot 93 in the same sale (Ker, *William Hunter*, p. 27, Appendix C).

BIBLIOGRAPHY: Young & Aitken, pp. 318-319; Oldham, *Notes on Bindings*, p. 16; R. Hanna, 'Two New Texts of More's *Dialogue of Comfort*', *Moreana*, 19, no. 74, 1982, pp. 5-11; cf. *New CBEL*, I, col. 1799; T. More, *A Dialogue of Comfort against Tribulation*, ed. L.L. Martz and F. Manley, New Haven, 1976 (The Yale Edition of the Complete Works of St. Thomas More, 12); Sotheby's, London, sale 10-11 July 1986, lot 9.

Decorated page with initial W; initial T.
MS Hunter 399, fols. 1 and 108v

Alchemists at work.
MS Ferguson 191, p. 21 and facing p. 41

46. Thomas Norton, The Ordinall of Alchemy

England, late 16th century.

MS Ferguson 191

Paper and vellum, 206 × 150 mm.; iv, 48, ii leaves; written space 105 × 168 mm., 32-43 long lines.

The tradition of the illuminated manuscript was kept alive in the new age of printing by the need for presentation volumes or for copies of a text not available in another form. Works of a highly controversial political and religious nature, such as More's *Dialogue* (no. 45) formed one group which circulated only in this clandestine way, and alchemical treatises were another.

The identity of the author of the *Ordinall of Alchemy*, written in English verse around 1477, is revealed in a couplet formed by taking the first syllable of the preface and each chapter and the whole of the first line of the last chapter:

> Tomas Norton of Briseto
> A parfect master ye may him trowe.

Member of Parliament for Bristol and occasional emissary for Edward IV, Thomas Norton became a pupil of the renowned philosopher George Ripley, Canon of Bridlington, and devoted most of his life to the hermetic art of alchemy. His *Ordinall* was written as a handbook 'for increasing riches for the needy and for putting poverty to flight' and provides an account of the general alchemical processes of his day. It was first published in a Latin translation in Germany in 1618 and was not printed in English until 1652.

The illustrations, which also appear in the printed texts, are diagrams of alchemical equipment and procedures. In this copy, sheets of vellum are interleaved with the main text, written on paper, to provide the traditional support for colours and liquid gold. But adherence to the illustrator's model was evidently more important than artistic finish, and these copies are stilted and naive. The volume is one of 330 manuscripts amongst some 7500 printed books on alchemy and related subjects collected by John Ferguson, sometime Regius Professor of Chemistry at the University of Glasgow.

PROVENANCE: Sir Roger Arundell of Trerice; sold by Thomas Osborne, catalogue of 16 December 1751; bought by Professor John Ferguson, 21 January 1890; acquired by the University of Glasgow in 1920.

BIBLIOGRAPHY: Cf. Michael Maier, *Tripus Aureus*, Frankfurt, 1618; Elias Ashmole, *Theatrum chemicum Britannicum*, London, 1652, pp. 1-106; J. Ferguson, *Bibliotheca chemica*, Glasgow, 1906, II, pp. 145-146; *New CBEL*, I, col. 692.

III · France

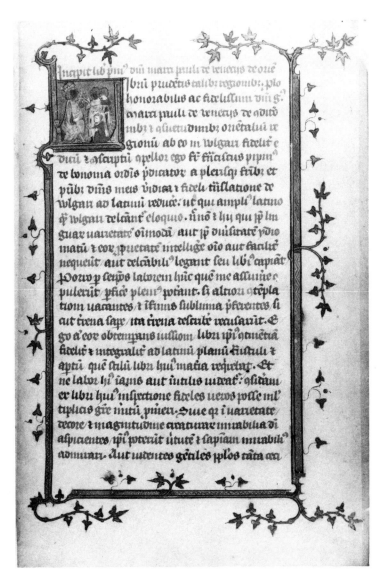

Decorated page. MS Hunter 458, fol. 1

47. Marco Polo, Travels in the East, and Orderic of Pordenone, Travels in Tartary and the East

Marcus Paulus, De orientalibus regionibus, translated into Latin by Brother Francesco Pipino of Bologna; Ordoricus, De mirabilibus Tartarorum et orientalium regionum.
France, second half of the 14th century.

MS Hunter 458 (V.6.8)

Vellum, 213 × 144 m.; [iv], i, 1-105, [ii], 106-133, i, [iii] leaves; written space 152 × 89 mm., 27-30 long lines.

During the 14th century, it became fashionable in French book production to pay greater attention to the framework and marginal decoration of manuscripts. Historiated initials, with their constantly recurring subject matter, tended to be less susceptible to change.

The initial introducing Marco Polo's *Travels* (fol.1) shows the author kneeling before a king seated on an oriental couch. The rather schematic figurework and background tracery have changed little since the time of St Louis. The frame itself, however, which is still in alternating bars of red and blue, now extends to the right-hand as well as the left-hand and bottom margins, and the ivy leaves, which had begun to appear a century or so earlier (cf. nos. 20-22), have sprouted into all the borders. The original brilliance of the silver used in the decoration has been lost; it would have equalled that of the gold which can still be seen.

A similar frame and initial introduce Orderic's work (fol. 107).

PROVENANCE: Guillaume de la Haye, 16th century; Hunter's source not traced.

BIBLIOGRAPHY: Young & Aitken, pp. 378-379.

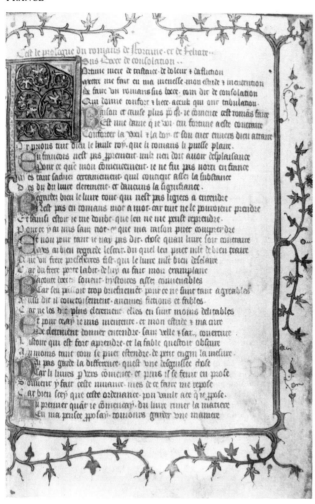

Decorated page. MS Hunter 439, fol. 1

48. Boethius, On the Consolation of Philosophy

Anicius Manlius Torquatus Severinus Boethius, De consolatione philosophiae, translated into French verse by Renaud de Louhans; Albertano di Brescia, Livre de Mélibée et de Prudence. France, c. 1400.

MS Hunter 439 (V.5.9)

Vellum, 255 × 179 mm.; [i], 70, ii, [i] leaves; written space 190 × 135 mm., fols. 1-12 with 36 long lines, fols. 12v-70v in double columns of 36 lines.

Of the thirteen different versions of the *Consolation of Philosophy* in medieval French, this adaptation by Renaud de Louhans, written in 1336 or 1337, was one of the most widespread: it survives in over thirty manuscripts. Renaud, a Dominican monk at Poligny, medievalizes the text with numerous additions that are uncomplicated by the higher literary and philosophical purposes of the original author.

The frame and ivy leaf decoration of the opening page (fol. 1) are very similar to the Marco Polo volume (no. 47). The illuminated initial is an early example of a decorative type that was to remain standard for most of the 15th century.

N. J. Foucault, to whom this manuscript belonged, also owned the splendid copy of the *Consolation* written in North Italy in 1385 (no. 71).

PROVENANCE: Nicolas Joseph Foucault (1643-1721).

BIBLIOGRAPHY: Young & Aitken, p. 362; A. Thomas and M. Roques, 'Traductions françaises de la *Consolatio philosophiae* de Boece', *Histoire Littéraire de la France*, 37, 1938, pp. 419-488; R. H. Lucas, 'Medieval French Translations of the Latin Classics to 1500', *Speculum*, 45, 1970, pp. 225-253; R. A. Dwyer, 'Manuscripts of the medieval French Boethius', *Notes and Queries*, 18, 1971, pp. 124-125; idem, *Boethian Fictions*, Cambridge, Mass., 1976, pp. 129-131; J. K. Atkinson, 'Some further confirmations and attributions of manuscripts of the medieval French Boethius', *Medium Aevum*, 47, 1978, pp. 22-29.

Caesar flanked by senators, soldiers and knights. MS Hunter 373, fol. 1

49. Life of Caesar

Vie de Cesar.
France, ?Paris, late 14th century.

MS Hunter 373 (V.1.10)

Vellum, 335 × 269 mm.; [ii], 226, [ii] leaves; written space 209 × 183 mm., in double columns of 34-35 lines.

This life of Julius Caesar is the first part of a compilation of Roman history from the works of Sallust, Suetonius and Lucan, known as *Le fait des Romains*.

By the end of the 14th century, the ivy-leaf pattern seen in the Marco Polo (no. 47) had grown to fill the whole margin with increasingly elaborate tracery. Figurative scenes were also commonly expanded from the confines of the historiated initial to occupy a large central panel in secular texts as well as religious books. The decoration of the first leaf of this volume owes much to the influence of Jacquemart d'Hesdin,

one of the foremost court painters of the period. The half-page miniature shows a seated figure who, despite the throne and the crown, is presumably meant to be Caesar, flanked by senators, numerous Roman soldiers and two knights on horseback. The modelling of the figures is carefully executed and is achieved by paint as well as by line-work; the drawing of the faces in particular is carried out with considerable delicacy and is characterized by the hooded eyelids and long nose. The predominance of blue and red in the colour scheme, the patterned background and the celebratory, statuesque quality of the composition all emphasize the traditions which the artist is following, but the differentiation of the figure types and the careful attention to dress mark a considerable development from more schematic scenes of a few decades earlier.

PROVENANCE: Château d'Anet sale, 1724, mark fol. 1; Guyon de Sardière sale, Paris, 1759, lot 1559; bought for Hunter in 1770, probably in Paris.

BIBLIOGRAPHY: Young & Aitken, pp. 299-300; Meyer, p. 113; Ker, *William Hunter*, p. 15, Appendix A, XI.

Portrait of the author. MS Hunter 385, fol. 3

Creation page. MS Hunter 8, fol. 10

50. Gaston de Foix, Pleasures of the Chase

Gaston III Phoebus, Comte de Foix, Miroir de Phébus, des deduicts de la chasse.
France, early 15th century.

MS Hunter 385 (V.2.5)

Vellum, 299 × 216 mm.; [ii], i, [ii], 97, [v], leaves; written space 180 × 126 mm., 29-30 long lines.

Gaston de Foix (1331-1391) owned 1600 dogs and 200 horses with which to pursue, after warfare and women, the third great love of his life: hunting. He began his famous book on the subject in 1387 to record the knowledge amassed over half a century; he died, on a hunt, four years later.

The portrait of the author (fol. 3) shows him seated in a field or garden giving directions to a kneeling huntsman who holds two white greyhounds on leashes, and with another huntsman holding a beagle or bloodhound behind. The Count in his costly robes is the most commanding figure in the composition, despite the effacement of his features; but the most notable aspect of the picture is the naturalism with which the scene is painted. Not only is the sky depicted, but the blue darkens towards the top, just as the impression of receding open ground is given by the darkening tone of the grass towards the horizon, evidence that notions of aerial perspective were finding their way north from Italy. The daisies may seem conventional, but the trees, for all their silver blossom, show considerable concern for verisimilitude. The manner of painting has also evolved from the turn of the century: although some outlines are emphasized in black ink, most of the contours are achieved by a delicate modelling, which is particularly noticeable in the silken sheen of the lining of the Count's cuffs and in the features of the central huntsman. It is interesting to note that the open-air feel is carried over into the decorated borders, where blue flowers on stems with oval green leaves give added life to the conventional ivy-leaf designs.

The volume still has its original binding of crimson velvet over wooden boards, with brass bosses, corner pieces and clasps.

PROVENANCE: Bought by Hunter at the Joseph Ames sale, London, 5 May 1760, lot 1008.

BIBLIOGRAPHY: Young & Aitken, pp. 307-308; Wardrop, 'Western Illuminated Manuscripts', p. 319; G. Tilander, *Gaston Phébus, Livre de chasse*, Karlshamn, 1971, p. 26; Ker, *William Hunter*, p. 13, Appendix A, II.

Bartholomew describing Trees and Plants.
MS Hunter 8, fol. 219v

51. Bartholomew the Englishman, Treatise on the Properties of Things

Bartholomaeus Anglicus, Le livre des propriétés des choses, translated into French
by Jean Corbichon.
France, second quarter of the 15th century.

MS Hunter 8 (S.1.8)

Vellum, 415 × 314 mm., [ii], 319, ii, [ii] leaves; written space 280 × 202 mm., in double columns of 49 lines.

Corbichon presents his Translation to Charles V. MS Hunter 8, fol. 9

This French version of Bartholomew's encyclopedia (see no. 22) was completed in 1372. It was one of many translations commissioned by Charles V of France. The original royal presentation copy opened with a miniature in four sections, showing three scenes of the Creation and one of the King and the translator. Donal Byrne has shown that this format was modernized in about 1415 by the Boucicaut Master in the copy of the work in Cambridge (Fitzwilliam Museum, MS 251, fol. 16); there the scene of Charles V and Corbichon was placed separately at the beginning of the preface, and the Creation panels were fused into a single half-page miniature of The Marriage of Adam and Eve. This updated layout is followed in the present copy. However, the content of the Creation picture (fol. 10) and that of the nineteen drawings which begin the different books are independent of the standardized French cycle of illustrations of the work, a fact that may be due to the absence of other illustrations in the exemplar, or to the influence of a patron. The Creation page shows instead a figure of Christ enthroned above two figures in academic robes discussing four volumes placed on a lectern. While the composition of the picture is complete, the unfinished colouring allows a glimpse of the painting and drawing techniques applied by the artist.

Although an English rather than a French source has been suggested for the miniatures and uncoloured drawings, their soft, limpid style, together with the costumes depicted and the background work in the painted scenes, would be unusual for English work; they are more likely to be from a provincial centre in France. The coat of arms of a Duke of Brittany, which appears repeatedly in the margins, is not part of the original decoration but suggests that the volume was in Brittany at an early date.

PROVENANCE: Arms of a Duke of Brittany, possibly François II, Duke from 1458-1488; ?Louis-Jean Gaignat; bought by Hunter in ?Paris in 1770.

BIBLIOGRAPHY: Young & Aitken, pp. 12-13; ?De Bure, I, p. 268, no. 1041; Meyer p. 114; D. Byrne, 'Two hitherto unidentified copies of the Livre des propriétés des choses, from the Royal Library of the Louvre and the Library of Jean de Berry', Scriptorium 31, 1977, pp. 90-98; idem, 'The Boucicaut Master and the Iconographical Tradition of the Livre des propriétés des choses', Gazette des Beaux-Arts, 91, 1978, pp. 149-164; Ker, William Hunter, p. 15, Appendix A, XI; D. Byrne, 'Manuscript ruling and pictorial design in the work of the Limbourgs, the Bedford Master and the Boucicaut Master', Art Bulletin, 66, 1984, pp. 117-135.

Decorated page. MS Hunter 468, fol. 1

52. Lapidary

Pseudo-Albertus Magnus, Liber lapidarius; (Anon.), Modus lapidum pretiosorum consecrandorum.
France, mid 15th century.

MS Hunter 468 (V.6.18)

Vellum, 206 × 144 mm.; [i], 33, [ii] leaves; written space 140 × 92 mm., 30 long lines.

From the early years of the 15th century it became increasingly common for the whole of the area bordering a page of text to be decorated with brightly coloured leaves and flowers within a supporting design of finely drawn hairline stems, or rinceaux, heightened with familiar shapes like gold discs, trefoils and wheat-ears. The space filled by this illumination was limited only by the need to stop short of the outer edges of the leaf which would be cut off when the volume was bound. This appealing invention was open to infinite variation to suit the purse of the owner and the style of the artist.

The arms on this volume suggest that it may have belonged to Charles d'Orléans, prince and poet (1394-1465). It is not listed in the inventories of his library, but he owned several scientific works as well as copies of the encyclopedias of his day, such as that of Bartholomew the Englishman (cf. nos. 22, 51). A work on precious stones would certainly have been of interest. The curiously unpractised humanistic hand of this manuscript is best explained as the work of a French scribe who may have had some familiarity with Italian models but no immediate copy on which to base his own script. The book is likely to have been written after Charles d'Orléans returned to France, in 1440, from his twenty-five years of imprisonment in England. Even if it dates from the 1450s, it is still a very early example of the use of a humanistic script in France.

PROVENANCE: Arms of Charles d'Orléans; Pierre Roussel, doctor to Jean, duc de Brabant; Charles de Montchal (1589-1651), Archbishop of Toulouse; bought for Hunter at the Louis-Jean Gaignat sale, Paris, 10 April 1769, lot 1022.

BIBLIOGRAPHY: Young & Aitken, pp. 390-391; De Bure, I, pp. 263-264, no. 1022; Ker, *William Hunter*, p. 14, Appendix A, VIII; cf. P. Champion, *La librairie de Charles d'Orléans*, Paris, 1910.

53. Cicero, Orator, Brutus, and Treatise 'On the Orator'

Marcus Tullius Cicero, Orator, Brutus,
De oratore.
France, second half of the 15th century.

MS General 334

Vellum, 258 × 186 mm.; [ii], 149, ii, [ii] leaves;
written space 165 × 116 mm., in double columns
of 38 lines.

A decorative pattern of acanthus leaf, flowers and
rinceaux occurs at the major text divisions. It is
similar to that in the lapidary (no. 52), although
the colour scheme is different and the decorations
cover only half the page. Some of the initials are
of conventional ivy-leaf work, but others (e.g.
fols. 1 and 127), contain well-observed naturalistic depictions of flowers.

The manuscript bears three coats of arms and
one additional mark of ownership. François Avril
has identified the arms on fol. 149v as those of
Antoine du Bois des Guerdes, Bishop of Béziers,
and the same arms appear in three other volumes
which, like this one, were in the Château d'Anet
sale in 1724 (Paris, Bibl. Nat., lat. 10637-10638,
and Vienna, Nationalbibliothek, Ink. 11.F.8).

PROVENANCE: Antoine du Bois des Guerdes, Bishop of Béziers
(1504-1537), arms on fol. 149v; Château d'Anet sale, 1724,
mark on fol. 1; Count Hoym, armorial stamp.

BIBLIOGRAPHY: Ker, *MMBL*, II, pp. 908-909.

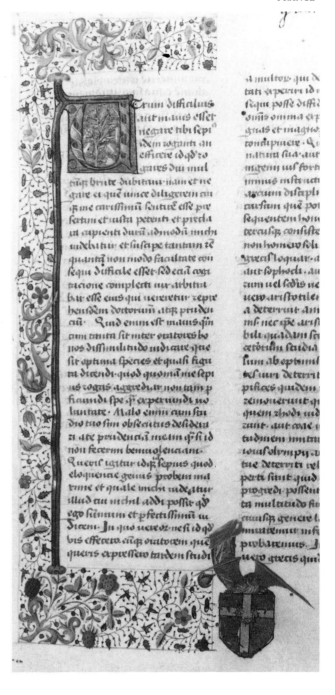

Initial U; initial I. MS General 334,
fols. 1 and 127

54. Boccaccio, Fall of Princes

Giovanni Boccaccio, De casibus virorum
illustrium, in French translation by
Laurent de Premierfait.
France, Paris, written by
Nicholas Saint Homme, 1467. 2 vols.

MSS Hunter 371-372 (V.1.8-9)

Vellum, 331 × 246 mm. and 327 × 246 mm.; I:
[ii], ii, 180, [ii] leaves, II: [v], 141, i, [ii] leaves;
written space 243 × 172 mm., in double columns
of 44-46 lines.

Laurent de Premierfait, secretary to Jean, duc de
Berry, made this translation of Boccaccio's peren-
nially popular work in 1409 (for an English
version see no. 41). Large numbers of copies
were made during the 15th century, many of
them richly illustrated.

This copy was written in Paris by Nicholas St.
Homme of the Order of St John in 1467 and
decorated there soon afterwards. The opening
picture shows Boccaccio pointing to Dame Fortune and the victims by her wheel. As identified
by Nicole Reynaud, it belongs to a group close to
the Coëtivy Master; other examples of this group
are in copies of the *Chronicles* of Guillaume de
Nangis in Paris (Bibl. Nat., fr. 2598) and Baltimore (Walters Art Gallery, W. 306). The figures
within the composition have been carefully indi-
vidualized. The kneeling king in the centre foreground in particular is carefully modelled, the
spiral movement of the body echoing the rotation
of the wheel. Unusual features include the setting
in an open landscape and the presence of a
woman on the wheel. The colour balance of the
composition is carefully controlled, matching the
colours used in the conventional flower and acanthus leaf borders.

The nine large paintings introducing the other
books are the work of a less skilful artist. The
full-page borders are executed in a standard
pattern throughout the volume, but it is interesting to note that from the middle of Book VI the
designs of the illuminated initials change from
ivy-leaf patterns to a series of more naturalistic
flowers.

PROVENANCE: Bought for Hunter at the Louis-Jean Gaignat
sale, Paris, 10 April 1769, lot 3489.

BIBLIOGRAPHY: Young & Aitken, pp. 298-299; De Bure, II, p.
233, no. 3489; Wardrop, 'Western Illuminated Manuscripts', p. 260; *Trésors*, p. 18, no. 31; *Treasures*, pp.
16-17, no. 44; Ker, *William Hunter*, p. 14, Appendix A,
VIII; V. Branca, P.F. Watson, V. Kirkham, 'Boccaccio
visualizzato', *Studi sul Boccaccio*, 15, 1985-86, p. 130.

Wheel of Fortune. MS Hunter 371, fol. 1. (*See also Colour Ill. 12*)

Boccaccio addresses Manutius and Followers (upper panel);
Phocinus murders Manutius (lower panel). MS Hunter 372, fol. 104v

111

55. Boccaccio, Fall of Princes

Giovanni Boccaccio, De casibus virorum
illustrium, in French translation by
Laurent de Premierfait.
France, Paris, fourth quarter of the 15th century.

MS Hunter 208 (U.1.12)

Vellum, 385 × 280 mm.; [ii], 376, [ii] leaves;
written space 260 × 178 mm., in double columns
of 42 lines.

The illustrative scheme of this second copy of
Premierfait's popular translation follows a different pattern from that in the earlier two-volume
copy (no. 54). It opens with a fully decorated
page, including a large miniature which shows
the translator offering his work to his patron,
Jean, duc de Berry. Thereafter, rather than
having other miniatures within full borders to
introduce each book, there are seventy-eight pictures, occupying from a third to a half of a single
column, which illustrate individual tales; spaces
for sixty-one others, including some at the beginning of books, remain blank.

The artist is a Parisian imitator of Maître
François who produced attractive work of consistent quality following conventional patterns and
styles. François Avril notes that the model of his
picture of Boccaccio and Fortune, for instance
(fol. 218v), is that used in another copy of the
work in the British Library (Add. MS 35321);
similar initials made of open tree trunks and
branches can be seen in a Paris Breviary in the
Bibliothèque Nationale (lat. 746). The decorated
ground to some of the initials is found also in a
French translation of Voragine's Golden Legend
(Bibl. Nat., fr. 244 and 245), which has miniatures by Jacques de Besançon, the chief associate
and successor of Maître François (see no. 60).

The artist of the present volume makes particular use of the spaces available for illustrations
at the top of a column to extend his pictures into
a lunette beyond the normal rectangle. This
became a popular shape, particularly in religious
manuscripts, in the early years of the 15th century. The result is a substantial increase in the
size of his pictures, and he often uses the extra
space to illustrate additional scenes in the story.

The almost full-page picture of Adam and Eve
(fol. 10) is of particular interest. The original leaf
here was removed at an early date and this is a
careful copy, made in the late 17th or early 18th
century, of a miniature in another illustrated
Premierfait, (Paris, Bibl. Nat., fr. 226, fol. 6),
and doubtless commissioned by a collector to
complete the volume. A comparison of the two
miniatures gives a fascinating view of how the
15th-century style is modulated when reproduced two centuries or more later: the colouring
is less vigorous overall, the volume both of
figures and architecture is indicated in more
painterly terms by the use of different tones of a
single colour for shading rather than by superim-
posing hatched lines, and there is a much greater
naturalism in the treatment of the human form
and in particular in facial expression.

PROVENANCE: Bought for Hunter at the Louis-Jean Gaignat
sale, Paris, 10 April 1769, lot 3490.

BIBLIOGRAPHY: Young & Aitken, pp. 151-156; De Bure, II, p.
233, no. 3490; Meyer, p. 114; Wardrop, 'Western Illumin-
ated Manuscripts,' pp. 259-260; Trésors, p. 19, no. 32;
Treasures, p. 17, no. 45; G. Wolf-Heidegger and A. M.
Cetto, Die anatomische Sektion, Basel, 1967, p. 140, no. 25;
Ker, William Hunter, p. 14, Appendix A, VIII; Baldwin,
William Hunter, p. 3, no. 4; V. Branca, P.F. Watson, V.
Kirkham, 'Boccaccio visualizzato', Studi sul Boccaccio, 15,
1985-86, p. 130.

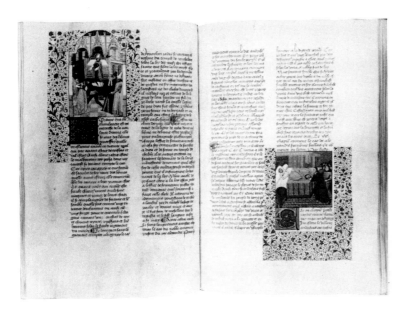

Opening showing the Doom of Joachim
the High Priest and the Head of Balas
presented to Ptolemy. MS Hunter 208,
fols. 206v-207. (See also Colour Ill. 14)

De adam et eue premier chapitre commençant en latin Maiorum nostrorum. et cetera.

Quant ie considere et pense en
diuerses manieres les ploura
bles maleurtez de noz predeces
seurs a celle fin que du grant nom

sare le arresterent deuant moy si tres
eagiez et si anciens quil sembloit que
ilz ne puissent trahiner les membres
tremblans. L'un de ces deux vieillar

Adam and Eve. MS Hunter 208, fol. 10

56. Chronicles of Saint-Denis

Chroniques de Saint-Denis, including Gilles Le Bouvier, Les chroniques du roi Charles VII. France, third quarter of the 15th century.

MS Hunter 203 (U.1.7)

Vellum, 345 × 246 mm.; [ii], 320, [ii] leaves; written space 240 × 160 mm., 41 long lines.

An account of the history of France from the reign of Philip IV to that of Charles VII, this is a continuation of *Les grandes chroniques de France*, the first important historical work in French which was completed about 1274 at the Royal Abbey of Saint-Denis. It begins in 1286 with the future King Edward III of England paying homage to Philip for Aquitaine, and ends with a major part of the *Chronicles of Charles VII* by Gilles Le Bouvier, known as the Berry herald. In this copy the chronicle covers Charles VII's reign from 1433 to 1453. The final gathering

containing an account of the closing years of his life is lost: he died in 1461.

The text is illustrated with four large pictures – a view of Paris (fol. 7); the homage of Edward III (fol. 15); Charles VI on his throne (fol. 165); and the coronation of Charles VII (fol. 266). The painting style and execution of the figures cannot be ascribed to any particular centre; however, the rather mannered execution indicates that it was not painted in Paris. An effaced crozier surmounting an obliterated coat of arms on fol. 15v and fol. 165v indicates that the copy was made for a bishop, presumably in the provinces.

PROVENANCE: Bought by Hunter at the David Mallet sale, London, 10 March 1766, lot 70.

BIBLIOGRAPHY: Young & Aitken, pp. 144-145; Meyer, p. 116; Ker, *William Hunter*, p. 14, Appendix A, V; cf. Gilles le Bouvier, *Les chroniques du roi Charles VII*, ed. H. Courteault, L. Célier, M. H. Jullien de Pommerol, Paris, 1979 (Société de l'Histoire de France).

Edward III paying homage to Philip IV. MS Hunter 203, fol. 15
(See also Colour Ill. 13)

57. Heinrich Seuse, Horologe of Wisdom

Henricus Suso, Horologium eternae sapientiae, translated into French.
France, Bourges, written by André Rousseau, 1470, with miniatures by Jean Colombe.

MS Hunter 420 (V.4.4)

Vellum, 269 × 184 mm.; [iv], 146, ii, [iii] leaves; written space 185 × 109 mm., 36 long lines.

The calm figures, modelled sculpture and idyllic landscape in the miniature of the Last Supper in this volume (fol. 94) are characteristic of the early work of the renowned illuminator Jean Colombe. Born in Bourges about 1435 into a prominent artistic family, Colombe formed an early and long-lasting partnership with the scribe André Rousseau, who was also librarian of the new University of Bourges (founded in 1467). This book, signed and dated by Rousseau, is an example of their collaboration. The rudimentary perspective of the pictures, the grouping of the figures, the handling of the robes and the faces of Christ and the Apostles, unchanging in the whole of Colombe's work, confirm its authorship. Another miniature by Colombe which begins the volume (fol. 1), showing the presentation of a book to a patron, has suffered some crude over-painting.

Two other works illustrated by Colombe and signed by Rousseau are the *Devotional Writings* in Paris (Bibl. Nat., lat. 1198) and a copy of Boethius's *De consolatione* in London (B.L., Harley MSS 4335-4339). The work of Colombe and the atelier which he established has been identified in more than sixty surviving volumes. He was commissioned to complete work begun by leading miniaturists of an earlier generation, Jean Fouquet (chief painter to Louis XI), Jean Bapteur and Perronet Lamy, in, for example, the Apocalypse begun in 1428 for the Dukes of Savoy. Duke Charles I of Savoy also engaged him to complete the famous *Très Riches Heures* of Jean, duc de Berry, left unfinished when the Limbourg brothers died of the plague in 1416. His own style changed from about 1472 to become more dramatic, verging sometimes on caricature, with a forceful use of colour. During his absence in Savoy from 1486 to 1489 he lent his house to André Rousseau. He died in the mid 1490s.

PROVENANCE: Arms of Jean de Vendôme, chamberlain of Louis XI and governor of Berry; Thomas de Balzac, seigneur de Montagu; Claude de Courbeton; bought for Hunter at the Louis-Jean Gaignat sale, Paris, 10 April 1769, lot 874.

Last Supper. MS Hunter 420, fol. 94
(See also Colour Ill. 17)

BIBLIOGRAPHY: Young & Aitken, pp. 344-346; De Bure, I, p. 229, no. 874; Meyer, p. 114; Claude Schaeffer, 'Les débuts de l'atelier de Jean Colombe', *Gazette des Beaux-Arts*, November 1977, pp. 137-150; Ker, *William Hunter*, p. 14, Appendix A, VIII; for Jean Colombe see also Jean Porcher, *L'enluminure française*, Paris, 1959, pp. 76-78, and C. Gardet, *L'Apocalypse figurée des ducs de Savoie* (MS Escurial E. Vitr. V), Annecy, 1969, pp. xiii, xiv, xxv; for Jean Colombe and B.L. Harley MSS 4335-4339 see Janet Backhouse, 'French Manuscript Illumination 1450-1530', in *Renaissance Painting in Manuscripts*, pp. 157-162.

Scenes at an inn; domestic interior with people in the bath.
MS Hunter 252, fols. 70 and 147. *(See also Colour Ill. 15)*

58. Les Cent Nouvelles Nouvelles

France, Tours school, fourth quarter
of the 15th century.

MS Hunter 252 (U.4.10)

Vellum, 255 × 187 mm.; [iv], 207, [iii] leaves;
written space 218 × 140 mm., 35 long lines.

This collection of burlesque tales, most of them
licentious, was modelled on Boccaccio's *Deca-
meron* and Poggio's *Facetiae*. It was presented to
Philip, Duke of Burgundy, in 1462. The tales are
supposedly recounted by various members of the
Burgundian court, but although their composition has been ascribed variously to Antoine de la
Sale and also to the Duke's chamberlain, Philippe
Pot, Seigneur de la Roche, their authorship
remains uncertain. This copy is the only surviving manuscript.

The one hundred miniatures in the volume,
each introducing a tale, give literal illustrations of
scenes of domestic and intimate life in provincial
France that are unknown on such a scale before.
The artist, while not of the first rank, is richly
inventive, with a good eye for telling narrative
detail and a lively sense of colour. The characters
are depicted in the bath, listening to music,
weaving, eating, receiving medical treatment,
undressing or lying naked in bed, as was the habit
of the time. Contrasting with these domestic
interiors with their rich draperies and bed hangings, there are also public scenes in churches, on
town streets and in the countryside. If the content of the pictures was too daring for the reputation of the grander miniaturists of the day, their
artist has succeeded in giving them much of the
full-blooded humour that made the tales themselves so popular.

PROVENANCE: D'Estrée family; bought for Hunter at the
Louis-Jean Gaignat sale, Paris, 10 April 1769, lot 2214.

BIBLIOGRAPHY: Young & Aitken, pp. 202-203; De Bure, I, p.
540, no. 2214; Meyer, p. 113; *Les cent nouvelles nouvelles*,
ed. T. Wright, Paris, 1858; *Les cent nouvelles nouvelles*,
ed. P. Champion, Paris, 1928; Wardrop, 'Western Illuminated Manuscripts', p. 260; *Trésors*, pp. 24-25, no. 42;
Treasures, p. 17, no. 48; *Les cent nouvelles nouvelles*, ed.
F. P. Sweetser, Geneva, 1966; Ker, *William Hunter*, p. 14,
Appendix A, VIII; Baldwin, *William Hunter*, pp. 3-4,
no. 5.

59. Apocalypse

Apocalypsis, in Latin, with French translation.
France, ?Provence, ?1480s.

MS Hunter 398 (V.2.18)

Vellum, 312 × 216 mm.; [ii], i, 62, i, [ii] leaves;
written space 220 × 184 mm., in double columns
of 28 and 33 lines.

In the middle years of the thirteenth century
there had been an extraordinary development of
artistic interest in St John's prophetic vision of
the end of the world in his Book of Revelation.
This arose substantially from the interpretation
of Joachim of Fiore and others that the new
world of the spirit would begin in 1260. The
cycles of half-page illustrations to the Book of
Revelation created at that time remained influential for more than two centuries as the scenes
were reproduced not only in manuscripts but also
in other mediums including stained glass and
tapestry.

The Hunterian Apocalypse has 48 half-page
miniatures illustrating Revelations I, v.1 – XIV,
v.7. The three gatherings of eight leaves (now
bound, out of order, with the second gathering
following the third) were doubtless originally
completed by two further gatherings of eight or
ten leaves containing the remaining forty or so
illustrations of the cycle. In their iconography the
miniatures correspond closely to the remarkable
series preserved in the Burckhardt-Wildt cuttings
(Sotheby's sale, 25 April 1983, lots 31-68), which
were painted in Lorraine around 1270 – 1280 and
originally contained 88 illustrations, and to the 84
scenes represented in tapestries made around
1370 for Louis I of Anjou for his palace at
Angers. For instance the same measured pace is
found at the beginning of Revelation VIII, containing separate scenes for the half-hour silence
in Heaven with the angels holding their trumpets
(vv. 1-2, fol.17v), the censing of the golden altar
(vv. 3-4, fol. 18), and the spilling of the censer
and the sounding of the first trumpet (vv. 5-7,
fol.18v); and in the illustration to Revelation XI
the witnesses are done to death by a single locust
ridden by Abaddon (vv. 7-8, fol. 24v).

This remarkable volume from Southern
France dates from a period when little is known
about the miniaturists and workshops of the
region. Its location may be established by the
prominent repetition of the arms of Aymar de
Poitiers, Grand Seneschal of Provence in 1484
and a noted bibliophile: he owned the Boucicaut
Hours (Paris, Musée Jacquemart-André) and the
great Bible moralisée begun by the Limbourg
brothers for Philip the Bold (Paris, Bibl. Nat.,
fr. 166). Aymar commissioned the completion of
many of the miniatures in the Bible moralisée
which had been left as drawings, and François
Avril notes that these additions appear to be
closely related to several aspects of the miniatures
of the Apocalypse: they include the colouring,
particularly the use of tones of pink, rose and
purple, and details of the architectural
framework such as sagging, bowed pillars. A
different artist painted the prefatory miniature of
St John on the Isle of Patmos, which is far more
archaic in style.

The initials in the French translation which
follows the Latin text are characteristic of the late
1480s, containing lively pictures of identifiable
flowers. The cadels (flourished strokes extending
into the top margin) of this section also contain
examples of the grotesque penwork faces which
were to become a prominent feature of calligraphic practice in the following decades.

PROVENANCE: Arms of Aymar de Poitiers, Seigneur de Saint-
Vallier; bought for Hunter at the Louis-Jean Gaignat sale,
Paris, 10 April 1769, lot 94.

BIBLIOGRAPHY: Young & Aitken, pp. 317-318; De Bure, I,
pp. 29-30, no. 94; Meyer, p. 114; M.R. James, The
Apocalypse in Art, London, 1931, p. 12, no. 47; Trésors, pp.
22-23, no. 38; Treasures, p. 17, no. 47; R. Hausherr, 'Eine
verspätete Apocalypsen-Handschrift und ihre Vorlage', Studies in Late Medieval and Renaissance Painting in Honor of
Millard Meiss, New York, 1977, pp. 219-240; Ker, William
Hunter, p. 14, Appendix A, VIII; cf. N. Morgan, 'The
Burckhardt-Wildt Apocalypse', Art at Auction 1982-83,
London, 1983, pp. 162-169; G. Henderson, 'The manuscript model of the Angers Apocalypse tapestries', Burlington Magazine, 127, 1985, pp. 208-219.

St John on Patmos. MS Hunter 398, fol. 1v
(See also Colour Ills. 18 and 20)

Woman taken in Adultery. MS Hunter 37, fol. 201 (originally misnumbered f. 185)
(See also Colour Ill. 19 of MS Hunter 39, fol. 97)

60. Ludolf of Saxony, Life of Christ

Ludolphus de Saxonia, Vita Christi,
in French translation by Guillaume Le Ménard.
France, Paris, 1490s, with miniatures
by Jacques de Besançon. 4 vols.

MSS Hunter 36-39 (T.1.4-7)

Vellum, I: 390 × 268 mm., II: 395 × 275 mm.,
III: 390 × 273 mm., IV: 406 × 280 mm.; I: [ii],
i, 204, i leaves, II: [ii], i, 242, i, [ii] leaves, III:
[ii], i, 238, ii, [ii] leaves, IV: [ii], i, 260, [ii]
leaves; written space 270 × 165 mm., in double
columns of 47 lines; 140 miniatures, I: 42, II:
42, III: 39, IV: 17.

This copy of Ludolf of Saxony's devotional
account of the *Life of Christ* is contained in four
sumptuous volumes with a rich succession of
miniatures. In the margins, the French royal
insignia recur in a constantly changing series of
decorated panels, and the inscription 'pour le roy'
at the beginning of each volume indicates that
they were intended for Charles VIII. The work is
indeed dedicated to the King, who is shown at
prayer in the first of the six fully decorated pages
in Vol. I and again in Vol. IV. His presence is
also felt elsewhere, for his features reappear in
representations of St John.

The 140 miniatures are chiefly the work of
Jacques de Besançon, who took over the workshop of the royal painter Maître François around
1480. Jacques de Besançon was the subject
almost a century ago of an important study by
Paul Durrieu, who sought to identify the style of
a substantial group of manuscripts produced in
the court circle in Paris in the latter part of the
15th century. More recent research has shown
that many of the manuscripts which Durrieu
ascribed to Jacques de Besançon are in fact the
work of Maître François, who is documented in
1473 and was active during the 1470s. Some
opinion has restricted Jacques de Besançon's
contribution simply to the provision of capitals
and border decoration. More recent study by
Nicole Reynaud, however, has reasserted the
importance of Jacques de Besançon, and identified him with the figure known hitherto as the
Chief Associate of Maître François: he is
documented in 1485 and his career was at its
height from then until the mid 1490s.

The extensive series of miniatures in this work
includes numbers of half-page or three-quarter-
page paintings set within fully decorated borders;
border decoration around smaller miniatures is
confined to a single margin or corner. They are
characterized by a regular drawing style and a
lively palette. While the miniatures normally
contain only a few figures within a restricted
space, the scene of the Feeding of the Five
Thousand (II, fol. 119) shows the painter's gift
for handling large numbers of people in a dyna-
mic way, with considerable differentiation and a
fine sense of colour and depth. These same
qualities appear in a more dramatic form in the
scene of the Woman taken in Adultery (II,
misnumbered fol. 185 by the original scribe, i.e.
fol. 201): the tension of the confrontation is
expressed in the movement of the Pharisees and
the warders holding the woman, and contrasts
well with the calm group of Apostles behind the
figure of Jesus. Particular prominence is given to
the Vision of Christ appearing to Charles VIII
(IV, fol. 97). It includes a volume lying open in
front of the King, noted by Roger Wieck as a
common but nonetheless significant indication of
the medieval function of the text as an aid to
meditation and prayer.

An artist at the head of a large workshop was
bound to use similar pictorial motifs repeatedly
in different settings, especially when he was
providing a number of extensive series of illustrations to different works. It is interesting to
compare, for instance, the picture of Christ's
lineage (I, fol. 36v) with a Tree of Jesse in a copy
in Paris of the *Légende dorée* also painted by
Jacques de Besançon (Bibl. Nat., fr. 244-245), in
which the overall design as well as the colouring
are very similar. Christ's forebears are seen
burgeoning from branches in a striking arrangement of horizontal loops which allow the scene to
be contained harmoniously within an almost
square space, and the lush green landscape provides a firm, earthly origin for the tribe whose
ultimate descendants in Joseph, Mary and the
Child are seen in ethereal splendour against the
deepening blue tones of the sky at the top of the
picture. While it has been claimed that Jacques
de Besançon was a man of modest achievement
whose reputation depended chiefly on the comparative weakness of his rivals, there is no doubt
that he was a thoroughly professional artist of
considerable skill.

PROVENANCE: Charles VIII, King of France, 1470-1498;
bought for Hunter at the Louis-Jean Gaignat sale, Paris, 10
April 1769, lot 126.

BIBLIOGRAPHY: Young & Aitken, pp. 38-46; De Bure, I, p.
39, no. 126; Meyer, pp. 113-114; Wardrop, 'Western
Illuminated Manuscripts', pp. 255-258; *Trésors*, p. 24, no.
41; *Treasures*, p. 18, no. 50; Ker, *William Hunter*, p. 14,
Appendix A, VIII; cf. P. Durrieu, *Un grand enlumineur
parisien au XVe siècle. Jacques de Besançon et son oeuvre*,
Paris, 1892; E.P. Spencer, 'Dom Louis de Busco's Psalter',
Gatherings in Honor of Dorothy Minor, ed. U.E. McCrack-
en, L.M.C. Randall and R.H. Randall, Baltimore, 1974,
pp. 227-240; J. Plummer and G. Clark, *The Last Flowering.
French Painting in Manuscripts 1420-1530 from American
Collections*, New York, 1983, pp. 68-71, nos. 89-91.

61. Avicenna, Canon of Medicine

Abû Alî Husain Ibn' Abd Allah, called Ibn Sînâ or Avicenna, De medicina, translated into Latin by Gerard of Cremona.
France, fourth quarter of the 15th century.

MS Hunter 9 (S.1.9)

Vellum, 415 × 294 mm.; [ii], 98, iii, [i] leaves; written space 294 × 175 mm., in double columns of 50 lines.

Avicenna's compendium, written originally in Arabic, remained the most influential single work on medicine throughout the later Middle Ages. In the first two of its five books, Avicenna (980-1037) deals with physiology, pathology and hygiene, in the third and fourth with methods of treating disease, and in the last with remedies and antidotes. The work was still in use as a textbook in the universities of Louvain and Montpellier in the mid 17th century.

The large picture which opens this copy shows the author lecturing to a group of students and colleagues in contemporary academic robes: the mace held by a gowned *bedellus* (a university official) confirms the university setting, which is enlivened by the presence of a dog in the foreground holding a bone, perhaps purloined from one of the anatomical classes. The practical side of medical instruction is illustrated in fifteen smaller miniatures in the text which include scenes of open-air dissections and of procedures of diagnosis, including uroscopy and pulse-taking.

The extensive use of gold paint to model both clothing and furniture became fashionable in the latter years of the 15th century, particularly in the North. The ground of the borders was also painted gold, rather than being left uncoloured. The rich ornamentation included, as in this manuscript, flowers, leaf-sprays, birds and grotesques. On the first leaf, the arms of a flint emitting sparks are those of the Order of the Golden Fleece, founded in 1429 by Philip the Good, Duke of Burgundy.

PROVENANCE: Hunter's source not traced.

BIBLIOGRAPHY: Young & Aitken, pp. 13-14; Meyer, p. 117; C. Singer, *The 'Fasciculo di medicina', Venice 1493*, Florence, 1925, pls. 88, 89; Wardrop, 'Western Illuminated Manuscripts', p. 322; *Treasures*, pp. 17-18, no. 49; MacKinney, pp. 127-128; G. Wolf-Heidegger and A. M. Cetto, *Die anatomische Sektion*, Basel, 1967, pp. 151-154, nos. 42-47.

Avicenna lecturing. MS Hunter 9, fol. 1 *(See also Colour Ill. 22)*

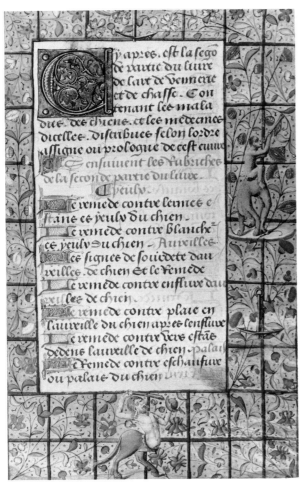

62. Guillaume Tardif, Art of Falconry, and Art of Hunting

Guillaume Tardif, Fauconnerie,
Venerie et la chasse.
France, c. 1494.

MS Hunter 269 (U.5.9)

Vellum, 226 × 147mm.; [ii], i, 98, i, [ii] leaves; written space 138 × 77 mm., 25 long lines.

Beautifully written and magnificently illustrated throughout by lifelike pictures of birds and dogs in the margins, this manuscript shows the perfection of book design achieved in France in the late 15th century. The illuminated initials follow the conventional pattern of ivy leaves on a solid gold ground which was used throughout the 15th century. Five full-page decorations on gold painted backgrounds include acanthus-leaf scrolls in blue and red with sprays of naturalistic flowers which are matched in other decorated initials; there is in addition a plentiful population of centaurs, mermen and monkeys. The range of subject matter and the delicate use of colour indicates an artist of considerable sophistication: the presence of the arms of France and Jerusalem on the first leaf suggests that this copy was made for Charles VIII, who commissioned Tardif to write the compilation, around 1494, when he was invested by Pope Alexander VI with the Kingdom of Naples and Jerusalem.

PROVENANCE: Charles VIII, King of France, 1470-1498; bought for Hunter at the Louis-Jean Gaignat sale, Paris, 10 April 1769, lot 1348.

BIBLIOGRAPHY: Young & Aitken, pp. 216-217; De Bure, I, p. 352, no. 1348; Meyer, p. 114; Wardrop, 'Western Illuminated Manuscripts', p. 319; *Trésors*, p. 25, no. 43; *Treasures*, p. 17, no. 46; Ker, *William Hunter*, p. 14, Appendix A, VIII [cited in error as De Bure, no. 64].

Decorated pages. MS Hunter 269
fols. 12 and 90. *(See also Colour Ill. 16)*

63. Seneca, Tragedies

Lucius Annaeus Seneca, Tragoediae.
France, 1490s.

MS Hunter 322 (U.7.16)

Vellum, 194 × 137 mm.; [i], iv, 287, ii, [ii] leaves; written space 120 × 77 mm., 21 long lines.

The French scribe who wrote this volume changed his hand into a good approximation of an Italian humanist script during the course of the early pages, perhaps because he was modelling his writing on that used by Italian Renaissance scribes for copying classical texts. The decoration, however, is resolutely French, resembling that of the Tardif (no. 62) in its floral and leaf sprays, the gold-painted ground and the population of birds, snails and grotesques among the vegetation.

Prominent on the first page is a heraldic Pegasus breathing fire and bearing the arms of Charles Guillard d'Epichelière, controller of finance at the Parlement of Paris; the arms are repeated in all save one of the nine other floreated pages. The Pegasus emblem also appears in a tapestry of Perseus woven for the Guillard family and is interesting evidence of the adoption of the outward forms of nobility by members of the upper professional classes of the day. Other manuscripts bearing the same arms and devices identified by Nicole Reynaud include Paris, Arsenal, MS 5068; Paris, Bibliothèque Mazarine, MS 3847; Paris, Bibl. Nat., lat. 6150; Caen, Bibliothèque Municipale, MS 181; and Dresden, MS Oct. 11. Such a collection reveals the prestige still attaching to manuscripts some decades after the introduction of printing.

The initial S which begins the text contains a picture of Hercules in full armour and wearing a lion-skin; he is carrying a spiked club over his shoulder and holds the three-headed hound Cerberus on a lead.

PROVENANCE: Arms of Charles Guillard d'Epichelière (1456-1537); Jean Balesdeus, French jurist, d. 1675; Jean and Théodore Maire, printers at Leyden and the Hague, ?1640s; bought by Hunter at the César de Missy sale, London, 18 March 1776, lot 1630.

BIBLIOGRAPHY: Young & Aitken, pp. 257-258; Oldham, *Notes on Bindings*, p. 15: 'English'; Ker, *William Hunter*, p. 15, Appendix A, XVII; for the Guillard tapestry see G. Souchal 'Un grand peintre français de la fin du XVe siècle, le Maître de la "Chasse à la Licorne"', *Revue de l'Art*, 1973, pp. 22-49.

Decorated page. MS Hunter 322, fol. 1
(below): Detail of decorated page. MS Hunter 322, fol. 218v

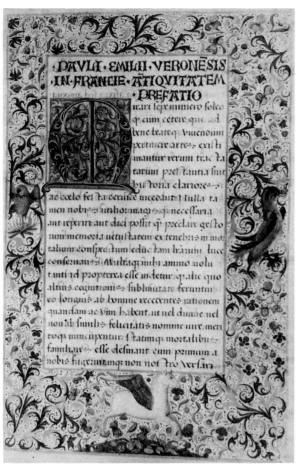

Decorated page. MS Hunter 98, fol. 1
(See also Colour Ill. 21)

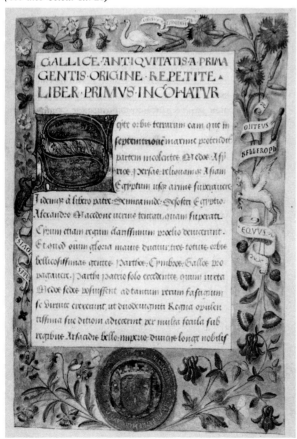

Decorated page. MS Hunter 11, fol. 7

64. Paolo Emili, French Antiquities

Paulus Aemilius Veronensis, In Franciae antiquitatem libri tres.
France, 1490s.

MS Hunter 98 (T.4.15)

Vellum, 276 × 198 mm.; i, 125, ii leaves; written space 178 × 107 mm., 24 long lines.

Paolo Emili of Verona was commissioned by Charles VIII to write a history of France, two copies of which are in the Hunterian collection. This copy, exquisitely written and decorated, has three emblems worked into the floreated border of the first leaf: a phoenix, a Pegasus, and a fire-breathing Alerion (a visual pun on the arms of Lorraine). The use of a plain background, contrary to the fashion of the time, allows the frame, the stems and many of the leaf scrolls themselves to be painted in gold.

PROVENANCE: Hunter's source not traced.

BIBLIOGRAPHY: Young & Aitken, pp. 106-107; Meyer, p. 117.

65. Paolo Emili, Antiquities of France

Paulus Aemilius Veronensis,
Galliae antiquitates.
France, written in the 1480s but decorated in the 1490s.

MS Hunter 11 (S.2.1)

Vellum, 256 × 176 mm.; iv, 55, v leaves; written space 150 × 105 mm., 19 long lines.

This copy of the *Antiquities* begins with dedications to Cardinal Charles Bourbon and to Charles VIII. The Cardinal's arms appear on the first leaf, but a note on a flyleaf recording that the volume belonged to Emili himself suggests that he regained possession of the volume after the Cardinal's death in 1488. The exquisite decoration of the first text-page (fol. 7), which includes the royal arms of France, dates from some years later. The flowers, berries, snail and butterflies of this page are painted with a concern for naturalistic representation which includes the casting of shadows from the objects onto the gold ground. Such illusionism was highly fashionable in Netherlandish decoration of the period and this page may have been the product of an artist from the Netherlands working in France.

PROVENANCE: Hunter's source not traced.

BIBLIOGRAPHY: Young & Aitken, pp. 14-15; Meyer, p. 117.

66. Jean Lemaire de Belges, L'Epistre du Roy

France, c. 1515.

MS Hunter 12 (S.2.2)

Vellum, 263 × 169 mm.; [i], i, 12, ii, [i] leaves; written space 175 × 100 mm., 30 long lines.

This allegorical poem, composed in 1511, refers to events in the reign of Louis XII – who is supposed to address it to his ancestor Hector – and deals rather roughly with Pope Julius II. In 1509, the Pope had joined the Emperor Maximilian and Louis XII in the League of Cambrai against the Republic of Venice; when France showed no sign of making peace after the Venetian defeat later that year, he formed a new alliance with Venice and Spain to counter French moves. The political intrigues and recourse to arms by the leader of the Christian Church attract sharp criticism in the poem. The preface mentions the accession of François I (in 1515) and is dedicated to Louis de Clèves, whose arms and motto appear on the first text-page (fol. 1).

The spirited decoration of the page includes a large picture of Louis de Clèves, fully armed, on horseback. Traditional French elements may be seen in the initial decorated with a strawberry, the gold highlights and the dramatic colours of the hills and trees of the landscape. In other respects it shows the influence of Italian book-design, which Lemaire would have seen at first hand on his visits to Italy. This includes the architectural framework, hung with garlands, which by this date had been taken over by printers from manuscript models, and also the illusionism by which the lines of text appear to have been written on a scroll supported within the arch (cf. no. 101).

PROVENANCE: Arms of Louis de Clèves, comte d'Auxerre, d. 1545; bought at P. Le Neve sale, London, 1730, by N. Hardinge (d. 1758); Hunter's source not traced.

BIBLIOGRAPHY: Young & Aitken, pp. 16-17; Meyer, p. 117; A. Adams, 'Le manuscrit Huntérien de L'Epistre du roy de Jean Lemaire de Belges et le manuscrit B.N. fonds français 1690', Bibliothèque d'Humanisme et Renaissance, 45, 1983, pp. 511-518; Ker, William Hunter, p. 26, Appendix C.

Louis de Clèves on horseback. MS Hunter 12, fol. 1
(See also Colour Ill. 1)

Title-page. Hunterian Collection, Bq 2. 11

67. Valerius Flaccus, Argonauts

Caius Valerius Flaccus, Argonauticon libri octo, cum Aegidii Maserii commentariis.
France, [Paris], printed by Josse Bade, 1519.

Hunterian Collection, Bq 2. 11

Vellum, 313 × 212 mm.; [ii], [8] , 114, [ii] leaves.

This copy of the Argonauticon, the third edition to be printed by Josse Bade within seven years, is remarkable for being printed on vellum and for being so richly decorated. In both respects it emulates its manuscript predecessors and demonstrates how the tradition of fine book production at this time tended to follow patterns established in manuscripts a generation or more earlier. Each of the eight books is introduced by a delicately painted woodcut picture, within a rich border of flowers and leaf scrolls on a gold ground. The name of Aegidius Maserius appearing on a scroll on the title-page suggests that this is the copy made for Gilles de Maizières, Rector of the University of Paris, who wrote the commentary in this edition.

The Argonauticon is an epic in eight books on the Quest of the Golden Fleece, imitated and partly translated from Apollonius of Rhodes in the latter part of the first century. The work is dedicated to the Emperor Vespasian and is in part intended to celebrate his achievements in establishing Roman rule in Britain. Another contemporary event alluded to is the eruption of Vesuvius in A.D. 79.

PROVENANCE: Gilles de Maizières; bought for Hunter at the Louis-Jean Gaignat sale, Paris, 10 April 1769, lot 1671.

BIBLIOGRAPHY: De Bure, I, p. 423, no. 1671; *Trésors*, p. 50, no. 84; P. Renouard, *Bibliographie des impressions et des oeuvres de Josse Bade Ascensius*, III, Paris, 1980, p. 316.

68. Thucydides, Peloponnesian War

Thucydides, Lhistoire de la guerre, qui fut entre les Péloponnésiens et Athéniens, translated into French by Claude de Seyssel.
France, Paris, printed by Josse Bade, 1527.

Hunterian Collection, Du 2. 9

Vellum, 310 × 198 mm.; [ii], [16] , 281, [i] leaves.

Thucydides' account of the war between Athens and Sparta, to 411 B.C., was written from first-hand knowledge of both sides. His aim was to give an accurate record of the events, not only because of their absorbing interest, but also for their value for the study of the science of government. This translation is one of a series made from the classics by Claude de Seyssel, and was presented in manuscript form to Louis XII. It was, appropriately, the first of the translations to be printed by order of François I, founder of the French Royal Library.

Bade's woodcut border to the title-page is derived from a Venetian border used in Niccolò de' Malermi's Italian translation of the Bible printed by Giovanni Ragazzo in 1490. It appears in several variations, depending on the space required to print the title words. In this copy, the usual central motif in the top border, a roundel showing a scribe at work supported by two heraldic lions, has been omitted to leave space for the king's emblem of a salamander. The royal arms, which appear five times on the first two leaves along with two other salamanders, suggest that this copy was a presentation volume to François I. The design of the border of the second leaf was completed independently of woodcuts: it is an interesting example of the design and painting skills still available for book decoration at this date.

Two other copies on vellum, also with painted borders, are recorded in Paris (Bibl. Nat., Vélins 699, and Bibliothèque Mazarine, 5541 C2) and a third was reported in Vienna in 1822. The standard edition on paper totalled 1225 copies.

PROVENANCE: François I, King of France, 1494-1547; ?Louis-Jean Gaignat sale, Paris, 10 April 1769, lot 2862.

BIBLIOGRAPHY: Van Praet, *Catalogue des livres imprimés sur vélin de la Bibliothèque du Roi*, Paris, 1822, V, pp. 44-46 and p. 377, no. 54; Mortimer, pp. 640-641, no. 522; P. Renouard, *Bibliographie des impressions et des oeuvres de Josse Bade Ascensius*, III, Paris, 1980, p. 304; Baldwin, *William Hunter*, p. 14, no. 29.

Title-page. Hunterian Collection, Du 2. 9

127

The Building of the Argo and the Argonauts' Departure from Iolcos.
Woodcut illustration. Hunterian Collection, Bq 2.11, fol. 1v

69. Pattern Book of Alphabets

France, c. 1526.

MS General 326

Paper, 260 × 182 mm.; folio; ii, 90, ii leaves.

Pattern books were in common use in the later Middle Ages and Renaissance, both for figurative work and for letters, but relatively few have survived. This example contains ten designs of alphabets and a number of single letters. The alphabets are chiefly variations on designs using pleated, folded or slashed scrolls, and motifs based on root stocks. Half the volume, however, is taken up by an alphabet of large, highly ornamented calligraphic initials with remarkable strapwork and grotesque faces and dragons. Dutch mottos accompanying the French text on some pages and including the date of 1526 may suggest that the calligrapher had a connection with the Low Countries.

PROVENANCE: Not traced.

Calligraphic initial M. MS General 326, p. 71

BIBLIOGRAPHY: For surviving pattern books see R.W. Scheller, *A Survey of Medieval Model Books*, Haarlem, 1963; H. Lehmann-Haupt, *The Göttingen Model Book*, Columbia, Mo., 1971; J. Backhouse, 'An Illuminator's Sketchbook [B.L., Sloane MS 1448 A]', *British Library Journal*, 1, 1975, pp. 3-4; eadem, *John Scottowe's Alphabet Books*, London, 1974 (Roxburghe Club).

Alphabet designs. MS General 326, p. 15

70. Petrarch, Canzone

Francesco Petrarca, Standomi un giorno solo a la fenestra, translated into French by Clément Marot.
France, second quarter of the 16th century.

Stirling Maxwell Collection, SMM 2

Vellum, 124 × 117 mm.; [iv], ii, 36, iv, [iv] pages.

Clément Marot (1496-1544) was a court poet to Marguerite de Navarre and François I and wrote a great variety of works, from epigrams and long allegorical poems to translations of the Psalms; he also translated Ovid, Virgil and Petrarch. This translation of Petrarch's *Canzone* was published in 1533 under the title *Visions de Pétrarque*.

The emblematic visions are of a succession of idylls being destroyed by the forces of nature. They include a hind being caught by two hounds; a galleon being wrecked in a storm; a laurel tree being struck by lightning; a group of nymphs and muses by a fountain being swallowed up in an earthquake; a phoenix pecking its heart out; and a beautiful woman being bitten by a snake.

Each of the six visions is illustrated in this volume by two watercolour pictures. The first of each pair depicts the idyllic scene described in the first half of each vision, and the second shows its annihilation. The artist has responded to the inherent drama of the poem in spirited drawings that dwell as much on its moral as on its artistic possibilities. Perhaps commissioned as an elegant gift, this volume shows one survival of the illustrated manuscript transformed here almost into a picture book. It may also reflect the design of early emblem books, such as Corrozet's *Hecatongraphie* (no. 143). The pictures in this volume were later the source of the illustrations in Jan van der Noot's emblem book *Het theatre* of 1568.

PROVENANCE: Sir William Stirling Maxwell; bequeathed to the Library by Sir John Stirling Maxwell in 1958.

BIBLIOGRAPHY: M. Bath, 'Pictorial Space and Verse Form in *The Theatre for Worldlings*', *Word and Visual Imagination*, ed. K.J. Höltgen, P. Daly and W. Lottes, Erlanger Forschungen, Reihe A, Geisteswissenschaften, Erlangen (forthcoming, 1988); cf. Clément Marot, *Oeuvres complètes. VI, Les traductions*, ed. C. A. Meyer, Geneva, 1980, pp. 215-219.

Opening with vision of galleon being wrecked in a storm.
Stirling Maxwell Collection, SMM 2, pp. 10-11

IV · Italy

71. Boethius, On the Consolation of Philosophy, with commentary by Nicholas Trivet

Anicius Manlius Torquatus Severinus Boethius, De consolatione philosophiae, cum commento. ?North-east Italy, written by Brother Amadeus, 1385.

MS Hunter 374 (V.1.11)

Vellum, 342 × 255 mm.; [ii], 110, [iii] leaves; written space 253/283 × 204 mm., text in 23 long lines, commentary in double columns of 43-57 lines.

Each of the five books of the *Consolation* is introduced in this copy by a beautifully floreated and gilt initial which, with a few lines of text, occupies the whole of a page. The historiated initial of Book I shows Boethius instructing students and is accompanied by another illustration showing the author in his prison at Ticinum (Pavia; cf. no. 4). The first of these scenes, contained within a large initial C, is a conventional medieval picture, and may be compared, for example, with the initials in the Augustine (no. 19) and the Seneca (no. 21). The present example shows greater interest in perspective and space, and a painterly concern for volume and surface texture. The free use of a large area for the prison scene follows a well-established pattern (cf. no. 13): here a typical North Italian detail is the V-shape terminating the castellation.

This manuscript was written for Gregorius of Genoa, whose name, preceded by a gold cross indicating an ecclesiastical position, appears in gold in the decoration of the first opening, with the date of 1385. It is signed in two places by Brother Amadeus who, while modestly claiming to be the least of all scribes ('ego enim sum minimus omnium scriptorum frater Amadeus': fol. 1 and again on fol. 3), has produced a volume of surpassing beauty. The first two leaves, containing alphabets and exemplary texts within decorated frames, are matched throughout the volume by initials embellished with distinctive penwork ornaments. In her current research, Marie-Thérèse Gousset has identified other examples of these ornaments in a manuscript from North-east Italy in Paris (Bibl. Nat., lat. 8955). A decade later Brother Amadeus may have written the text of the celebrated Visconti Hours

Initial P. MS Hunter 374, fol. 25v
(See also Colour Frontispiece of fol. 4)

(Florence, Biblioteca Nazionale, BR 397 and LF 22, written before 1395) which shows many of the same characteristics; if so, it is likely that he was one of the foremost scribes working for Giangaleazzo Visconti, who became sole ruler of the County of Milan in the year this manuscript was written. Since a French influence can be seen in the design of the gold shapes of the spraywork decoration, it may be possible to connect the scribe with North-west Italy by this date.

PROVENANCE: Gregorius of Genoa; arms of Nicolas Joseph Foucault (1643-1721); bought for Hunter at the Pieter Burmann sale, Leyden, 27 September 1779, lot 1223.

BIBLIOGRAPHY: Young & Aitken, pp. 300-301; Meyer, p. 113; Wardrop, 'Western Illuminated Manuscripts', pp. 322-325; *Trésors*, pp. 10-11, no. 14; *Treasures*, p. 8, no. 22; B. Wolpe, 'Florilegium alphabeticum: Alphabets in Medieval Manuscripts', in *Calligraphy and Palaeography. Essays presented to Alfred Fairbank*, ed. A.S. Osley, 1965, pp. 69-74; P. Courcelle, *La Consolation de philosophie dans la tradition littéraire*, Paris, 1967, pl. 18; Alexander, 'Italian Illuminated Manuscripts', p. 116; Ker, *William Hunter*, p. 17, Appendix A, XIX; Baldwin, *William Hunter*, p. 5, no. 8.

72. Jerome, Letters

Hieronymus, Epistolae.
North-east Italy, second half of the 15th century,
with initial by the Master of the Brussels Initials,
c.1400-1410.

MS Hunter 202 (U.1.6)

Vellum, 348 × 256 mm.; i, 386, ii leaves; written
space 240 × 151 mm., 36 long lines.

117 letters survive from the correspondence of
Jerome (c. 345-419/420), probably the most
learned man of his age, and certainly the most
prolific in literary output. He wrote saints' lives
and other biographies, and reference books as
well as extensive biblical commentaries; he also
translated the canonical books of the Hebrew Old
Testament. Pictures of Jerome in manuscripts of
his works often show him writing in his study.

When this manuscript was written in the latter
years of the 15th century, space was left for an
introductory initial which was in all probability
intended to contain a portrait of Jerome. The
present initial, however, is a Nativity, dating
from the first decade of the century, which has
been stuck onto a rewritten sheet (fol. 8). This
initial, measuring 63 × 49 mm., is by the Italian
artist known as the Master of the Brussels Initials, after a series of historiated initials which he
executed in the *Très Belles Heures* of the duc de
Berry, now in Brussels (Bibliothèque Royale,
MS 11060-61); he was formerly called Zeno or
Zanobi da Firenze after an inscription in the
Hours of Charles the Noble in Cleveland
(Museum of Art, 64.40), which is his most lavish
production. He is the only miniature painter
known to have moved from Italy to France at the
turn of the 14th and 15th centuries.

This small example of his work shows his
characteristic dynamism in the flow of space and
form within a small compass: it seems to have
served as a standard image for use in many of his
illuminated manuscripts. The apparent lack of
writing on the reverse of the initial does not
necessarily mean that it was cut out of a completed manuscript. Its presence here indicates a
readiness to incorporate earlier styles when the
initial was given its new setting.

PROVENANCE: ?From the Pieter Burmann sale, Leyden, 27
September 1779, lot 1208.

BIBLIOGRAPHY: Young & Aitken, p. 143; cf. M. Meiss, *French
Painting in the Time of Jean de Berry. The Limbourgs and
their Contemporaries*, London, 1974, p. 377; R. Calkins,
Illuminated Books of the Middle Ages, Ithaca, 1983, p. 253;
E.F. Rice, *Saint Jerome in the Renaissance*, Baltimore,
1985.

Initial O with Nativity. MS Hunter 202, fol. 8. (See also Colour Ill. 25)

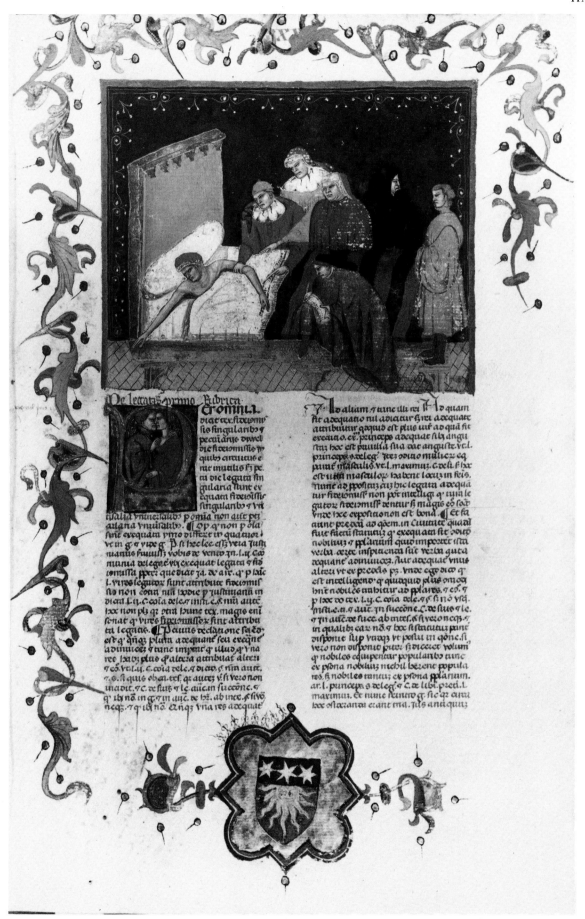

Decorated page with death-bed scene. MS Hunter 6, fol. 1
(See also Colour Ill. 27)

73. Bartolo da Sassoferrato, Treatise on 'Infortiatum'

Bartolus de Saxoferrato,
Lectura super infortiato.
Italy, Bologna, c. 1400.

MS Hunter 6 (S.1.6)

Paper, 418 × 283 mm.; [ii], 189, [ii] leaves; written space 289 × 180 mm., in double columns of 65 lines.

Bartolo da Sassoferrato (1314-1357) wrote a monumental commentary on the whole of the Corpus Juris and was the greatest of 14th-century civil lawyers. The late date of his writings and their wide diffusion led to many copies being written on paper rather than vellum, which was unusual for an illuminated manuscript. There is a slightly later Index of Bartolo's work in Edinburgh also on paper (National Library of Scotland, Adv. 10.1.5). The Infortiatum – a term for which there is no English equivalent – was the middle section of the Corpus Juris Civilis (or Civil Law) established by the Emperor Justinian in the 6th century. It extends from Book 24,3 to Book 38,17, between the Old Digest and the New Digest, but scholars have found no satisfactory explanation of these divisions. The arrangement of the text in two columns differentiates this treatise from a glossed text, the other major form of legal writing in this period, which was in four columns.

The miniature which introduces the volume is a strongly drawn picture of a man in bed making his will (fol. 1). The death-bed scene, and particularly the making of a will, occurs in most illuminated Bolognese law manuscripts since it is one of the most common legal transactions, concerning civil and ecclesiastical authorities alike. Sometimes a priest or a friar and a doctor are shown. The dying man is isolated from the colour of the bystanders and the coverlet by the pallor of his skin and by the white bed linen; he is being restrained by one of the three men on the further side of the bed as he turns away from them in a strong diagonal movement that extends beyond the lower corner of the miniature to include the young couple embracing within the confines of the historiated initial beneath. The domestic nature of the scene is emphasized by the brick floor and the simple bed, while the absence of further specific details of interior furnishings allows the scene to be interpreted as a general view of preparation for death. However, the family, as represented by the grieving woman, already dressed in black, and the stoical young man at the foot of the bed, are kept at a distance to allow room for the lawyers to do their work.

The picture, the figured initials at the beginning of each book, and the other decoration of this manuscript were painted in Bologna, the centre of both law studies and the book trade at this period. The upper half of the coat of arms at the foot of the page is found in many Bolognese armorials. The colours, facial types and decorative elements within the picture and in the garlands of leaves and gold discs in the margins all point to a date at the turn of the 14th and 15th centuries, which is corroborated by the fashionable high collars of the two younger men. The sharp re-entrant angles of the foliage normally appear at the corners; this border is very conservative in its elements but more repetitive than in earlier 14th-century examples. Robert Gibbs notes that the figure style is representative of the minor Bolognese workshops of the late 14th century, closer to the painter Jacopo di Paolo than to the major illuminators, Niccolò and Stefano Azzi. The sharp jawlines of the figures on the frontispiece occur in a more primitive form in the Statutes of the Barbers of 1376 (Bologna, Archivio di Stato, cod. min. 17), but there is also a suggestion of the crisper technique of the Master of the Brussels Initials (cf. no. 72), particularly in the initials of the other chapters. The high viewpoint, unusual in Bolognese illumination, can be paralleled in the celebrated market scene of 1411 in the Register of the Drapers (Bologna, Museo Civico MS 93).

PROVENANCE: Hunter's source not traced.

BIBLIOGRAPHY: Young & Aitken, p. 9; for Bartolo da Sassoferrato see J.A. Clarence Smith, *Medieval Law Teachers and Writers*, Ottawa, 1975, pp. 81-82.

Decorated page. MS Hunter 91, fol. 1

74. Leonardo Bruni, Lives, and other works

Leonardo Bruni, Vitae antiquorum, Vita Demosthenis; Basilius Magnus, De vera institutione; Xenophon, Hiero.
North-east Italy or Veneto, early 15th century (after 1415).

MS Hunter 91 (T.4.8)

Vellum, 281 × 204 mm.; [i], 108, i, [i] leaves; written space 198 × 129 mm., in double columns of 46-47 lines.

The decorative scheme for the initials and borders in this manuscript is based on swirling leaf forms set against generous gold grounds, with multiple large gold discs in the border foliage. The unusual bird design in the lower margin of fol. 1, with its long scrolled neck, is similar to one found in a copy of Boccaccio's *De geneaologia deorum* in Paris (Bibl. Nat., lat. 7877); the orange colouring and a similar style of pattern is also found in Bibl. Nat., lat. 364 (see E. Pellegrin, *La bibliothèque des Visconti et des Sforza, ducs de Milan, au XVe siècle*, Paris, 1955, Supplément, 1969, p. 18, pls. 76, 101). Although the leaf forms and the bird design are stylized shapes on a flat surface, there is a hint of more representational work in the two flower forms and stems in the top margin. The heavy black outline to the gold surfaces may be compared with that of the slightly earlier Brussels Master initial in the Jerome (no. 72): it has however been omitted from the last disc of the floral border, where the gesso ground for the gold can be seen. Initials at the beginning of each work are treated in a similar way.

Leonardo Bruni (1370-1444), was secretary to the papal chancery from 1405 and chancellor to the republic of Florence from 1427 until his death. He was a fine classical scholar and wrote the first history of Florence based on a critical examination of sources. The texts in this collection include his lives of Cato written in 1408, Sertorius (1408-9), Demosthenes (1412), Cicero (1415) and other classical figures, as well as his translations of works by St Basil and Xenophon.

PROVENANCE: Hunter's source not traced.

BIBLIOGRAPHY: Young & Aitken, p. 98.

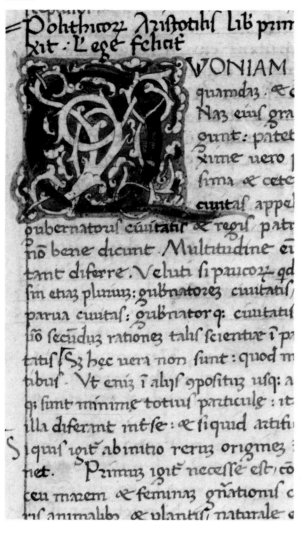

Initial Q *(enlarged)*. MS Hunter 245, fol. 3

75. Aristotle, Politics, and Ethics

Aristoteles, Politica, Ethica, translated into Latin by Leonardo Bruni.
Italy, Florence, 1440.

MS Hunter 245 (U.4.3.)

Vellum, 270 × 195 mm.; [ii], 119, i, [ii] leaves; written space 176 × 118 mm., 42 long lines.

Bruni's translations of the Greek classics greatly advanced the knowledge of Greek literature. This dated copy of his translation of works by Aristotle was made during the Council of Florence (1439-1443) which achieved a union, albeit temporary, between the Greek and Roman Churches. It bears extensive annotations in a contemporary humanist hand.

The initials are elegant examples of the 'white-vine' or 'vine-scroll' style, a Carolingian design developed by the humanists in the mistaken belief that it was a motif used in classical times. It was based on the decoration of initials of central Italian manuscripts of the 11th and 12th centuries (cf. no. 4), which had developed a schematized foliage scroll used in Carolingian manuscripts of the late 9th century and in 10th-century Ottonian manuscripts from Southern Germany. The coils of uncoloured vine stems enclosing a gold initial letter on a square ground, which was coloured mainly blue but had panels in contrasting colours such as red, yellow and green, became a distinctive feature of Florentine book decoration during the early years of the 15th century. This manuscript contains twenty-three of these initials, varying in size from four to sixteen lines. Other works (nos. 76, 80-87, 93) show some of the luxuriantly inventive designs that were developed in Florence and elsewhere from this basic pattern.

The Italian humanist script used in this volume was developed around 1400 by the humanist scholars who were establishing the study of the classics on a firm textual basis and looked to classical models for a more appropriate form of writing than the Gothic hand in contemporary use. The earliest example of this script to be identified so far is a copy of Valerio Massimo's *Opera*, written in Florence in 1397 (Vatican Library, Pal. lat. 903; see G. Billanovich, 'Alle origini della scrittura umanistica: Padova 1261 e Firenze 1397', *Medioevo e Umanesimo*, 44, 1981, pp. 125-140); it also contains white-vine initials.

PROVENANCE: Charles Montagu, first Earl of Halifax, 1702; bought by Hunter from Foulis catalogue, 1771, item 8.

BIBLIOGRAPHY: Young & Aitken, pp. 197-198; Ker, *William Hunter*, p. 21, Appendix A, XXII; for the white-vine style see J.J.G. Alexander, *Italian Renaissance Illuminations*, London, 1977, pp. 12-13.

76. Lactantius, Treatises

Lucius Caecilius Firmianus Lactantius, De ira
Dei, De opificio Dei.
Written in Basel, 1444.

MS General 338

Vellum, 181 × 126 mm.; [i], ii, 80, [i] leaves;
written space 120 × 75 mm., 24-25 long lines.

An initial A on fol. 1 is painted in liquid gold at
the centre of a large white-vine design, delicately
drawn and with red and green panels against a
gold ground. This manuscript, which is dated
May 1444, was doubtless written by an Italian
attending what remained of the Council of Basel
after Pope Eugene IV transferred the Council to
Ferrara in 1437. The Council of Basel was inau-
gurated in 1431 and agreed on a number of
measures concerning church organization and
finance but was split over its attitude to the
papacy itself. The continuance of a section of the
Council in Basel from 1437 saw in 1439 the
election of an antipope, Felix V, but this council
decreed its own dissolution in 1449. The Italian
decoration of the initial may indicate that this
work was added after the owner's return to Italy.

Lactantius (c. 240 – c. 320) had little to say of
Christian doctrine and institutions. He is of more
value as a stylist than a theologian. His style is the
most classical among the Early Christian Latin
authors and he was known in the Renaissance as
the 'Christian Cicero'.

Decorated page with initial Q. MS General 338, fol. 43

PROVENANCE: Abbot Nicholas de la Place, 18th century; in
the Library before 1828.

BIBLIOGRAPHY: Ker, *MMBL*, II, p. 912.

Decorated page with initial N. MS Hunter 425, fol. 131

77. Lactantius, Treatises

Lucius Caecilius Firmianus Lactantius,
Divinarum institutionum libri VII,
De ira Dei, De opificio Dei.
Italy, Bologna, mid 15th century.

MS Hunter 425 (V.4.9)

Vellum, 265 × 183 mm.; [ii], 261, [ii] leaves;
written space 163 × 105 mm., 31 long lines.

The flower and leaf decorations of the initials in this copy of Lactantius link it with a small group of manuscripts now in Paris (Bibl. Nat., lat. 1668, lat. 2969, lat. 8261 and lat. 4769, the last of which is dated Bologna, 1442). François Avril suggests that they were probably produced in or near Bologna around the middle of the 15th century. The flowers in the margins are a simple, flat design based on a scarlet pimpernel, with gold centres and either blue or red petals, like the flower itself. The supporting leaves and stems are treated in a similarly schematic way, with an emphasis on the free use of strong colour.

One initial stands out from the others in containing a delicately modelled profile bust of an elegant young woman, painted in light mauve with white highlights against a dark background (fol. 131). The broad swirls of her dress echo those of the initial, as if to indicate that the whole initial is a matter of design only, but the sense of immediacy in the face is consistent with the possibility that it is in fact a portrait.

PROVENANCE: Hunter's source not traced.

BIBLIOGRAPHY: Young & Aitken, pp. 350-351.

78. Livy, History, Books XXI-XXX

Titus Livius Patavinus, Decas Tertia.
Italy, Milan, written by Laurentius Dolobella,
c. 1450, with miniatures by the Master
of the Vitae Imperatorum.

MS Hunter 370 (V.1.7)

Vellum, 338 × 235 mm.; [ii], 307, ii leaves;
written space 206 × 115 mm., 32 long lines.

The Master of the Vitae Imperatorum was one of
the foremost miniaturists working at the court of
Milan in the early and mid 15th century. He
takes his name from a copy of an Italian translation of Suetonius's *Lives of the Twelve Emperors*,
which he illustrated for Filippo Maria Visconti in
1431 (Paris, Bibl. Nat., it. 131). His surviving
work, identified on stylistic grounds, includes
some fifty books and fragments, divided between
classical and religious texts, and there are over a
dozen related volumes which may be workshop
products. He worked squarely within the Lombard traditions of the late 14th and early 15th
centuries, in a conservative style which remained
remarkably homogeneous throughout his long
career. His work in this volume of Livy has not
been recorded hitherto.

All ten books in the volume are introduced by
large two-compartment initials set against an
incised gold background. The illustrations are
scenes of battles and other military deeds in the
following narrative and are exceptional, not only
in their quality, but also because Livy was not
normally illustrated; as Albinia de la Mare
observes, he 'was generally considered in Italy as
a serious author, not to be treated as a picture-
book'. Landscape and perspective are subordinated to the narrative context and to the artist's
interest in detail: the pointed nimbus surmounting some of the warriors, for instance, is of
Castilian origin and echoes the shape of the gold
background outside the letter form. The figures
themselves are small and firmly drawn with
elaborate modelling of the draperies, and the
representation of emotion in the faces of the
participants is extended into the general anima-
tion of his scenes. There is nonetheless a painterly concern for volume which helps to articulate
the crowded scenes, and the overall designs are
unified with a precise awareness of tonal values.

The scribe who executed this volume, Laurentius Dolobella, also wrote the splendidly illuminated Plutarch in London (B.L., Add. MS
22318).

PROVENANCE: An effaced coat of arms on fol. 1 with the
initials I.A. suggests that the manuscript was written for
someone whose name, in the custom of the time, began with
those letters (?Jacobus) and who may have been a friend of

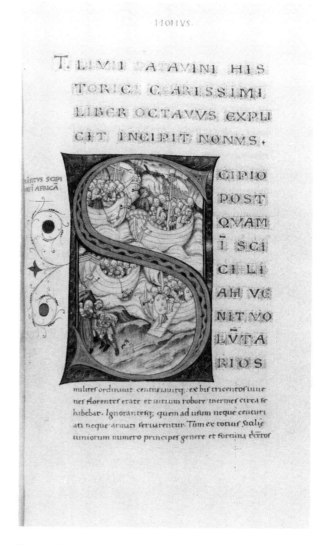

Decorated page with initial S showing Scipio
crossing into Africa. MS Hunter 370, fol. 253
(See also Colour Ill. 32)

Pier Candido Decembrio; bought for Hunter at the Louis-
Jean Gaignat sale, Paris 10 April 1769, lot 2886.

BIBLIOGRAPHY: Young & Aitken, pp. 296-297; De Bure, II, p.
89, no. 2886; *Treasures*, p. 19, no. 54; Alexander, 'Italian
Illuminated Manuscripts', p. 116; Ker, *William Hunter*, p.
14, Appendix A, VIII; Baldwin, *William Hunter*, pp. 5-6,
no. 9; cf. E. Pellegrin, *La bibliothèque des Visconti et des
Sforza, ducs de Milan, au XVe siècle*, Paris, 1955, Supplément, 1969, p. 38; C. Mitchell, *A Fifteenth-Century Italian
Plutarch*, London, 1961; Alison Stones, 'An Italian Minia-
ture in the Gambier Barry Collection', *Burlington Maga-
zine*, 111, 1969, pp. 7-12; A.C. de la Mare, 'Florentine
Manuscripts of Livy in the Fifteenth Century', *Livy*, ed.
T.A. Dorey, London, 1971, pp. 187, 195; E. Cappugi,
'Contributo alla conoscenza dell' "Inferno" Parigi-Imola e
del suo miniatore detto il Maestro del Vitae Imperatorum',
*La Miniatura Italiana tra Gotico e Rinascimento. Atti del II
Congresso di Storia della Miniatura Italiana*, ed. E. Sesti,
Florence, 1985, pp. 285-296; L. Stefani, 'Per una storia
della miniatura Lombarda da Giovanni de' Grassi alla scuola
Cremonese della II metà del Quattrocento: appunti bibliog-
rafici', ibid., Appendice, 'Codici ascritti al 'Magister Vitae
Imperatorum', pp. 821-874, Appendice pp. 875-881: the
Glasgow manuscript is not listed in this Appendix.

Roman and Carthaginian Battles. MS Hunter 41, fol. 1

79. Niccolò da Ferrara, Roman History

Niccolò da Ferrara, Polistorio, Books III and IV.
Italy, Ferrara, 1450s.

MS Hunter 41 (T.1.9)

Vellum, 395 × 266 mm.; [ii], 406, [ii] leaves; written space 278 × 185 mm., in double columns of 48 lines.

Books III and IV of Niccolò's history of Rome cover the long period from the first Punic War to the war between the Conte di Romagna and Ricardo Manfredi of Faenza. In this copy, references to Este and Modena are marked out in the margin for special attention. In addition to its historiated and illuminated initials the volume is remarkable for two large panels packed with narrative and pictorial detail. The first panel, introducing Book III (fol. 1), depicts land and sea battles of the Romans and Carthaginians against a background of the coasts and waters of the Mediterranean; the foot soldiers and cavalry of both sides wear contemporary Italian costume and armour, and the walled cities are defended by moats with drawbridges.

The panel introducing Book IV (fol. 149) shows Augustus on his triumphal entry into Rome being welcomed by a group of senators on the drawbridge. The spirited scene appears to be based on contemporary processions, from the hangings on the chariot to the presence of the jester in a fool's cap making an unclassical gesture of impudent contempt (*far le fiche*) towards the emperor. Although the background details of landscape, city wall, moat and sky are rather schematic, the figure groups are vigorous and recall the forceful designs of panels on *cassoni* (wooden chests) of the period. The miniature is also notable for its tonality, with the juxtaposition of strong colours and a sparing use of outline. The miniaturist makes ample use of the opportunity for gay armorial displays on the shields of the soldiers, the banners of the trumpeters and the pennant floating above the knights; his interest in abstract design is demonstrated in the patterns made by the red harness on the white horses pulling the emperor's chariot.

Each panel is set at the head of a page which is fully decorated in all margins with armorial bearings, medallions, putti, candelabra and floral designs, completed by elaborate penwork within a broad frame of gold. Medallions tended to be used in Ferrarese work at an earlier date than elsewhere (cf. no. 85, from Milan, and no. 102, from Rome or Naples). The apparent shadow cast by the coat of arms is an early instance of this use of *trompe l'oeil*.

PROVENANCE: Arms of Strozzi of Ferrara, fols. 1 and 149; bought by Hunter at the Joseph Ames sale, London, 5 May 1760, lot 1014.

BIBLIOGRAPHY: Young & Aitken, pp. 46-48; Wardrop, 'Western Illuminated Manuscripts', p. 322; Ker, *William Hunter*, p. 12, Appendix A, II.

Augustus entering Rome in Triumph. MS Hunter 41, fol. 149
(See also Colour Ill. 31)

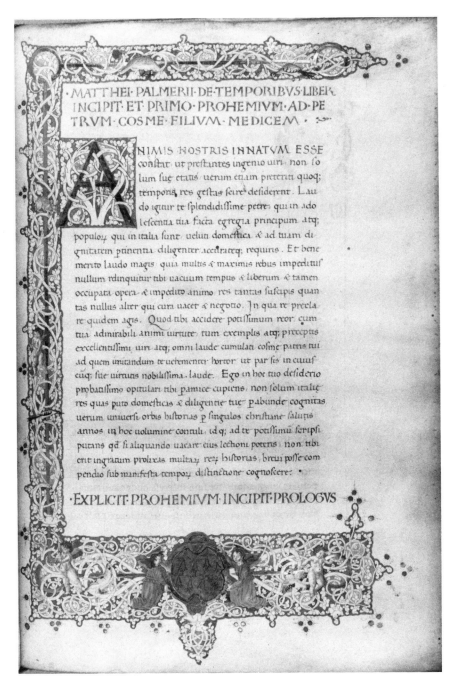

Decorated page. MS Hunter 198, fol. 1

80. Matteo Palmieri, Annals

Matteo Palmieri, De temporibus.
Italy, Florence, written by Ser Giovanni
di Piero da Stia, 1450-60.

MS Hunter 198 (U.1.2)

Vellum, 369 × 257 mm.; [ii], ii, 84, ii, [iii]
leaves; written space 235 × 145 mm., 31 long
lines.

Ser Giovanni di Piero da Stia (c.1405-1474) was
a Florentine notary, who copied works on commission for humanists such as Manetti or Vespa-
siano and also for stock in his shop. Albinia de la
Mare has attributed some forty manuscripts to
his hand. The rich white-vine decoration of the
first leaf sets this volume apart from the general
run of his more simply embellished books. The
gold shafts are less intricately arranged than in
the Cicero (no. 86) but there is a similar population of angels, putti, birds and animals. The coat
of arms is a later addition.

The *Annals* of the historian Palmieri (1405-
1475) give an account of world events from the
birth of Christ to 1448.

PROVENANCE: Hunter's source not traced.

BIBLIOGRAPHY: Young & Aitken, p. 141; de la Mare, 'New
Research', pp. 425-426, 499-500.

Decorated page. MS Hunter 441, fol. 1 *(See also Colour Ill. 34)*

81. Cicero, Letters to his Friends

Marcus Tullius Cicero, Epistolae ad familiares. Italy, Florence, 1450-60.

MS Hunter 441 (V.5.11)

Vellum, 256 × 166 mm.; [iii], 192, [ii] leaves; written space 172 × 90 mm., 30 long lines.

This magnificent copy of Cicero's letters is written in a cursive humanistic script with numerous gold initials surrounded by white-vine decoration. The vine scrolls which festoon the splendid initial and borders of the first leaf are inhabited by a population of cherubs, birds and insects, and are supported by a trellis-like framework of gold shafts which also includes a medallion portrait. The style has been identified as close to that of Francesco d'Antonio del Cherico (see no. 83).

The design demonstrates a tension between the stylized decoration of a flat surface and the attention to naturalistic detail that was introduced in Florence during the 1450s under the influence of Piero de' Medici's commissions for the decoration of books for his library in the Palazzo Medici. The new style was developed by illuminators availing themselves of the modelbooks which by then were in general use in the workshops of panel- and fresco-painters.

PROVENANCE: The effaced blazon on fol. 1, which bears traces of a cross, may have been the arms of Piccolomini, or perhaps those of Savoy; Hunter's source not traced.

BIBLIOGRAPHY: Young & Aitken, p. 364; Bodleian Library, *Italian Illuminated Manuscripts from 1400 to 1500*, Oxford, 1948, no. 80; *Treasures*, pp. 19-20, no. 56; for the use of modelbooks by Florentine illuminators see F. Ames-Lewis, 'Modelbook Drawings and the Florentine Quattrocento Artist', *Art History*, 10, 1987, pp. 1-11.

82. Bartolomeo Cipolla, Treatise on the Selection of a Military Commander

Bartolomeus Cepolla, De imperatore
militum deligendo.
Italy, Verona, late 1450s, with illumination and
lettering by Felice Feliciano of Verona.

MS Hunter 275 (U.5.15)

Vellum, 233 × 157 mm.; [iii], ii, [i], 161, [iii]
leaves; written space 140 × 85 mm., 23 long
lines.

The exuberant designs in this remarkable volume
are the work of Felice Feliciano of Verona
(c.1432-1480), a forceful individual characterized
in his various activities by J. Wardrop as 'anti-
quary, doggerel poet, calligrapher, printer, al-
chemist and immoralist'. The full-page white-
vine illuminations are among the richest examples of his skills, displaying a splendid inventive-
ness in the initials and borders, such as the
exuberant capital A which begins the text (fol. 3;
colour ill. 33) and in the whole-page decorations
made independently of the text.

The epigraphic lettering and accompanying
monumental designs are of equal importance in
showing the growth of interest at this period in
classical inscriptions. Feliciano, with the painter
Andrea Mantegna and the scribe and scholar
Bartolomeo Sanvito, was at the forefront of this
activity, recording for instance in his *Jubilatio* an
excursion made with Mantegna and others along
the shore of Lake Garda in September 1464
which, to the accompaniment of music and wine,
yielded twenty-two inscriptions. All his manuscript designs give evidence of his direct observation of these antiquities, and other scribes were
quick to follow the conventions of classical Roman lettering. Other pages in the volume are
tinted in green or purple, possibly in the manner
of Ciriaco Pizzicolli of Ancona (1391-1452), a
scarcely less colourful epigrapher, whose business interests caused him to travel extensively in
Greece and Asia Minor.

Cipolla (c.1420-1475), Professor of Law at
Padua, was one of the most distinguished lawyers
of his time. His *Treatise on the Selection of a
Military Commander* was written in 1453-54,
when the leadership of the Venetian army was
being hotly debated, and this copy has a dedication to Bartolomeo Colleoni, in whose favour the
issue was decided. The presence of Cipolla's
arms indicates that this was his own copy. It is
likely therefore to have been decorated for him
before he left Verona in 1458, and is important
evidence for the interest in epigraphic designs at
an early date.

PROVENANCE: Bartolomeo Cipolla; Hunter's source not
traced.

BIBLIOGRAPHY: Young & Aitken, pp. 222-223; J.J.G. Alexander, *Italian Renaissance Illuminations*, London, 1977, pp.
19-20; idem, 'Italian Illuminated Manuscripts', p. 116; cf.
J. Wardrop, *The Script of Humanism*, Oxford, 1963, pp.
16-18; R. Avesani, 'Felice Feliciano artigiano del libro
antiquario e letterato', *Verona nel Quattrocento. La civiltà
delle lettere. Verona e il suo territorio*, VII, 2, Verona, 1984,
cap. 4, pp. 113-144.

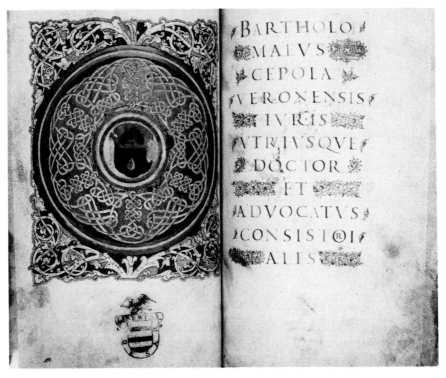

Decorated opening. MS Hunter 275, fols. 1v-2
(See also Colour Ill. 33 of initial on fol. 3)

83. Servius, Commentary on Virgil

Servius Honoratus Grammaticus, Expositio in Vergilium.
Italy, Florence, written by Ser Piero di Bernardo Cennini, 1464, and illuminated by Francesco d'Antonio del Cherico.

MS Hunter 219 (U.2.10)

Paper, 333 × 232 mm.; [i], 288, xvi leaves; written space 224 × 130 mm., 37 long lines.

The major decoration in this volume is the work of Francesco d'Antonio del Cherico, goldsmith and miniaturist in Florence. He became a member of the Compagnia di S. Paolo in 1452, serving as governor eleven times before his death in 1484, and he has been described as the most elegant decorative artist of the Florentine Renaissance. The importance of his influence can be measured by the fact that it was in his workshop that the generation of miniature painters active from 1470 to the end of the century was trained (cf. nos. 81 and 91).

The putti and half-length portrait in the historiated initial (fol.1) are modelled in a painterly manner, the flesh tones being worked in a distinctively dramatic way. The elaborate white-vine design is one version of a style that was freely used in different arrangements – for initials alone (no. 75), for a complete border (no. 81), for three connected margins (no. 80), or in the pattern in this manuscript of a single design embracing the inner and top margins and initial, with a separate panel below including a coat of arms – that of the Benivieni family – within a wreath. The text contains gold initials with white-vine decoration on grounds of two or three colours.

The script is an elegant humanistic cursive written by Ser Piero di Bernardo Cennini (c. 1445-1484), a humanist and professional notary whose earliest surviving dated manuscript was written in 1460, when he was only about fifteen. He wrote the present manuscript four years later, and it is particularly interesting to note that Servius's *Commentary* was the first work to be printed in Florence, in 1471-72, by Piero's father, the goldsmith Bernardo Cennini.

Greek annotations in the text have been identified by Dieter Harlfinger as being in the hand of the scholar Johannes Skutariores.

PROVENANCE: Benivieni family of Florence; Hunter's source not traced.

BIBLIOGRAPHY: Young & Aitken, p. 163; de la Mare, 'New Research', pp. 445, 526-529, no. 12; cf. M. Levi d'Ancona, *Miniatura e miniatori a Firenze dal XIV al XVI secolo*, Florence, 1962, pp. 108-116.

Decorated page with initial B. MS Hunter 219, fol. 1

Decorated page. MS General 193, fol. 1

84. Diodorus Siculus, Historical Library

Diodorus Siculus, Bibliotheca Historica, translated into Latin by Poggio Bracciolini. Italy, ?Rome, third quarter of the 15th century.

MS General 193

Vellum, 243 × 170 mm.; [ii], ii, 152, ii, [ii] leaves; written space 149 × 111 mm., double columns of 30-34 lines.

The white-vine decoration on fols. 1, 19 and 93 is more organic than the Florentine examples in the collection (nos. 75, 80, 81, 83). The same colours of red, green and blue are used for the infill and background, and the clusters of triple white dots are similar; but the overall angularity of the design is not within the broadly linear frame of the Florentine work. The modelling of the putti is rather heavier than of those painted by Francesco d'Antonio del Cherico (no. 83).

Diodorus's work, written c. 60-30 B.C., is a compendium of sources for the history of the world from the earliest times to Caesar's Gallic War in 54 B.C. Poggio's translation was one of many commissioned by the humanist Pope Nicolas V: it was started towards the end of Poggio's long career with the Curia in Rome and was completed in the early 1450s in Florence, with the help of the noted Florentine humanist Pier Candido Decembrio, when Poggio retired there to the post of chancellor and historiographer to the Republic.

PROVENANCE: College of Arras, Louvain, early 17th century; in the Library by 1828.

BIBLIOGRAPHY: Ker, *MMBL*, II, p. 903.

85. Justinus, Epitome of Trogus's History

Marcus Junianus Justinus, Epitoma historiarum
Philippicarum Pompei Trogi.
Italy, Milan, third quarter of the 15th century.

MS Hunter 282 (U.5.22)

Vellum, 243 × 169 mm.; [ii], 246, [ii] leaves;
written space 145 × 85 mm., 23 long lines.

The historical writings of Trogus Pompeius (59
B.C.-17 A.D.) are lost except for this 3rd-
century abridgement by Marcus Junianus Justinus and a few excerpts in Pliny. Its forty-four
books contained a general history of the world,
and even in its fragmentary state it is often an
important authority for the ancient history of the
states bordering the Eastern Mediterranean. The
work was widely read in the Middle Ages and was
first printed in Rome c.1469.

The illuminated first page of this copy has a
gold initial and a complete border of white-vine
decoration, with a medallion and figurative
scenes as well as a coat of arms. Except in the
frame bars, the gold of the border is used to fill
segments of the vine-stem pattern rather than as
part of the formal structure of the design. The
width of the main vine stems gives them a flat
banner-like appearance, quite distinct from their
Florentine counterparts, and the stems are further characterized by having hair-line collar decoration at the bifurcations. Both these features
appear also in a manuscript written in Ferrara in
1469 now in New York (Lucius Junius Modera-
tus Columella, *De re rustica*, written by Hen-
riecus Roffinus de Murialdo, Pierpont Morgan
Library, M. 139, formerly owned by the Duke of
Hamilton; see M. Harrsen and G.K. Boyce,
*Italian Manuscripts in the Pierpont Morgan Lib-
rary*, New York, 1953, p. 33, no. 59) and in a
copy of Livy's *Third Decade* written by Johannes
Maguntinus in 1449 and illuminated for Leonello
d'Este (cf. C. de Hamel, *A History of Illuminated
Manuscripts*, Oxford, 1986, pp. 229-230). The
skilfully painted cameo medallion portrait of
Philip of Macedon is evidence of the antiquarian
interests of the period, which extended beyond
the classical texts themselves to an interest in
architecture, armour and the decorative arts. The
medallion motif itself is imitated from Ferrarese
work (cf. no. 79) and is uncommon in Milan.
François Avril notes that the elaborate arms,
which appear with similar decoration also on
Paris, Bibl. Nat., lat. 5771, may be those of the
Sforza family of Pesaro.

PROVENANCE: Hunter's source not traced.

BIBLIOGRAPHY: Young & Aitken, p. 228; Ker, *William Hunter*, p. 27, Appendix C.

Decorated page. MS Hunter 282, fol. 1
(See also Colour Ill. 35)

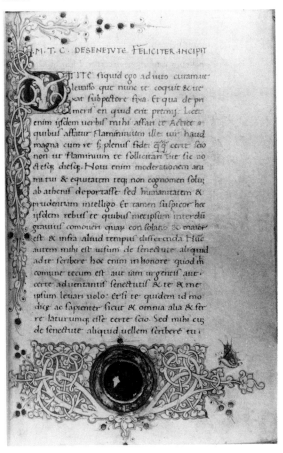

Decorated page. MS Hunter 459, fol. 1

Decorated page. Hunterian Collection, Bf 1. 13, fol. 4

86. Cicero, Treatises

Marcus Tullius Cicero, De senectute, De amicitia, De paradoxis, De somno Scipionis. Italy, Florence, written by Michael de Ghuardavillis of Volterra, third quarter of the 15th century.

MS Hunter 459 (V.6.9)

Vellum, 215 × 145 mm.; [i], 70, ii, [i] leaves; written space 140 × 91 mm., 25 long lines.

The first leaf has an initial in gold with white-vine decoration in three borders, including a winged insect. The manuscript is one of ten identified by Albinia de la Mare as having been written by Michael de Ghuardavillis of Volterra. This is his formal hand: it was used in six of the manuscripts, and the others were written in a humanistic cursive hand.

PROVENANCE: Arms of ?Bartolomaeus Scala; Hunter's source not traced.

BIBLIOGRAPHY: Young & Aitken, pp. 379-380; de la Mare, 'New Research', p. 514.

87. Pope Leo I, Sermons

Leo I, Sermones, edited by Johannes Andreae, Bishop of Aleria. Italy, Rome, printed by Giovanni Filippo da Legname, c. 1470.

Hunterian Collection, Bf 1. 13

Paper, 331 × 229 mm.; folio; [ii], i, 158, i, [ii] leaves.

The introduction of printing did not at first have a significant impact on book design. In fact printed volumes were intended to resemble the more prestigious manuscripts as closely as possible, and they were decorated in the same way. This book and others from later in the same decade (nos. 93, 94, 96, 97) show variations of the white-vine and other foliate patterns which continued to be used in the early years of printing in Italy.

The unidentified coat of arms on this volume appears also with similar decoration in a companion work in Hunter's collection, Ambrose's *De officiis*, printed in Rome by the same printer c. 1471; it was also in the Gaignat Library (sale, 1769, lot 226).

PROVENANCE: Bought for Hunter at the Louis-Jean Gaignat sale, Paris, 10 April 1769, lot 248.

BIBLIOGRAPHY: Goff, L 131; De Bure, I, p. 69, no. 248.

88. Lactantius, Treatises, and other works

Lucius Coelius Firmianus Lactantius, De divinis institutionibus, De ira Dei, De opificio Dei, De Phoenice carmen; Ovid, De Phoenice; Dante Alighieri, Della Fenice; Venantius Fortunatus, Carmen de Pascha.
Italy, [Venice], printed by Adam de Ambergau, 1471.

Hunterian Collection, Bf 3. 2

Vellum, 394 × 205 mm.; folio; [ii], 219, [ii] leaves.

The general framework of the first page of text with gold shafts, the wreath for the armorial, the alternating background panels of blue and red with triple white dots, the putti, the hair-line sprays round the gold discs, and the form of the gold initial M, all suggest a strong Italian influence. The drawing, however, from the shapes of the foliage to the figures of animals, birds and grotesques, is of northern inspiration, probably Dutch. The finished flower in the initial and the half-length figure with a hat in the lower half of the right-hand margin are particularly northern in character. The wash modelling given to most of the uncoloured elements of the design may indicate that the decoration has been taken as far as was intended rather than that it was left incomplete. It must have been difficult to combine the two traditions, and possibly this is why the page as a whole gives the impression of having been finished rather hurriedly.

The eight illuminated initials in the text which introduce chapters and different works are more firmly in the Italian manner, with different colours of leaf design and gold initials; several contain vignettes of birds and other figures.

The work of Lactantius (cf. no. 76) has the honour of being the earliest extant dated book printed in Italy; it was produced by Konrad Sweynheim and Arnold Pannartz in Subiaco six years previously, in 1465.

PROVENANCE: Bought for Hunter at the Louis-Jean Gaignat sale, Paris, 10 April 1769, lot 220.

BIBLIOGRAPHY: Goff, L 4; De Bure, I, p. 63, no. 220.

Decorated page. Hunterian Collection, Bf 3, 2, fol. 13

ad calcem uix ufque perduxi opus magn
fanctitati a qua uelut fonte omnia mea l
quidem ut inftitutionibus grammaticis
indigeat: qui caeteros in doctrinis oibus (
felicitate praecellis:Sed ut i tua illa biblic
tiffimam comparas aliquo pacto colloca

Initial C. Hunterian Collection, Bg 1. 9, fol. 1

89. Giovanni Tortelli, On Orthography

Giovanni Tortelli, De orthographia.
Italy, Venice, printed by Nicolaus Jenson, 1471.

Hunterian Collection, Bg 1. 9

Paper, 379 × 269 mm.; folio; [ii], 269, [iii] leaves.

This volume is one of two copies of Tortelli's work known to have been decorated by the same artist; the other is in the Library of Trinity College, Dublin (SS.aa.32). In both copies the faceted initial C contains a classical figure subject. The Hunterian figure is of a semi-draped man holding a bunch of grasses and making a libation of wine from a bowl onto an altar fire, while the Trinity College subject is of a centaur in an open landscape. These two initials are characterized by the delicate modelling of the figures and the stipple colouring of the ground and sky, combined with a drawing technique which is quite loose in some details. Although neither subject is specifically related to Tortelli's work, they are in complete harmony with the classical character of Jenson's printing.

Lilian Armstrong has identified five other incunables with initials by the same artist, in addition to the Trinity College volume. They range in date from 1469 to 1478 and include another book printed by Jenson, a copy of his Plutarch of 1478 which was formerly in the Olschki collection.

PROVENANCE: Bought for Hunter at the Louis-Jean Gaignat sale, Paris, 10 April 1769, lot 1405.

BIBLIOGRAPHY: Goff, T 395; De Bure, I, p. 371, no. 1405; cf. L.S. Olschki, 'Incunables illustrés imitant les manuscrits', *Bibliofilia*, 15, 1913, p. 325, no. 38.

90. Petrarch, Works

Francesco Petrarca, Canzoniere, Trionfi,
Memorabilia de Laura; Leonardo Bruni,
Vita di Petrarca.
Italy, Padua, printed by Bartolomeo Valdezochio
and Martinus de Septem Arboribus,
6 November 1472, and illustrated by the Master
of the London Pliny.

Hunterian Collection, Bg 2. 12

Paper, 265 × 163 mm.; folio; [ii], 188, [ii]
leaves; binding by J. Derome of Paris (d. 1761).

The Master who executed the initials and other
illustrations in this volume has been named from
the historiated initials in the Jenson Pliny of 1472
now in London (B.L., IC 19662). He was the
principal associate of the Master of the Putti who
was active in Venice between 1469 and 1473, and
together they established the *all'antica* style in
the Veneto in the early 1470s. This copy of
Petrarch shows him working at the outset of his
career in close collaboration with the Putti Master, and it is interesting to note that another copy
of this edition of Petrarch, now in Milan (Biblioteca Trivulziana, Inc. Petr. 2) was illustrated
by the Putti Master himself.

The score of volumes which have been identified as containing the London Pliny Master's
work span the years from 1472 to 1482. His
understanding of anatomy, perspective and the
antique is evident in the frontispiece to this copy
of Petrarch: Lilian Armstrong recently established it as his earliest full frontispiece, and it is
additional to the works she lists in her account of
the Master's *oeuvre*. The main architectural elements of the pillar and candelabra are supported
on a base which includes a frieze of male and
female sea creatures with putti riding on their
tails; these figure designs are used also in a
manuscript of the *Descriptio originis mundi et
urbis Romae* in Venice (Biblioteca Marciana, MS
lat. X, 231 [3731]) formerly owned by the Agostini family. The pen drawing is heightened by
wash, as in the other initials in the book; the page
has a frame of liquid gold, used also for the large
initial, and the composition is discreetly enlivened by the colours of a bowl of flowers. The
original coat of arms, perhaps of the Capello
family of Venice, has been overpainted with the
arms of France.

In later years, particularly when he worked,
probably in Rome, for Cardinal Giovanni of
Aragon (see no. 97), the London Pliny Master
moved away from the use of architectural designs
for his frontispieces, favouring painted scenes
rather than monochrome linework.

Frontispiece. Hunterian Collection, Bg 2. 12, fol. 1

PROVENANCE: ?Capello family of Venice bought by Hunter at
the Louis-Jean Gaignat sale, Paris, 10 April 1769, lot 1979.

BIBLIOGRAPHY: Goff, P 373; De Bure, I, p. 492, no. 1979;
Oldham, *Notes on Bindings*, p. 4; cf. G. Mariani Canova,
La miniatura veneta del rinascimento 1450-1500, Venice,
1969, pp. 34, 149, no. 45; L. Armstrong, *Renaissance
Miniature Painters and Classical Imagery. The Master of
the Putti and his Venetian Workshop*, London, 1981; de la
Mare, 'Florentine Scribes', p. 251; L. Armstrong, 'The
Agostini Plutarch: an Illuminated Venetian Incunable in the
Fagel Collection', *Treasures of the Library, Trinity College
Dublin*, ed. P. Fox, Dublin, 1986, pp. 86-96.

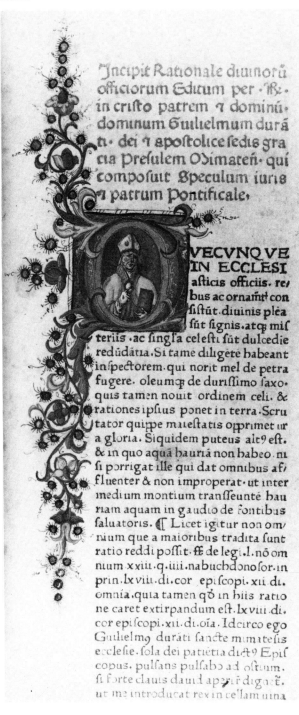

Initial Q. Hunterian Collection, Bg 1. 6, fol. 6

91. Guillaume Durand, Manual for the Holy Offices

Guillaume Durand, Bishop of Mende, Rationale divinorum officiorum, edited by Johannes Baptista de Lanciis.
Italy, Rome, printed by Ulrich Han and Simone Cardella de Luca, 23 June 1473.

Hunterian Collection, Bg 1. 6

Paper, 383 × 264 mm.; folio; [iii], 282, [iv] leaves.

The frontispiece initial, with a portrait of Bishop Durand (1237-1296), is painted in the style of Francesco d'Antonio del Cherico of Florence (see no. 83). The treatise contains eight books relating to church symbolism in subjects like vestments and architecture and the organisation of services throughout the year. It became a standard work on the subject and was first printed by Johann Fust and Peter Schoeffer in Mainz in 1459.

PROVENANCE: 'Ex-libris Ad. R.P. Magistri Francisci Tibaldi T.', printed label on fol. 2; Hunter's source not traced.

BIBLIOGRAPHY: Goff, D 406; Oldham, Notes on Bindings, p. 4: 'Elliott and Chapman, London'; cf. M.B. Stillwell, The Beginning of the World of Books, New York, 1972, p. 15, no. 26.

92. Gratian, Decretum

Johannes Gratianus, Decretum, with commentary of Bartholomaeus Brixiensis, edited by Alexander de Novo and Petrus Albinianus Trecius. Italy, Venice, printed by Nicolaus Jenson, 28 June 1474.

Hunterian Collection, Bw 1. 12

Paper, 425 × 285 mm. ; folio; [iii], [1], 388, [iii] leaves.

The Decretum, or ordinances, of Gratian was composed in the first half of the 12th century. It is one of the most important canonical collections in the history of Canon Law, although it was never given papal authority as an official source. It is a vast compilation of some four thousand chapters, divided into three parts, and deals with pastoral problems, aspects of ecclesiastical discipline, the administration of the Church and the conduct of monks, and also includes a treatise on the Sacraments. It quickly won a universal recognition that had not been enjoyed by any previous canonical compilation. One hundred and fifty of the four hundred surviving manuscripts listed by A. Melnikas are illustrated, some twenty of them with a series of between thirty and forty miniatures.

In addition to the completed decorative scheme of large painted initials on gold grounds and small gold initials on painted grounds, this imposing printed volume has a series of thirty-three drawings illustrating scenes from the examples of Canon Law described in the text. As the drawings are uncoloured and a larger space across both columns of text has been left for a frontispiece, it may be assumed that they are designs for miniatures that were left unpainted. Another copy of this edition with an extensive series of completed miniatures, produced for Lorenzo Roverella, Bishop of Ferrara, is in the Museo di Schifanoia in Ferrara (cf. G. Mariani Canova, *La miniatura Veneta del Rinascimento 1450-1500*, Venice, 1969, p. 52 and p. 152, no. 63).

PROVENANCE: Phillip Carteret Webb, 1700-1770; Hunter's source not traced.

BIBLIOGRAPHY: Goff, G 363; cf. A. Melnikas, *The Corpus of the Miniatures in the Manuscripts of the Decretum Gratiani*, (Studia Gratiana XVI-XVIII), 3 vols., Rome, 1975.

Detail of decorated page. Hunterian Collection, Bw 1. 12, fol. 186

93. Petrarch, Trionfi

Francesco Petrarca, Trionfi,
edited by Bernardo Lapini.
Italy, Bologna, printed by Annibale Malpigli, 27 April 1475.

Hunterian Collection, Bf 1. 1

Paper, 332 × 225 mm.; folio; [ii], 244, [ii] leaves.

An imposing gold framework which surrounds the first page of text provides an elaborate trellis for the white-vine decoration. The tight curls of the vine stems and the multiplicity of leaves are characteristic of Bolognese work. The design incorporates the arms of the Bentivoglio family of Bologna, where the work was printed. Other white-vine initials occur throughout the text.

PROVENANCE: Bought for Hunter at the Louis-Jean Gaignat sale, Paris, 10 April 1769, lot 1989.

BIBLIOGRAPHY: IGI, no. 7543; BMC VI, p. 811; De Bure, I, p. 494, no. 1989.

94. Bible

Biblia latina, ed. Johannes Andreae, Bishop of Aleria; Aristeas, De septuaginta interpretibus, translated by Mathias Palmerius.
Nürnberg, printed by Andreas Frisner and Johann Sensenschmidt, 9 December 1475. Vol. I (of II).

Hunterian Collection, Bv 1. 10

Paper, 456 × 320 mm.; folio; [ii], 212, [ii] leaves.

The first of two volumes of this impressive Bible. Although most of the initials are in red and blue penwork of German origin, the first text-page has an ebullient floral design covering all the borders and the centre margin as well, which suggests that it was decorated for an Italian owner. Vestiges of conventional white-vine design, present in the lower left-hand margin, appear curiously out of place in this newly-developed design with its greater emphasis on natural forms and softer tonalities of colour. The gentle shades of green, pink and blue are heightened by a liberal use of gold in the background to the initial, the frame itself and the plentiful gold discs, as well as by the occasional use of red which reflects the printed rubric at the top of the page. The trees which appear in the roundels of both the inner and the outer margin may be a device of the original owner. (Cf. no 95)

PROVENANCE: Bought for Hunter at the Louis-Jean Gaignat sale, Paris, 10 April 1769, lot 23.

BIBLIOGRAPHY: Goff, B 544; De Bure, I, pp. 9-10, no. 23.

95. Bible

Biblia latina, ed. Johannes Andreae, Bishop of Aleria; Aristeas, De septuaginta interpretibus, translated by Mathias Palmerius.
Nürnberg, printed by Andreas Frisner and Johann Sensenschmidt, 9 December 1475. Vol. I (of II).

Euing Collection, Dn – b. 7

Paper, 464 × 327 mm.; folio; [ii], 212, [ii] leaves.

Another copy of the same edition of this Nürnberg Bible as no. 94, however decorated for the German market. German decoration tended to be more restrained than Italian work, being often limited, as here, to a carefully worked initial and sprays of leaves with long tendrils in the margins, heightened by a modest use of gold and silver. It is interesting to note that the whole decorative scheme down to the flourishing of capital letters in the text is varied in the two copies: the Italian work uses a light yellow wash while the German one has the more common bar-lines in red ink.

PROVENANCE: Jesuits of Teplitz, Bohemia (now Teplice, Czechoslovakia); Royal Academy of Prague; bought by William Euing, 6 July 1844, and bequeathed by him to the Library in 1874.

BIBLIOGRAPHY: Goff, B 544.

96. Pliny, Natural History

Caius Plinius Secundus, Historia naturalis, translated into Italian by Cristoforo Landino.
Italy, Venice, printed by Nicolaus Jenson, 1476.

Euing Collection, BD12 – a. 11

Paper, 387 × 253 mm.; folio; [iii], 409, [ii] leaves.

Both in colouring and design, the decorated page introducing Book II (fol. 21) is typically Venetian. Flower and leaf forms are enclosed within a regular pattern of swirling hair-lines; a putto's head is included in the centre of the top border in a similar fashion to the cameo portrait in Hunter's copy of the Livy of 1478 (no. 100); and the red and green column of overlapping leaves in the inner margin is another regular feature of Venetian work of this period.

For more fully illuminated copies of this edition of Pliny by the artist of Hunter's *Breviarium Romanum* of 1478 see the entry for no. 101.

PROVENANCE: Donated to the Library by William Euing in 1872.

BIBLIOGRAPHY: Goff, P 801.

Decorated page. Hunterian Collection, Bf 1. 1, fol. 5
(See also Colour Ill. on Half-title)

Decorated page. Euing Collection, Dn – b. 7, fol. 9

Decorated page. Hunterian Collection, Bv 1. 10, fol. 9

Decorated page. Euing Collection, BD12 – a. 11, fol. 21

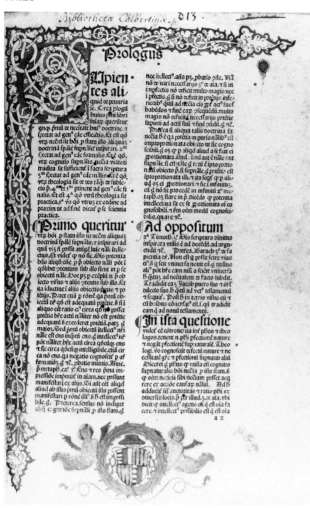

Decorated page. Hunterian Collection, By 2. 3, fol. 1

97. Duns Scotus, Commentaries on the Sentences of Peter Lombard

Johannes Duns Scotus, Quaestiones in quattuor libros Sententiarum Petri Lombardi, edited by Thomas Penketh and Bartholomaeus Bellatus. Part I (of IV).
Italy, Venice, printed by Johann of Cologne and Johann Manthen of Gerresheim, 26 July 1477, and illuminated by Matteo Felice in Naples.

Hunterian Collection, By 2. 3

Paper, 296 × 197 mm.; folio; [ii], 242, i, [ii] leaves.

Although this volume was printed in Venice, the gold initial and white-vine decoration was added in Naples by Matteo Felice for the renowned collector Cardinal Giovanni of Aragon, whose arms appear on the first page. All of Cardinal Giovanni's incunables that have been identified so far were decorated by the same artist.

The press of Johann of Cologne and Johann Manthen was a continuation of the first press established in Venice by Johann of Speier in 1469, which seems to have broken down in 1473, with the types passing to his successors by 1474. Another work printed by them is no. 104.

PROVENANCE: Cardinal Giovanni of Aragon (1456-1485); Jean-Baptiste Colbert, Marquis de Seignelay (1609-1683); bought for Hunter at the Louis-Jean Gaignat sale, Paris, 10 April 1769, lot 264.

BIBLIOGRAPHY: Goff, D 379; De Bure, I, p. 75, no. 264; Oldham, *Notes on Bindings*, p. 8; for other books written or decorated for Cardinal Giovanni see de la Mare, 'Florentine Scribes', Appendix I.

98. Appian, History of Rome

Appianus, De bellis civilibus, translated by Pier Candido Decembrio. Vol. II (of II).
Italy, Venice, printed by Bernhard Maler and Erhard Ratdolt with Peter Löslein, 1477.

Hunterian Collection, Bw 2. 15

Paper, 281 × 207 mm.; quarto; [i], 212, [ii] leaves.

This is the second part of Appian's *History of Rome*. The elegant three-sided block on the first page of this volume was made for this edition by Bernhard Maler. The arabesque design is based on a symmetrical and regular version of the white-vine pattern: at the same time as being one of the most typical examples of the influence of the tradition of illumination on the printed page, it is the most successful design achieved in the process of replacing hand decoration by printed ornamentation. This is one of a number of copies in which the block is printed in red, and here it has also been partly coloured in. Volume I of the work, *Historia romana*, begins with a four-sided block of similar design, which in Hunter's copy is printed in black and has also been coloured by hand. These two blocks exercized a lasting influence on the design of the printed book in the Renaissance.

The busy partnership of the three printers – though Peter Löslein was generally referred to as 'corrector et socius' – lasted only from late 1476 until some time in 1478, when a part of their stock of type and capitals passed to Franz Renner, who printed no. 99.

PROVENANCE: Hunter's source not traced.

BIBLIOGRAPHY: Goff, A 928; Sander no. 482; Hoepli, no. 2.

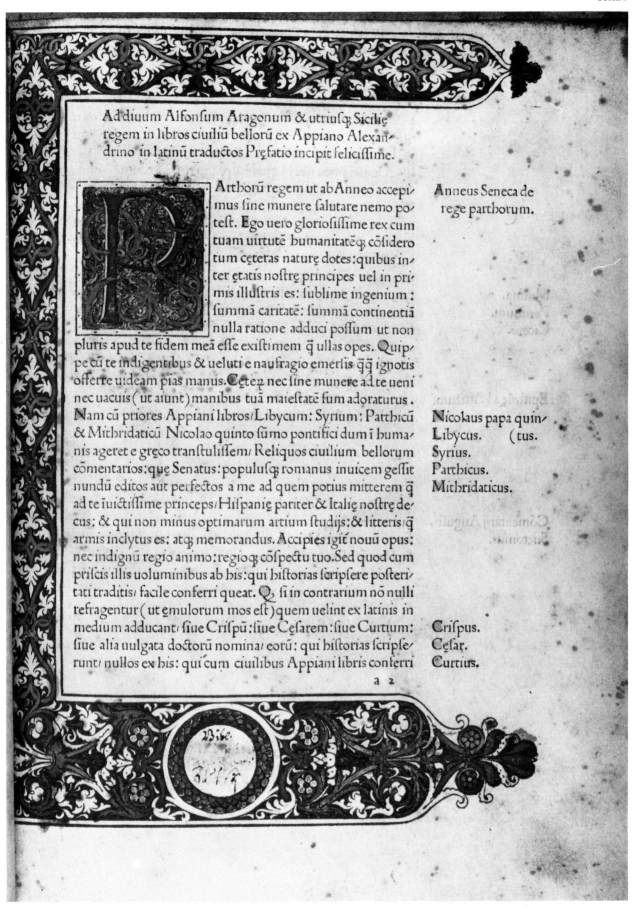

Ad diuum Alfonfum Aragonum & utriufq3 Sicilię
regem in libros ciuiliū belloru ex Appiano Alexan-
drino in latinū traductos Prefatio incipit feliciffime.

Arthorū regem ut ab Anneo accepi-
mus fine munere falutare nemo po-
teft. Ego uero gloriofiffime rex cum
tuam uirtutē humanitatēq3 cōfidero
tum cęteras naturę dotes: quibus inter ętatis noftrę principes uel in pri-
mis illuftris es: fublime ingenium:
fummā caritate: fummā continentiā
nulla ratione adduci poffum ut non
pluris apud te fidem meā effe exiftimem q̄ ullas opes. Quip-
pe cū te indigentibus & ueluti e naufragio emerfis q̄q̄ ignotis
offerre uideam pias manus. Cętez nec fine munere ad te ueni
nec uacuis (ut aiunt) manibus tuā maieftatē fum adoraturus.
Nam cū priores Appiani libros/Libycum: Syrium: Patthicū
& Mithridaticū Nicolao quinto fūmo pontifici dum i huma-
nis ageret e greco tranftuliffem/ Reliquos ciuilium bellorum
cōmentarios: quę Senatus: populufq3 romanus inuicem geffit
nundū editos aut perfectos a me ad quem potius mitterem q̄
ad te iuictiffime princeps/ Hifpanię pariter & Italię noftrę decus: & qui non minus optimarum artium ftudijs: & litteris/ q̄
armis inclytus es: atq3 memorandus. Accipies igiť nouū opus:
nec indignū regio animo: regioq3 cōfpectu tuo. Sed quod cum
prifcis illis uoluminibus ab his: qui hiftorias fcripfere pofteri-
tati traditis/ facile conferri queat. Q̄ fi in contrarium nō nulli
tefragentur (ut ęmulorum mos eft) quem uelint ex latinis in
medium adducant/ fiue Crifpū: fiue Cęfarem: fiue Curtium:
fiue alia uulgata doctorū nomina/ eotū: qui hiftorias fcripfe-
runt/ nullos ex his: qui cum ciuilibus Appiani libris conferri

Anneus Seneca de
rege parthorum.

Nicolaus papa quin-
Libycus.   (tus.
Syrius.
Parthicus.
Mithridaticus.

Crifpus.
Cęfar.
Curtius.

a 2

Decorated page. Hunterian Collection, Bw 2. 15, fol. 1

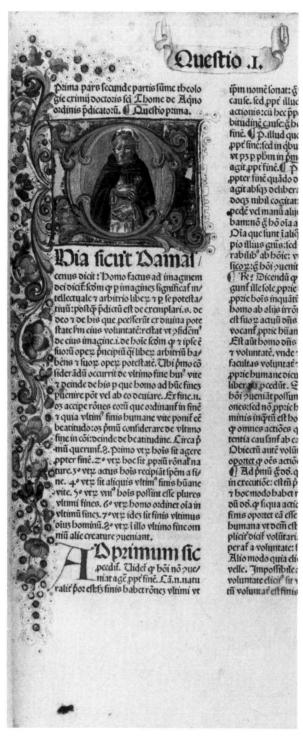

Detail of decorated page. Hunterian Collection, Bg 3. 11, fol. 1

99. Thomas Aquinas, Summa

Thomas Aquinas, Summa theologica. Part II (i)
Italy, Venice, printed by Franz Renner of
Heilbronn and Pietro da Bartua, 1478.

Hunterian Collection, Bg 3. 11

Paper, 285 × 198 mm.; folio; [i], i, 279, i, [i]
leaves.

The historiated portrait initial on fol. 1 was
painted in Florence, like the similar historiated
initial in Durand's *Rationale* (no. 91). Although
the modelling of the face and hands is more
mannered, the conventional border decoration of
flower and leaf motifs and gold discs with hair-
line penwork is of good quality.

Franz Renner began printing in Venice on his
own in 1471. Pietro da Bartua was his second
partner, with whom he printed four works in
1477-1478; he then made a fresh start alone,
continuing to print regularly until 1483.

PROVENANCE: Bought by Hunter at the sale of Joseph Smith
(1682-1770), British Consul at Venice, 25 January 1773, lot
1813.

BIBLIOGRAPHY: Goff, T 204.

100. Livy, History, Books XXI-XXX

Titus Livius, La terza decha; Leonardo Bruni,
De primo bello Punico.
Italy, Venice, printed by Antonio di Bartolom-
meo da Bologna (Miscomini), 11 April 1478.

Hunterian Collection, Bh 1. 19

Paper, 326 × 229 mm.; folio; [i], [10], i, 142,
[ii] leaves.

The frontispiece decoration of this volume is
probably Venetian. The column of overlapping
leaves recalling the trunk of a palm tree in the
centre margin was a design known to Venetian
printers since at least 1470. Jenson himself had
used a woodblock of it in an edition of the *Vitae
imperatorum* by Cornelius Nepos in 1471 (BMC
V p. 167, copy also in the Euing Collection,
BD9-d.10); perhaps he was imitating a similar
woodblock in a Cicero printed in Venice probably by Wendelin of Speier in 1470 (Hunterian
copy Bg 2. 9). The column is surmounted by a
cameo bust of a man in profile. In the lower
margin an armorial shield within a laurel wreath
is supported by dragons and putti with liquid
gold hair and bodies modelled in silver which has
since oxidized. The greater use of hair-line scrolls
in the floral design of the inner margin is found in
Ferrarese as well as Venetian work.

PROVENANCE: Bought by Hunter at the sale of Joseph Smith
(1682-1770), British Consul at Venice, 25 January 1773, lot
1150.

BIBLIOGRAPHY: Goff, L 252.

FINITA LA PRIMA DECA DE TI
TO LIVIO PATAVINO HISTO
RICO DAL COMINCIAMENTO
DE LA CITA DE ROMA: SEGVI
TA LA TERZA DE LA SECON
DA BATTAGLIA CARTHAGI
NESE CAPITVLO PRIMO.

N QVESTA PARTE DE
la mia opera e licito a me de par
lare spontaneamente prometten
do quello che la magior parte de
li scriptori hanno promisso nel
pricipio de tutta la summa de lo
pera loro. Cioe che io scriuero
una guerra maximamete degnia
de memoria intra tutte laltre che
mai siano state p tempo alcuno. La quale Hā
nibale duca de Carthagiesi hebbe col populo
Romano. Imperoche mai non combatterono
intra loro alcune citade: o gente piu ualide et
forte de richeze: ne a quelle medesime fu mai
tāto de uirtu o forza dato quāto a queste: Le
quale nō cōbatteuano intra loro ignorantemē
te ma sempre comparauano a la battaglia com
quelle arte puate nella prima guerra Cartha
ginese. Et fu tanto uaria la fortuna de la guer
ra et dubiosa la battaglia che piu uicini fuoro
al periculo li uincitori che glialtri. Costoro an
cora cōbatterono piu quasi p magior odio che
forze luno contra laltro: sdegnādosi li Roma
ni che li uinti spontaneamente portasseno lar
me contra li uicitori. Et li Carthagiesi credē
do che cō superbia et auaramente sopra loro:
che erano uinti fusse usato da Romani lo impe
rio. Ancora e fama che Hānibale i etade qua
si de noue anni essendo puerilmente lusingato
il Padre Hamilcare: a cio che lo menasse i his
pania: conciofussecche finita la battaglia Africa
na deuesse conducere la tutto lo exercito: quan
do ello sacrificaua se accosto al Altare et missa
la mano sopra le cose sacre, pmisse cō iuramen
to che come ello fusse i etade apta aguerra chel
sarebbe inimico al Populo Romano.

Come p la morte de Hamilcare si
plongo la seconda guerra intra li
Carthaginesi et li Romani. C. ii.

A perdita de Sicilia et de Sardignia
I sule: cōstringeuano et tormētauano
Hamilcare homo sauio et de grādissi
mo ingenio. Perche Sicilia per troppo subita
desperatione de le cose era stata cōcesa. Sardi
gnia nel mouimento de Africa era stata tolta p
inganno da Romani agiunto a queste cose il
soprapposto stipendio. Affanato per questa sol
licitudine lo excellente capitaneo si porto non
dimēo si et itale modo nella battaglia Africa
na: laquale fece p cinque anni sotto speranza

de la nuoua pace Romana: et si ācora dapoi p
noue anni in Hispagnia crescendo lo imperio
Carthaginese: chel mostro chiaramente haue
re nel animo una assai magior guerra de quel
la chel faceua alhora. Et se Hamilcare fusse du
rato in uita li Africani bauerebbeno portato
larme loro in Italia combattēdo sotto la guida
sua: che poi sotto Hanibale ci combatterono.
La morte de Hamilcare molto opportūa a ro
mani et la pueritia de Hannibale plongaro la
guerra.

Come et pche Hasdrubal succedette
ad Hamilcare et come il dicto Has
drubal fu morto da uno seruo. C. iii.

A sdrubal mezo itra il Padre et il fi
glio tenne quasi per octo anni lo Im
perio nel exercito. Costui nel fiore
de la etade: si come si dice primamente fu con
ciliato ad Hamilcare et fu suo genero p la sua
nobile indole et per che era de perito animo et
perche era de la secta Barchina potente appres
so li Caualieri et la Plebe certamente ello nō
tēne lo imperio de cōsētimento de principi. El
lo facendo le sue cose piu p consiglio che per
forza: et piu com auspicio di Reguli: et recon
ciliando le noue genti per amicicia de Princi
pi acrebbe piu la potētia de Carthaginesi che
per guerra o per armi. Ma nō gli fu la pace p
tanto piu secura. Vno Barbaro adirato p caso
ne che il Signore suo era stato morto da lui:
in presentia de molti lo assalto et occiselo. Et es
sendo preso da li circōstanti: non cō altro uol
to stette a tormenti che sel fusse scampato et cō
quel habito medesimo de faccia perseuero lace
rādolo quelli che superati li dolori da la letitia
quasi ancora mostrō a tutti similitudine de ho
mo ridēte. Com questo Hasdrubale: peroche
mirauliosamente fu artificioso in sollicitare le
gente et agiungerle al suo imperio haua il
populo de Roma renouato li pacti de la nuoua
pace i questo modo cioe che lo termine de luno
impio et de laltro fusse el fiume hibero: et che
li Sagútini che erāo i mezo uiuessēo i liberta

Come Hānibal fu misso i loco de Has
drubale: et dalcuna disputatione gia fa
cta intra li Carthaginesi. C. iiii.

Erta cosa e: che i loco de Hasdrubale
morto p la militare progatiua il gio
uene Hannibale fu portato nel pro
rio: peroche cō grandissimo rumore et cōsenti
mento di tutti era stato chiamato Impadore del
exercito. Costui essendo ancora giouenetto fu
chiamato p lettere da Hasdrubale et era stato
cōcluso nel senato da Carthagiesi: maxime p
fauore de la Secta Barchina: che Hānibale si
deuesse accostumare et auezare a larte de la

2

Decorated page. Hunterian Collection, Bh 1. 19, fol. a1

Resurrection. Hunterian Collection, Bf 1. 18, fol. 146v
(See also Colour Ill. 29 of fol. 14)

101. Breviary

Breviarium Romanum, edited by Georgius de Spathariis.
Italy, Venice, printed by Nicolaus Jenson, before 6 May 1478.

Hunterian Collection, Bf 1. 18

Vellum, 328 × 234 mm.; folio; [ii], i, [6], 396, i, [ii] leaves.

This magnificent volume, printed on vellum in red as well as black, is one of the typographic masterpieces of Nicolaus Jenson. A Frenchman from Sommevoire, near Troyes, Jenson trained as a die-cutter before learning the art of printing, almost certainly in Germany. During his career in Venice (1470-1480) he designed not only the most beautiful Roman type of the period, but also the splendid Gothic rotunda used in this Breviary.

As the foremost printer of the Venetian republic, Jenson produced many sumptuously decorated copies of books from his press, numbers of them printed like the Breviary on vellum. The volume has nine full-page decorations with miniatures by the same Venetian or Paduan artist who painted the major pictures in a manuscript Breviary from Ferrara now at Harvard (Houghton Library, MS Typ. 219). Lilian Armstrong has identified further examples of his work in a copy of Jenson's Pliny of 1476 in Manchester (John Rylands University Library, no. 3380, printed on vellum), and in a detached folio from another copy of the same edition formerly in the Kann collection (see J. Mannheim and E. Rahir, *Catalogue of the Rodolphe Kann Collection. Objets d'Art. Vol. I. Middle Ages and Renaissance*, Paris, 1907, Pt. I, p. 66, no. 84; for the Glasgow copy of this edition of Pliny see no. 96).

The subjects of the miniatures include figures from the Old and New Testaments in open landscapes characterized by sudden outcrops of rock formations and by a regular distribution of smaller stones. Classical figures and decorations are accorded equal, and occasionally greater, importance in the designs, with putti and candelabra prominent. Filigree penwork in many of the borders, characteristic of Ferrarese work, encloses medallions that contain studies of birds and animals as well as Biblical figures. A strikingly naturalistic portrait bust of a man is included in one of the designs.

The most remarkable feature of the fully decorated pages is the virtuoso illusionism in which the text columns appear to be set on leaves suspended in front of the landscape scenes of the borders. The effect, at first subdued, becomes increasingly exuberant through the volume. In two early pages (fols. 14 and 39) the bottom of this 'leaf' appears to be roughly torn, with sky – and on the first page a glimpse of the Almighty – visible through the holes. At the beginning of the Easter Mass (fol. 146v) the 'leaf' is suspended in front of monumental pillars and an architrave framing a landscape in which Christ rises from the tomb. Holes painted on the surface of the 'leaf' reveal elements of all the levels of the background, from the hills and the flush of sunrise to the purple tones of the higher firmament and the bas-relief figures on the architrave. The Breviary opens with a Calendar, bearing on every page roundels in violet ink with a series of classical heads: they are chiefly in profile, and many are wearing fantastic helmets. Other penwork in the Calendar resembles that in the Harvard Breviary.

The coat of arms of the Du Prat family, which appears on the full-page frontispiece (fol. 1) and at the beginning of the Temporale (fol. 39) is painted over another blazon, presumably that of the original owner, whose name is indicated by the abbreviations LEO and BO on each side of the shield. Lilian Armstrong has identified the owner of the volume as one Leonardus by noting the appearance of this name written in full in a humanist hand at the foot of fols. 34 and 309. The printer seems to have reserved certain lots of parchment for particular clients, as she has observed in the case of volumes printed for B. Agostini; the inference is that the vellum of the Hunterian Breviary was similarly reserved in advance. Other copies printed on vellum are in the National Library of Scotland in Edinburgh and in the Victoria and Albert Museum, London.

PROVENANCE: Ex-libris of Martinus Spifanius; arms of Du Prat family of Auvergne; bought for Hunter at the Louis-Jean Gaignat sale, Paris, 10 April 1769, lot 174.

BIBLIOGRAPHY: Goff, B 1112; De Bure, I, p. 51, no. 174; *Trésors*, p. 35, no. 59; *Treasures*, pp. 22-23, no. 66; Alexander, 'Notes', no. 4; cf. Harvard College Library, *Illuminated and Calligraphic Manuscripts*, Cambridge, Mass., 1955, p. 25, no. 81; Roger S. Wieck, *Late Medieval and Renaissance Illuminated Manuscripts 1350-1525 in the Houghton Library*, Cambridge, Mass., 1983, pp. 70-71, no. 34; L. Armstrong, 'The Illustration of Pliny's Historia naturalis in Venetian Manuscripts and Printed Books', *Manuscripts in the Fifty Years after the Invention of Printing*, ed. J.B. Trapp, London, 1983, pp. 97-106; eadem, 'The Agostini Plutarch: an Illuminated Venetian Incunable in the Fagel Collection', *Treasures of the Library*, Trinity College Dublin, ed. P. Fox, Dublin, 1986, pp. 86-96.

Decorated page. MS Hunter 47, fol 1.
(See also Colour Ill. 28)

102. Quintus Curtius, History of Alexander the Great

Quintus Curtius, Historia.
Italy, Written by Rodolfo Brancalupo probably in Naples, c.1480, and illuminated by the Master of the Vatican Homer.

MS Hunter 47 (T.2.5)

Vellum, 314 × 223 mm.; [ii], ii, 187, iii, [ii] leaves; written space 197 × 115 mm., 28 long lines.

The frontispiece to this copy of Quintus Curtius is a fine example of the work of a contemporary of Mantegna, or one of his followers, who in 1477 painted the miniatures in a manuscript of Homer written for Cardinal Francesco Gonzaga which is now in the Vatican (Vat. Gr. 1626). Though clearly of the Paduan school, he appears to have been active mainly in Rome, and work in some forty manuscripts has now been identified as by his hand.

The design of the frontispiece is wholly classical in inspiration, from the architectural structure of the pillars and the trophies of arms to the cornucopiae and vases and the medallion portrait of Alexander the Great in gold chiaroscuro. The brilliance of the execution is to be seen in the illusionism of the historiated initial. It contains a square author-portrait, apparently in relief, of a scribe writing at a desk, and appears to be set within a framework of sculpted panels painted in blue chiaroscuro. This cameo may show the influence on the artist of the Master of the London Pliny (see no. 90) who seems to have gone to Rome or Naples to work for Cardinal Giovanni of Aragon, son of the King of Naples, in about 1480. The whole composition, in which the cameo initial appears to rest on the page of text which itself is made to hang in front of the supporting pillars against a further background of delicately shredded shades of blue, is a work of great refinement brilliantly achieved. Fine epigraphic initials appear throughout the text.

PROVENANCE: Cardinal Giovanni of Aragon; Hunter's source not traced.

BIBLIOGRAPHY: Young & Aitken, pp. 53-54; *Treasures*, p. 20, no. 57; Alexander, 'Notes', no. 8; Baldwin, *William Hunter*, p. 6, no. 10; de la Mare, 'Florentine Scribes', pp. 245-293, Appendices I, no. 38 and III, no. 34.

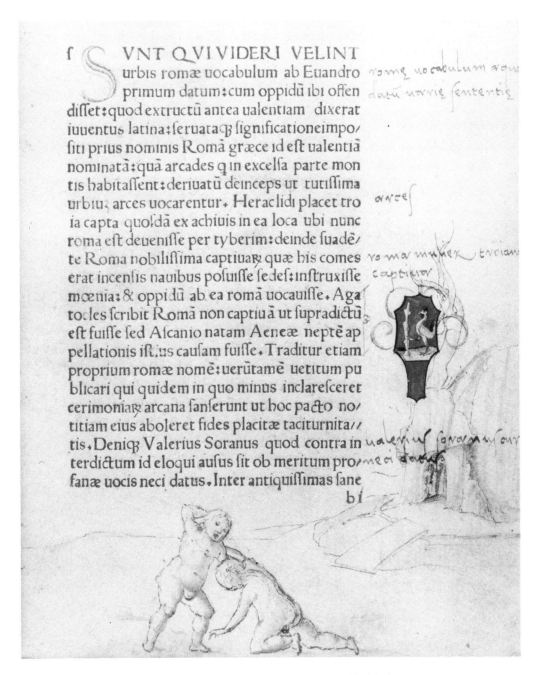

Decorated page. Euing Collection, BD7 – e. 13, fol. 4

103. Solinus, Wonders of the World

Caius Julius Solinus, Polyhistor,
sive De mirabilibus mundi.
Italy, Parma, printed by Andrea Portilia, 20
December 1480.

Euing Collection, BD7 – e. 13

Paper, 203 × 144 mm.; quarto; [ii], 100, [ii]
leaves.

Quarto volumes, which were intended for a wider
market, were far less likely to be illustrated by
hand than the large folio volumes destined for the
libraries of the wealthy. This small volume,
containing a collection of curious and memorable
facts about early peoples and distant lands begins
with an account of the founding of Rome. The
first page is embellished by the owner's coat of
arms on a shield hanging in a tree above a cave,
with Romulus and Remus as putti wrestling in
the foreground. Although the pen and wash
drawing is no more than a rapid sketch, it shows
that classical models and contemporary fashions
of illustration had their influence on volumes
destined not only for the libraries of princes,
prelates and merchants, but also for the growing
audience of less wealthy and influential readers.

PROVENANCE: Given to the Library by William Euing in 1872.

BIBLIOGRAPHY: Goff, S 619.

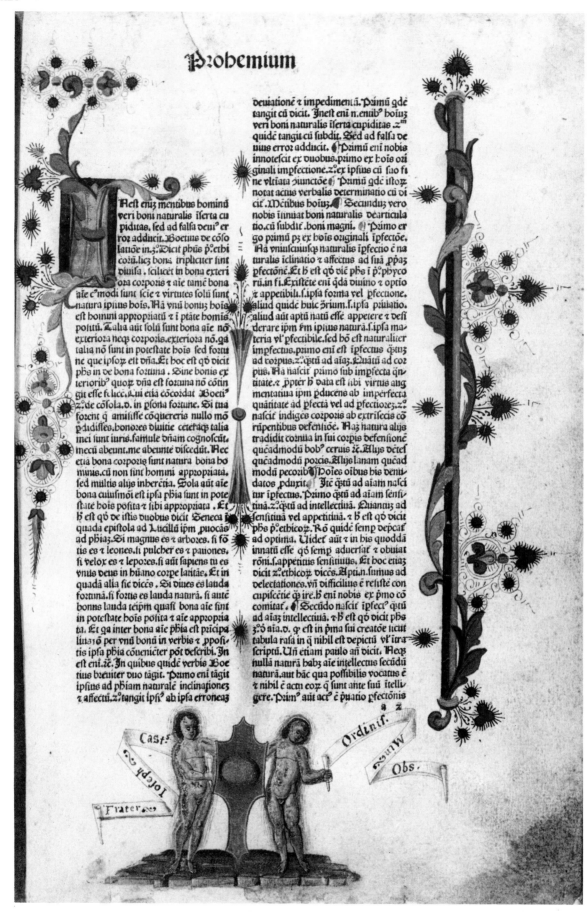

Decorated page. Euing Collection, BD9 – c. 7, fol. 2

104. Johannes de Gandavo, Commentary on Aristotle

Johannes de Ianduno, Quaestiones super tres libros de anima Aristotelis.
Italy, Venice, printed by Johann of Cologne and Johann Manthen of Gerresheim, 18 June 1480, and illuminated by the Master of the Pico della Mirandola Pliny.

Euing Collection, BD9 – c. 7

Paper, 302 × 206 mm.; folio; [ii], 158, [i] leaves.

The stylish decoration of the frontispiece of this volume is the work of an artist recently named by Lilian Armstrong as the Pico Master, after a manuscript of Pliny which he illuminated in 1481 for Giovanni Pico della Mirandola (1463-1494); that volume is now in Venice (Biblioteca Marciana, MS Lat. VI, 245=2976). He was active from at least 1469 to about 1505 and there are some sixty or more works by him in Venetian incunables; another more richly illustrated example is no. 105.

The object on the shield held by two putti in the lower margin has not been identified. The accompanying banderoles bear the name of 'Joseph Casts.', and identify him as an Observant Franciscan friar, probably in Venice. While the most obvious assumption is that this is the name of the owner, Lilian Armstrong has raised the possibility that it is instead the name of the artist.

The book is one of the last printed by Johann of Cologne and Johann Manthen, whose recorded activity ceased in October 1480.

PROVENANCE: ?Joseph Casts; bought by William Euing from Mr Arthur, bookseller, 17 February 1870 (MS Euing 49, p. 361, no. 4576) and donated by him to the Library in 1872.

BIBLIOGRAPHY: Goff, J 352.

105. Avicenna, Canon of Medicine

Abû Alî Husain Ibn' Abd Allah, called Ibn Sînâ or Avicenna, Canon medicinae, translated by Gerard of Cremona; De viribus cordis, translated by Arnoldus de Villa Nova.
Italy, Venice, printed by Pierre Maufer, 1486, with illuminations by the Master of the Pico della Mirandola Pliny.

Hunterian Collection, Bw 3. 24

Paper, 227 × 165 mm.; quarto; in five parts.

This printed copy of Avicenna's great work on medicine (for a manuscript copy see no. 61) is remarkable for its six full-page illuminations, identified by Lilian Armstrong as the work of the Pico Master (see no.104). The illuminations vary considerably in overall design. The frontispiece has a chiefly decorative pattern of circular leaf forms and tendrils with medallion studies of birds and a deer, together with echoes of classical motifs such as cornucopiae and candelabra, all within a framework of gilded and painted bars and with a coat of arms supported by two owls. The illumination introducing Book IV of the work on the other hand has a classical architectural framework of pillars, arch and pediment seen against a sketchy mountain background, but with elements of fancy such as the sea creatures surmounting the pillars. Book II opens with a design that is a combination of architectural and decorative motifs: pediments at the foot of the page frame a landscape with a centaur holding medicinal herbs, the side margins are decorated with medallions, peacocks, pearls and gold sprays, and the figure of Avicenna in the initial introducing the text is balanced by that of a disciple facing him. All the pages contain an author-portrait in an historiated initial, generally of a figure in robes and a turban similar to that used by the artist in a Venetian Bible of 1482-1483 now in the Vatican (Stamp. Ross. 1158).

The work is characterized by the predominance of gold sprays highlighting leaf patterns on a strongly painted ground of red, green or blue, with pearls and cameos prominent in the design. The use of jewellery, particularly of gemstones and pearls, was apparently introduced into the decoration of illuminated borders by Girolamo da Cremona, a Lombard illuminator whose work is recorded from 1461 to 1483. Since Venice, through the captaincy of Jacopo Antonio Marcello (see no. 107), had taken over the rule of Ravenna at this period, it is interesting to note that many of these elements appear in the mosaics there – for example in the borders to the panels of Justinian and the Empress Theodora in San Vitale and also in the vaulting of the Archbishop's Chapel – and the Pico Master may have used them for their imperial overtones. The designs of some pages refer also to the illusionistic practice of making the text appear to be hanging in front of the painted scene, a motif used in a number of the artist's other works. Pico himself owned both printed and manuscript copies of Avicenna's work.

PROVENANCE: Bought by Hunter at the Anthony Askew sale, London, 13 February 1775, lot 1006.

BIBLIOGRAPHY: Goff, A 1422; for Pico's printed Avicenna see P. Kibre, The Library of Pico della Mirandola, New York, 1936, p. 124, no. 39: no. 527 in the inventory of 1498.

Decorated page. Hunterian Collection, Bw 3. 24, Bk. IV, fol. 1
(See also Colour Ill. 30 of Bk. II, fol. 1)

106. Bible

Biblia Latina, Genesis-Ecclesiasticus.
Italy, Genoa, c. 1490, with miniatures by Michele da Genova.

MS General 1060

Vellum, 430 × 306 mm.; [i], 278, [i] leaves; written space 270 × 177 mm., in double columns of 50 lines.

The decoration of this volume of the historical and didactic books of the Bible gives a fascinating view of the early career of the illuminator Michele da Genova. Four fully illuminated pages which introduce Jerome's general preface (fol. 1) and the books of Genesis (fol. 4), Exodus (fol. 23) and Leviticus (fol. 39), are strongly based in the *all'antica* tradition established by the Master of the Putti and the Master of the London Pliny in the 1470s (see no. 90). In addition, however, to the conventional classical motifs of architectural surrounds, cameos and extensive leafscroll and candelabra patterns, there are large historiated initials and extensive pictorial scenes in the borders, organized in a different manner on each page; these show an inventive mind exploring a range of other possibilities in a search for new solutions to the problems of book illustration.

The Genesis page has scenes mainly of the Creation. The first four panels arranged down the centre of the page form the initial 'I' of 'In principio', five further scenes fill the outer margin, and the lower margin contains a large representation of the Last Judgement. These rectangular panels are each set within a border, largely of jewels, gold and interlaced threads which appear to be lying on the surface of the page. The scenes are harmonized by a uniform treatment of figures and landscape, except in that of the First Day when all is darkness. In the Exodus page the architectural framework gives a sense of the scene of the crossing of the Red Sea taking place behind the decorated surface, and this impression is heightened in the Leviticus page, where one scene blends into another on a continuous landscape along the lower and outer margins within the architectural frame. The two columns of text appear to be on a sheet suspended from the architrave in the upper margin, a motif which had been popular since the 1470s (see no. 101).

Both the design and the general atmosphere of these scenes becomes increasingly naturalistic rather than antique as the volume progresses. The drawing, costume and faces of the principal figures are handled in an observant manner, with much attention to modelling, and the miniaturist appears to have taken particular care to differ-

Genesis page. MS General 1060, fol. 4
(See also Colour Ill. 36)

entiate the features of his female figures, as in for example a group in the lower margin of the Leviticus page. Anna de Floriani has suggested that one of the two figures kneeling before the Almighty in the lower margin of fol. 50 is in fact a portrait of the man who commissioned the volume.

The full-page sketch on fol. 50 marks the beginning of the Book of Numbers and is the first of five unfinished designs; the others introduce the Books of Deuteronomy (fol. 65), Judith (fol. 199v), Job (fol. 211), and the Psalms (fol. 222). The degree of completion varies in each page, the first of the five having substantial areas where all aspects of figurework and landscape are finished, while the Judith page has only the underdrawing of a scene in an army camp with a group of tents and numbers of cannons in the foreground. An interesting feature of the whole sequence is the movement towards illusionism, not only in the way in which the 'page' with the two columns of text in the centre of the leaf is made to appear as an independent surface, with curling corners and tears in the edges through which the background can be seen, but also in the search for a harmonious space unifying the different sections of the pictorial area.

The drawing style of the faces and drapery in these pages is repeated in an Antiphonary of San Giovanni Evangelista at Parma (P, N.4), which was made in 1492 and is one of four antiphonaries completed in Parma by Michele da Genova between 1492 and 1497. The same arms of a member of the Fregoso family, with the devices of a pair of compasses and a wolf and the motto 'Per non fallir', appear on a manuscript of Gior-

gio Stella's *Annals* of 1396-1435 (Genoa, Archivio di Stato, MS restituito dalla Francia no. 4) which was written in 1490. Although it seems that Michele left his native Genoa for Parma in the early 1490s, no reason is yet known for the Bible decoration to have been discontinued.

PROVENANCE: Arms of Fregoso (or Campofregoso) of Genoa; John Callendar of Craigforth, 18th century; in the Library by 1828.

BIBLIOGRAPHY: Ker, *MMBL*, II, p. 916; Alexander, 'Italian Illuminated Manuscripts', p. 116; Anna de Floriani, 'Michele da Genova, miniatore: le tappe di uno sviluppo', in *Sisto IV e Giulio II mecenati e promotori di cultura*, forthcoming [conference at Savona, 3-6 November 1985].

Opening page to Book of Job. MS General 1060, fol. 211.

107. Niccolò Sagundino and others, On the Death of Valerio Marcello

Nicolaus Secundinus et al.,
De obitu Valerii Marcelli.
North-east Italy, written c.1463 but decorated in the 1480s.

MS Hunter 201 (U.1.5)

Vellum, 366 × 245 mm.; [iii], 213 (paginated as 426), [iii] leaves; written space 246 × 130 mm., in single columns of 40 lines.

This volume contains texts by a number of authors written for Jacopo Antonio Marcello (1398/1399 – 1464/1465), member of a long-established noble Venetian family and captain of the city's army as well as a humanist and scholar. It was commissioned to commemorate the death of his son Valerio on New Year's Day, 1461, just before his ninth birthday. In addition to Niccolò Sagundino, the authors include, amongst others, the Greek grammarian George Trebizond of Crete, the philosopher Francesco Filelfo, the poet Lodovico Carbone, the poetess Isotta Nogarola, the mercenary soldier Carlo Fortebracci da Montone, and one of Valerio's own teachers, Pietro Perleone. The last work, identified by Margaret King, is the *Excusatio adversus consolatores in obitu Valerii filii*, which was supposedly written by Marcello to René, Duke of Anjou, but was actually composed by Marcello's aide Giorgio Bevilacqua da Lazise at his request: King René had invested Marcello as a knight of his newly established Order of the Crescent in 1449, and five translations which were commissioned by Marcello, chiefly of classical texts, have dedicatory letters from Marcello to King René.

Several of the texts in this collection include the date of 1463, and this manuscript was apparently copied not long afterwards, in a most beautiful hand. The script is similar to that of the copy of Strabo's *Geography*, given to Marcello by King René in 1458-59 (Albi, Bibliothèque Rochegude, MS 4; cf. M. Meiss, *Andrea Mantegna as Illuminator*, New York, 1957, and Bibliothèque Nationale, *Dix siècles d'enluminure italienne*, Paris, 1984, pp. 128-130, no. 112). Margaret King has suggested that the volume was intended as a presentation copy to King René. However, the spaces left for illumination were not filled until some twenty or twenty-five years later, and even then three spaces, including a whole leaf to introduce the final text (p. 309), were left blank. The exquisitely painted epigraphic capitals are set against a variety of coloured backgrounds, including violet, mauve,

Initial M. MS Hunter 201, p. 134
(See also Colour Ill. 24 of p. 269)

grey and black, but also blue, red and green in a less funereal register. They contain delicate studies of flowers, animals, butterflies, figures, jewels and other objects in a style that dates from the 1480s. The full-page frontispiece, sadly damaged by damp, includes a portrait vignette of a youth, doubtless representing Valerio, who is listening as St Mark, the patron saint of Venice, reads to him from the further border of the page.

PROVENANCE: Arms of Pisani of S. Marina; bought by Hunter at the César de Missy sale, London, 18 March 1776, lot 1662.

BIBLIOGRAPHY: Young & Aitken, pp. 142-143; Ker, *William Hunter*, p. 15, Appendix A, XVII; J. Monfasani, *George of Trebizond*, Leiden, 1976, pp. 174-175; M.L. King, *Venetian Humanism in an Age of Patrician Dominance*, Princeton, 1986, pp. 395-396.

Decorated page. MS Hunter 344, fol. 2

108. Festus Rufus or Rufius, Summary of Roman History

Festus Rufus, Breviarium; Giulio Pomponio Leto, Compendium historiae Romanae.
Italy, Rome, written by Giuliano Ceci and another scribe, late 15th century, and decorated in Florence.

MS Hunter 344 (U.8.12)

Vellum, 151 × 99 mm.; [iii], 81, ii, [iii] leaves; written space 102 × 52 mm., 14-15 long lines.

This copy of a mid 4th-century compendium of Roman history is written in two hands. The second of these (fols. 35v-81v) has been attributed by Albinia de la Mare to Giuliano Ceci, a pupil of the distinguished scribe and classical scholar Pomponio Leto (1427-1497), who wrote the work copied here by Ceci. Although the manuscript was written in Rome, the decoration is Florentine. The full border on fol. 2 has floral designs and penwork typical of the late 15th century; both the blank wreath supported by two putti and a gold circle in the outer margin, containing a sketch of a dog, show the ink centre line of the marginal framework which controlled the design. The panel at the top of the page was prepared with a magenta ground for figurative work or a title which was never begun.

PROVENANCE: Bought for Hunter at the Pieter Burmann sale, Leyden, 27 September 1779, lot 3647.

BIBLIOGRAPHY: Young & Aitken, pp. 279-280; Ker, *William Hunter*, p. 17, Appendix A, XIX.

109. Treatises on Engines and Weapons

Poliorcetici Graeci (Athenaeus, Biton, Heron, Philon, etc.) in Greek.
Italy, c.1510.

MS Hunter 220 (U.2.11)

Paper, 332 × 225 mm.; [ii], 80, [iii] leaves; written space 220 × 125 mm., 30 long lines.

Italians of the late 15th and early 16th centuries were fascinated by works on military machines, not only for their antiquarian interest but also as a source for modern inventions, to be used alongside such authorities as Valturio (no. 133). This manuscript contains six complete treatises, and other extracts, mostly concerned with siege warfare, by classical authors including Athenaeus (second century B.C.), Heron of Alexandria and Apollodorus of Damascus (first century A.D.).

The pen and watercolour drawings in the volume are working diagrams designed to elucidate the text. Some are plans of machines in which different parts are identified by different colours for clarity; other larger pictures show a skilful use of perspective in an artist well able to handle three-dimensional objects in a naturalistic way on this relatively small scale.

PROVENANCE: Jean-Jacques Chifflet, 1588-1660; bookplate of Nicolas Joseph Foucault, 1643-1721.

BIBLIOGRAPHY: Young & Aitken, pp. 164-165; *Trésors*, p. 28, no. 48; I.C. Cunningham, *Greek Manuscripts in Scotland*, Edinburgh, 1982, no. 42; cf. *Veterum mathematicorum opera*, Paris, 1693; *Philon*, ed. R. Schöne, Berlin, 1893; others, ed. C. Wescher, *Poliorcétique des Grecs*, Paris, 1867.

Design for a siege engine; design for naval grappling irons.
MS Hunter 220, fols. 4v and 6

Two women beating a man. MS Hunter 29, fol. Bv

110. Boccaccio, The Old Crow

Giovanni Boccaccio, Il corbaccio.
Italy, Venice, c.1510.

MS Hunter 29 (S.2.19)

Paper, 221 × 164 mm.; [iv], ii, 114, i, [iv] leaves; written space 144 × 85 mm., 19-22 long lines.

In *Il Corbaccio*, written around 1354-1355, the middle-aged Boccaccio (1313-1375) takes a sharply ironic though anti-feminist look at the relationship between the sexes. The narrator is a man of his own age who is transported with passion for a Florentine widow a year or two younger. In the midst of his pangs of unrequited love, he is visited in a dream by the shade of the woman's former husband who, by revealing the truth (as he sees it) about her wanton behaviour, supposedly cures him of his passion; but the process of his spiritual enlightenment is far from complete at the end of their dialogue.

The first of two full-page pictures in this copy shows the narrator encountering the widow's departed husband (fol. ii). In the second picture (fol. 1v) he is being attacked by two women who beat him to the ground in an illustration of the way a man can expect to suffer at the hands of women. The pictures are set within floral borders containing landscape vignettes, and a similar full border in contrasting colours surrounds the first text-page. The border designs are in the Venetian tradition exemplified by the Pico Master (see no. 105) and followed by the printers of the city (e.g. no. 138). The different medium and support, watercolour on paper, give the illustrations a more fluid quality than their predecessors on vellum.

PROVENANCE: Richard Humfrey and Anne Humfrey, 17th century; Hunter's source not traced.

BIBLIOGRAPHY: Young & Aitken, pp. 28-29; V. Branca, *Tradizione delle opere di Giovanni Boccaccio*, Rome, 1958, p. 26; cf. T. Nurmela, 'Manuscrits et éditions du *Corbaccio* de Boccace', *Neuphilologische Mitteilungen*, 54, 1953, pp. 102-134; G. Boccaccio, *Il Corbaccio*, ed. T. Nurmela, Helsinki, 1968; G. Boccaccio, *The Corbaccio*, trans. and ed. A.K. Cassell, Urbana, 1975; P.G. Ricci, *Studi sulla vita e le opere del Boccaccio*, Milan, 1985, pp. 87-96 ('Per il testo del Corbaccio'), pp. 97-114 ('Ancora sul testo del Corbaccio').

111. Pietro Lando, Ducal Commission to Paolo Delfino

Pietro Lando, Commissione a Paolo Delfino.
Italy, Venice, 30 August 1543.

MS Hunter 28 (S.2.18)

Vellum, 235 × 165 mm.; 24 leaves; written space 162 × 110 mm., 25 long lines.

Formal documents of appointment, such as this one issued by Pietro Lando, Doge of Venice from 1539-1545, were decorated in a conservative style for many years. The design of the frame on the first page has scarcely altered from that of the vignettes within a floral background seen not merely thirty years before in the Boccaccio (no. 110), but also thirty years before that in the Pico Master (no. 105). The execution has accordingly lost much of its freshness; but it is interesting nonetheless for the glimpse it gives of the more fluid painting style of its time, both in the figurework of the Virgin and Child and of St Paul, as well as in the landscape in the bottom vignette. The upper border vignette shows the lion of St. Mark, emblem of the Republic.

PROVENANCE: Hunter's source not traced.

BIBLIOGRAPHY: Young & Aitken, pp. 27-28.

Opening page. MS Hunter 28, fol. 1

112. Battista Agnese, World Maps

Baptista Agnese, Atlante portolano.
Italy, Venice, 25 September 1542.

MS Hunter 492 (V.7.19)

Vellum, 185 × 129 mm.; iii, 15, ii leaves; 12 maps preceded by astrological tables.

The high quality of Agnese's maps, which survive in more than seventy sets, has led some commentators to value their art more than their accuracy. Although he was a copyist rather than an original cartographer, Agnese was nonetheless at pains to keep his maps up to date and was the first mapmaker known to have depicted the discoveries on the north-west coast of America by Francisco de Ulloa in 1539 and 1540.

Of Genoese origin, Agnese was active c.1535-1564. He worked in Venice, then the centre of European trade, and produced maps of the whole of the known world. Several maps in each set, chiefly of European regions, are drawn in the traditional style of a portulan, or book of sailing directions. They show complete coasts and waterways and bear characteristic direction lines from the thirty-two points of the compass. His technique of colouring remained virtually the same throughout his career: coast-lines are in blue, names are black or red, islands often green or gold, the Red Sea and the Gulf of California always red. The maps at Glasgow are among the earliest to portray the California peninsula, which appears in Agnese's work from 1542 on. Closer to home, it is perhaps surprising to find that Scotland is shown as being separated from England by a considerable strait, a feature which remained in his work until 1553. The maps were not used for navigational purposes, but they reached a wide audience. This set has windhead points annotated in Spanish, and other copies are known to have been made specifically for German or Dutch owners as well as Italians.

PROVENANCE: Hunter's source not traced.

BIBLIOGRAPHY: Young & Aitken, p. 405; H.R. Wagner, 'The Manuscript Atlases of Battista Agnese', *Papers of the Bibliographical Society of America*, 25, 1931, p. 52 and p. 69 no. XXIII; Baldwin, *William Hunter*, pp. 7-8, no. 13; cf. M. Harrsen and G.K. Boyce, *Italian Manuscripts in the Pierpont Morgan Library*, New York, 1953, p. 54, no. 96, set of maps dated 15 May 1542, including the earliest known example of an atlas by Agnese delineating Lower California; M. de La Roncière, M. Mollat du Jourdin, *Les portulans*, Freiburg, 1984, p. 227, no. 41.

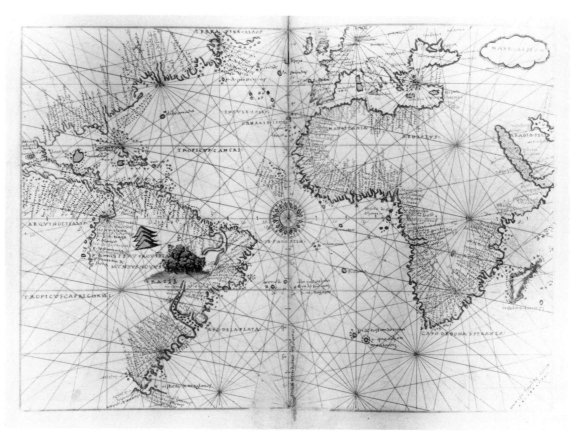

Opening with Atlantic chart. MS Hunter 492, fols. 4v-5

V · The Netherlands

113. Giovanni Balbi, Treatise on Latin Grammar, and Glossary

Giovanni Balbi da Genova, Catholicon.
Netherlands, Brabant, 26 November 1407.

MS Hunter 1 (S.1.1)

Vellum, 445 × 316 mm.; [ii], 342, [ii] leaves; written space 312 × 218 mm., in double columns of 58 lines.

This volume displays the vigorous decorative penmanship that was a feature of books large and small produced in the Netherlands throughout the 15th century (see also nos. 115 and 126). In addition to two full-page calligraphic borders, the volume contains decorated initials of all the letters of the alphabet in characteristic fretwork designs of blue and red against a ground of closely worked filigree patterns of red, blue and purple. The date of this copy, one of two owned by Hunter, is given on the last leaf. The name of the monastery where it was written has been effaced.

The Dominican monk Giovanni da Genova (d. 1298) completed this vast Latin glossary in 1286. With its grammatical digressions and observations on etymology and syntax it remained an essential work of reference well into the 16th century: after the Bible and other religious works it was one of the first texts to appear in print, perhaps from the press of Johann Gutenberg in Mainz in 1460, and two dozen editions had appeared before the end of the century.

PROVENANCE: Bought for Hunter at the Pieter Burmann sale, Leyden, 27 September 1779, lot 1233.

BIBLIOGRAPHY: Young & Aitken, pp. 1-2; Ker, *William Hunter*, p. 17, Appendix A, XIX; cf. M.B. Stillwell, *The Beginning of the World of Books*, New York, 1972, p. 17, no. 30.

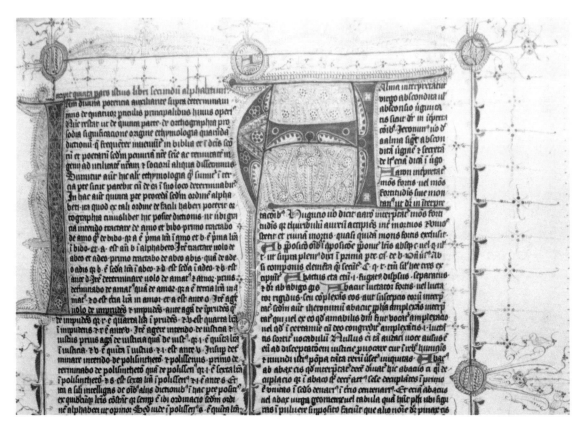

Detail of decorated page with initials I and A. MS Hunter 1, fol. 57

Detail of decorated page with Advent miniature.
MS General 1111, fol. 6v

114. Jacobus de Voragine, Golden Legend

Jacobus de Voragine, Legenda aurea. 2 vols.
Flanders, probably Bruges, c.1405-1410.

MS General 1111

Vellum, 320 × 230 mm.; I: [ii],193, [ii], II: [ii],
181, [ii] leaves; written space 231 × 151 mm., in
double columns of 53 lines.

The Glasgow *Legenda aurea* is one of the most
important Flemish illuminated manuscripts of
the early 15th century, yet only recently has it
become the subject of scholarly attention. It is an
exceptional copy of the text, with 102 miniatures
surviving from the 106 originally present. The
original Latin text was seldom illustrated, though
illuminated copies of the French version by Jean
de Vignay are not uncommon.

The *Golden Legend* was probably the most
popular non-liturgical work of the late Middle
Ages, with some 500 copies extant. The 182
chapters of Voragine's original text were intended
for regular devotional readings in Chapter
Houses and refectories of monastic institutions.
In this copy, the text has been expanded to 248
chapters, one of the longest of which is devoted
to St Antoninus of Piacenza. Since the introductory miniature here is the largest in the book (123
× 70 mm., fol. 368), it is likely that the volume
was made for the Augustinian canons of S.
Antonio in Piacenza, and Italian annotations
indicate that it was still in Italy in the 17th
century. The fact that some of the other additional chapters contain material of Spanish origin
suggests that the model for the Glasgow copy was
a version produced for the Catalan merchant
colony of Bruges and Ghent.

Nicholas Rogers has identified three Flemish
artists at work in the manuscript. He has named
them the Litany Master, the Deacon Master and
the Helen Master. Although the normal size of
the miniatures, some 75 × 65 mm., restricts their
scope for including much narrative detail, the
artists' work is marked by their concern for the
natural appearance of people and for the minutiae
of their daily life, exemplified by Joseph preparing gruel in the scenes of the Nativity and
Epiphany. Stylistically, the Helen Master is the
most individual and expressive of the three. His
work is characterized by the white highlighting of
people's faces and their sharp eyes; he is responsible for the second largest miniature in the
book, the Death and Coronation of the Virgin
(fol. 146v). The backgrounds of the miniatures
are red or blue with gold flourishing or geometric
patterns. The miniature of St Anthony on fol.
39v, however, places the saint against a background of blue sky growing paler towards the

St Antoninus of Piacenza. MS General 1111, fol. 368
(See also Colour Ill. 37)

115. Bible

Biblia, Proverbs-Maccabees.
Netherlands, written by Albertus de Heenvliet,
20 July 1446.

MS General 1119

Vellum, 304 × 212 mm.; [ii], 168, [i] leaves; written space 220 × 142 mm., in double columns of c. 53 lines.

Each of the eighteen books and their accompanying prologues are introduced by large penwork initials with decoration extending into the margins and on occasion filling the whole page. The fretwork patterns of the blue and red initials are handled more broadly than in the earlier Glossary (no. 113), and filigree linework has been replaced by a heavier and looser design based on calligraphic flourishes, with liberal indications of leaf shapes emphasized by green wash.

PROVENANCE: Gift of Lord Archibald Campbell to Lachlan Campbell, Utrecht, 1702, by whom it was presented to the Library about 1705.

BIBLIOGRAPHY: Ker, *MMBL*, II, p. 923.

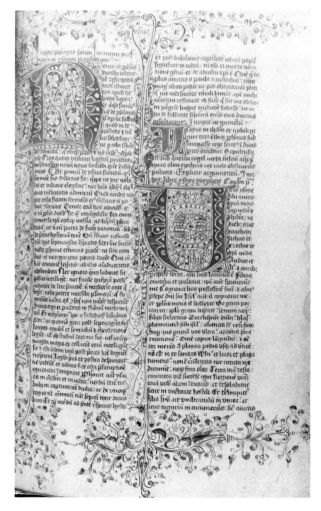

Decorated page. MS General 1119, fol. 58

horizon, and the single appearance of this naturalistic background suggests experimentation with a new idea, which can be expected at this period from the influence of the Limbourgs and the Boucicaut Master (see nos. 51, 57 and 59). Nicholas Rogers has noted that the three surviving miniatures in Downside Abbey MS 26530 appear to be the work of the Litany Master at a slightly later stage in his career. This would place the present manuscript nearer to 1405 than to 1410; a date within these limits is confirmed by other Flemish parallels for the minor decoration and the script.

PROVENANCE: Donated to the Library by Archibald Philip, Earl of Rosebery, in 1918.

BIBLIOGRAPHY: Ker, *MMBL*, II, pp. 916-919; *Flemish Art 1300-1700*, no. 563; N.J. Rogers, *The Glasgow 'Legenda aurea' and its place in Flemish art*, University of Glasgow, Stone Lecture in Bibliophily, 17 March 1982 (text deposited in Glasgow University Library, MS General 1580).

116. Mirror of Man's Salvation

Miroir de l'humaine salvation.
Flanders, Bruges, 1455.

MS Hunter 60 (T.2.18)

Vellum, 305 × 213 mm.; ii, 61, iv leaves; written space 194 × 134 mm., in double columns of 37 lines.

The anonymous *Speculum humanae salvationis*, written in the early years of the 14th century, enjoyed a popularity almost as great as that of the *Legenda aurea* (no. 114). In contrast to the *Golden Legend*, however, the majority of these 350 surviving manuscripts are illustrated. The pictures are indeed an important part of the work, for they give visual emphasis to the relationship between the Old and New Testaments in the work's central concern with the doctrine of the Fall and Redemption. In this copy, forty-two panels depict these typological connections, each with a coloured scene from the New Testament and three scenes in grisaille showing prefigurations of it in the Old Testament.

Four French translations of the *Speculum* are known to have been made in the 15th century, including this version, which was made in 1448 by Jean Miélot for Philip the Good, Duke of Burgundy. Although the wording of the Hunterian copy does not precisely follow that of the original paper draft of the translation, which still survives in Brussels (Bibliothèque Royale, MS 9249-9250), the frontispiece miniature shows the presentation of the volume to a patron, who may be the Duke. This thoroughly professional painting has been attributed to one of the leading miniaturists of the day, William Vrelant, who had moved to Bruges from Utrecht in 1454 following restrictions imposed in Bruges on the importation of Dutch miniatures. The statement in the colophon that the manuscript was written in Bruges in 1455 gives this attribution some plausibility, but further stylistic analysis is necessary before all the works supposedly from his hand can be seen as authentic.

The frontispiece is a subtle blend of naturalism and symbolism. The patron and the translator are fashionably dressed and placed in an elaborate architectural setting. They are accompanied by two female figures beyond the pillars of the throne room who seem scarcely less real but who in fact represent the Church (in the guise of a nun holding a patriarchal cross and the Chalice and Host), and the discredited Synagogue (with broken lance and her crown falling from her head). The painting is characterized by a bright palette, dignified spaciousness, the fusion of landscape and interior, and a delicate handling of faces and flesh tones. These elements appear less forcefully in the typological panels, but the small scale of the panels and the likelihood that they were modelled on existing designs may explain the difference in overall effect. The panels have been attributed to the work of assistants of the Master who painted the frontispiece; but the close similarity in the handling of specific features such as modelling, clothing, architectural detail, landscape and sky suggests that they are the less painstaking work of the same artist, who was able to expand in the frontispiece the skills cramped by the multiplicity of small scenes in the rest of the book. Nicholas Rogers has suggested that the miniatures could well be by the artist of Brussels, Bibliothèque Royale, MS 11104-5; the same model appears to have been used for the translator in the frontispiece of the present manuscript and for a messenger on fol. 66 of the Brussels manuscript.

Miniatures in grisaille, which had been popular a century earlier, particularly in Paris, seem largely to have disappeared in the early 15th century, but they had recently reappeared at the court of Philip the Good, in a Book of Hours illustrated in 1454 by Jean Le Tavernier (The Hague, Royal Library, MS 76). The extensive use of the technique in this manuscript is certain to have been influenced by this renewed interest.

Betrothal of the Virgin with Old Testament prefigurations (Tobit's Betrothal to Sarah. Tower of Baris, David's Tower and Shields). MS Hunter 60, fol. 9

Presentation of Book to Patron. MS Hunter 60, fol. 1
(See also Colour Ill. 38)

PROVENANCE: Bought for Hunter at the Louis-Jean Gaignat sale, Paris, 10 April 1769, lot 117.

BIBLIOGRAPHY: Young & Aitken, pp. 68-71; De Bure, I, p. 36, no. 117; Meyer, p. 114; J. Lutz and P. Perdrizet, *Speculum humanae salvationis*, Mulhouse, 1907, I, p. 105, no. 243; *Flemish Art 1300-1700*, p. 152, no. 567; *La miniature flamande*, p. 107, no. 106; *Trésors*, pp. 17-18, no. 29; *Treasures*, p. 16, no. 42; Ker, *William Hunter*, p. 14, Appendix A, VIII; Baldwin, *William Hunter*, pp. 6-7, no. 11; A. Wilson and J.L. Wilson, *A Medieval Mirror: Speculum humanae salvationis 1324-1500*, Berkeley, 1985, pp. 73-76; cf. J.D. Farquhar, 'The Vrelant Enigma: is the Style the Man?', *Quaerendo*, 4, 1974, pp. 100-108; idem, *Creation and Imitation*, Fort Lauderdale, Florida, 1976, pp. 24-33.

117. Book of Hours, Psalter, etc.

Horae, Psalterium, etc.
Flanders, Bruges, c.1450-1460.

MS General 288

Vellum, 221 × 155 mm.; [i], 296, [i] leaves; written space 123 × 82 mm., 21 long lines.

Books of Hours were the personal prayerbooks of the laity and they formed the largest single category of illuminated manuscript. Since they were free from clerical control, they could be decorated according to the requirements and the purse of the owner. Demand was so great that mass production methods were common, particularly in the Netherlands where the trade was concentrated.

This combined Book of Hours and Psalter has eighteen full-page pictures on single leaves with blank versos, painted separately and inserted into the completed volume at the beginnings of major sections of the text. The border decoration of the pictures is matched on the facing page in a single unified design, and the presence of six other text-pages with full borders suggests that pictures were meant to be included at those places also. The illustrations are the work of two artists, the major one from the circle of William Vrelant (see no. 116). His portraits of the Evangelists in particular (e.g. St Mark, fol. 275v) show his skill in modelling the body in a variety of poses; his drawing of hands and faces is closely observed and many of his figures are realistic character studies. Several of the miniatures in the Psalms include delicately detailed views of single houses and larger groups of buildings, the presence of which is emphasized by a deliberately schematic representation of landscape, and the general atmosphere is one of heightened naturalism. The richly coloured borders include leaf patterns, daisies and gold highlights, with tendrils in distinctive knot patterns. Large areas of incised gold leaf in numbers of the miniatures and the use of liquid silver, still well preserved, in details such as window panes and sword blades, indicate the high standards expected by an exacting patron.

PROVENANCE: Presented to the Library by Archibald Philip, Earl of Rosebery, in 1918.

BIBLIOGRAPHY: Ker, *MMBL*, II, pp. 905-907; *Flemish Art 1300-1700*, no. 575.

King David playing bells; King David with a fool.
MS General 288, fols. 183v and 156v
(See also Colour Ill. 42)

118. Book of Hours

Horae.
Flanders, ?Ghent, c.1460.

MS Euing 3

Vellum, 117 × 88 mm.; ii, 138, ii leaves; written space 61 × 47 mm., 18 long lines.

The eight full-page pictures in this pocket-sized copy of a Book of Hours were also painted on single leaves, like those of much more luxurious copies such as the Rosebery volume (no. 117), since the production of pictures was separate from that of the rest of the book. The pictures come from the same milieu, though their small scale makes them more schematic than the Rosebery miniatures, and the artistry is far less accomplished. They are accompanied by fourteen even smaller pictures, 25 × 25 mm., chiefly in the Gospel sequences and the memorials of saints. The borders of swirling acanthus-style leaves are typical of much Ghent and Bruges decoration, though the content of the Calendar points to Ghent rather than Bruges.

PROVENANCE: Bought by William Euing on 25 June 1853 and bequeathed by him to the Library in 1874.

BIBLIOGRAPHY: Ker, *MMBL*, II, p. 873.

Opening with Flight into Egypt. MS Euing 3, fols. 92v-93

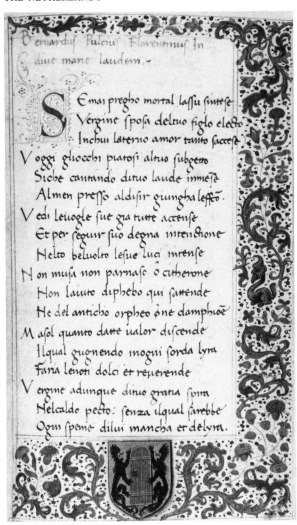

Decorated page. MS Hunter 483, fol. 1

119. Bernardo Pulci, Poems on the Virgin and on Christ's Passion

Bernardo Pulci di Firenze, Lodi della Vergine Maria, Della Passione del Domino; Antonio Mattei de Cardinis, Salve Regina, Ave Maria. Written in Italy and decorated in Flanders, third quarter of the 15th century.

MS Hunter 483 (V.7.10)

Vellum, 185 × 118 mm.; [ii], 23, i leaves; written space 125 × 65 mm., 21 long lines.

Written in Florence in a fine Italian humanistic hand, this small volume of devotional poems belonged to Giovanni Batista Portinari and his brother Tommaso, members of an important Florentine merchant family which had traded in Bruges since the 14th century. Tommaso (d.1501) was assistant manager of the Medici bank in Bruges from the mid 1450s and became manager ten years later. He commissioned the Portinari altarpiece, now in the Uffizi Gallery in Florence, from Hugo van der Goes in the early 1470s and had his portrait and that of his wife painted by Memling.

The manuscript, which bears the Portinari arms on the first page, has borders decorated in typical Bruges style (cf. no. 118) with blue acanthus-leaf scrolls and a variety of flower patterns interspersed with liquid gold discs and modest hair-line sprays, all on a plain ground. Amongst the foliage lurks a small grotesque of a type which came to be common in later 15th-century decoration in the Netherlands and France (see nos. 61-63). The volume is also noteworthy for its original blind-stamped binding which was probably also made in Bruges: in addition to panels of St Margaret and the dragon, there are two larger panels of bird and animal figures, with two devotional texts, of which no other example was known to J.B. Oldham.

PROVENANCE: Portinari family; arms of Francesco Sassetti drawn on inside front cover, with his motto 'A Mon Povoir': Sassetti was head of the Medici bank in Florence; Hunter's source not traced.

BIBLIOGRAPHY: Young & Aitken, pp. 401-402; Oldham, *Notes on Bindings*, p. 16; for Tommaso Portinari see R. de Roover, *Money, Banking and Credit in Medieval Bruges*, Cambridge, Mass., 1948.

120. Book of Hours

Horae.
French Flanders, c.1460.

MS Euing 4

Vellum, 224 × 158 mm.; i, 130, iv leaves; written space 105 × 65 mm.; 16 long lines.

Entries in the Calendar, which has a saint for every day in the French manner, show that this Book of Hours was written for the use of Saint-Omer in North-east France: the saint's festival on 9 September and, of especial interest, the feast of 'Saint Omer en fleurs' on 8 June, are both marked in red.

The twelve miniatures in this volume are painted in spaces left in the text-pages, rather than being inserted on additional single leaves, as was the practice further north (see nos. 117 and 118). Two of the miniatures are in an earlier style than the others: these are the Annunciation, introducing the Hours of the Virgin, and King David, introducing the Penitential Psalms. Such entries were often reserved for the head of a workshop and are likely here to be the late work of a miniaturist trained in the 1420s.

The other ten miniatures are in the more interesting style developed by Simon Marmion in the 1450s. The landscapes (cf. The Flight into Egypt, fol. 55) are more sharply detailed, often with extensive buildings in the middle distance; the poses of the characters are more dramatic, and the painting more fluid. The artist's manner of painting trees, his walls of large pink blocks, the wooden-pegged panelling and characteristic details of faces, such as the emphasis given to cheeks by firm diagonal strokes and to eyes drawn with bistre, has led Nicole Reynaud to suggest that he is to be identified with the painter responsible for the miniatures in the first volume of the *Chronicles of Hainaut* now in Boulogne (Bibl. mun. MS 149); this was produced for the Créqui family and subsequently passed to the Abbey of Saint Bertin at Saint-Omer.

The variable quality of some of the miniatures in this Book of Hours is consistent with a painter experimenting with new styles early in his career. It suggests too a combination of French and Netherlandish influences, particularly noticeable in the delicate border decoration which is the same both in the Chronicles and the Hours. A particular feature of the decorative work is the linear stylization of the acanthus leaves and tendrils, which in some borders take on regular geometric forms.

Annunciation to Shepherds. MS Euing 4, 45v
(See also Colour Ill. 41 of fol. 55)

PROVENANCE: Bequeathed to the Library by William Euing in 1874.

BIBLIOGRAPHY: Ker, *MMBL*, II, pp. 873-874; *Flemish Art 1300-1700*, no. 571; *La miniature flamande*, p. 38, no. 32; *Trésors*, p. 12, no. 17; *Treasures*, p. 15, no. 39.

Woman kneeling before St Peter.
MS Euing 9, fol. 14v

121. Psalter, and Prayer Book

Psalterium, etc.
French Flanders, c. 1470.

MS Euing 9

Vellum, 157 × 107 mm.; i, 229, ii leaves; written space 87 × 59 mm., 17 long lines.

This well-produced book of prayers and psalms, with alternating gold and penwork initials throughout, was written for use in the diocese of Arras. The Psalter opens with a half-page initial of St Jerome (fol. 15), who was possibly the patron of the church where the book was used. The large miniature on the facing page, which has been inserted, shows a woman in black kneeling before St Peter and is perhaps a representation of the owner who had a devotion to this saint (fol. 14v). The two pictures are conventional workshop images, competently drawn though lacking in vigour; they are gaily coloured in harmony with the blue, red, green and gold border of acanthus leaves and rinceaux.

PROVENANCE: Bought by William Euing from Knight, a bookdealer, on 21 June 1860 and bequeathed by him to the Library in 1874.

BIBLIOGRAPHY: Ker, *MMBL*, II, p. 875.

Decorated page with initial B showing St Jerome.
MS Euing 9, fol. 15

122. Missal

Officium missae, etc.
Northern Netherlands, ?Utrecht, c. 1460.

MS Euing 7

Vellum, 172 × 127 mm.; [i] , 30, [i] leaves;
written space 116 × 86 mm., in double columns
of 31 lines, fols. 21-23 with 28 long lines.

Miniature painting in the Northern Netherlands
followed traditions that were largely independent
of those of the southern provinces. Dutch techniques of representation were more objective
than in the South and in France; they were
coupled with a simplicity and seriousness derived
from the reforming religious movement of the
devotio moderna, which originated in the
Netherlands at the end of the 14th century.

These qualities are evident in the miniature of
the Trinity in this small volume, one of two
full-page miniatures on single leaves inserted into
the text. The figure of God the Father is a study
of solemn dignity, wise yet not remote from the
humanity of Christ, whose body bears the evidence of his suffering only too visibly. The dove
of the Holy Spirit scarcely obtrudes upon the
grimly real portrait of the Father and Son, the
strength of which lies in its concentration upon
simple rhythmic forms, its avoidance of distract-
ing detail in contrasting the frailty of man with
the strength of the Almighty, and the painterli-
ness of the robes, body forms and faces, all of
which are present in volume as well as in outline.
The ready transfer of iconographic elements between Dutch miniatures and panel paintings is
echoed here in the artistry with which the miniature resembles a panel painting laid on the page.

The second painting is a portrait of a young
bishop by the same artist. It may be connected
with the translation of David of Burgundy, one of
the many natural sons of Philip the Good, from
the bishopric in Thérouanne to that of Utrecht in
1457. The rich decoration of initials of borders
elsewhere in the volume is also of northern
origin, though it contrasts with the simplicity of
the borders of the miniature pages.

PROVENANCE: Bought by William Euing on 27 April 1864 and
bequeathed by him to the library in 1874.

BIBLIOGRAPHY: Ker, *MMBL*, II, pp. 874-875.

The Trinity; a bishop. MS Euing 7, fols. 20 and 12
(See also Colour Ill. 40 of fol. 20)

Annunciation. MS Hunter 465, fol. 6v

123. Cardinal Bonaventura, Spur of Divine Love

Eustachius Bonaventura, Stimulus amoris, translated into French by Jean Charlier de Gerson. Flanders, third quarter of the 15th century.

MS Hunter 465 (V.6.15)

Vellum, 203 × 158 mm.; [iv], 164, [iv] leaves; written space 146 × 100 mm., 24 long lines.

Illustrators of manuscripts in the Netherlands did not confine themselves to painting in colours. They used techniques like painting in grisaille (see no. 116) or in other monochrome colours, as in the *Composition de la sainte écriture* illustrated by Dreux Jean in Brussels in 1462 (Brussels, Bibliothèque Royale, MS 9017). They also made pen and wash drawings such as those in a Bible of 1439 now in Munich (Staatsbibliothek, MS Germ. 1102), and line drawings, as in this manuscript. The three drawings in this volume are of the Annunciation (fol. 6v), the Nativity announced to the Shepherds (fol. 23), and the Crucifixion (fol. 82v). In their architecture, linework, draperies and definition of space, they have marked similarities with the woodcut tradition of the blockbook, and it is interesting to see a manuscript imitating the appearance of a printed page at the same time that printing was itself in general modelling itself on the more prestigious manuscript forms.

Most of the gold initials are decorated with penwork leaf and flower patterns, but there are also pen drawings of the face of God (fols. 62v and 132v), as well as a forceful picture of a face representing Pride (fol. 74v). In the lower margin of fol. 162 there is in addition a finely drawn portrait of a man dating from the late 16th or early 17th century.

PROVENANCE: 'Georgius ?Gagaus' fol. 1; Hunter's source not traced.

BIBLIOGRAPHY: Young & Aitken, pp. 386-387.

124. Plato, Phaedrus and Phaedo, with Commentaries

Plato, Phaedrus, Phaedo, translated into Latin by Leonardo Bruni; Marsilio Ficino, Giovanni Cavalcanti, Heros, Christoforo Landino, Carlo Marsuppini, Tommaso Benci, Commentarium in Platonis Convivium, etc.; Marsilio Ficino, De voluptate, De divino furore, De magnificentiae laude, De quattuor sectis philosophorum. Southern Netherlands, 1483.

MS Hunter 206 (U.1.10)

Vellum, 364 × 265 mm.; [i], iv, 102, iv, [i] leaves; written space 261 × 175 mm., 38 long lines.

This substantial volume of philosophical texts and commentaries belonged to Raphael de Marcatellis, Abbot of St Bavon's in Ghent, whose coat of arms appears along with the monogram L.Y.S. in several of the illuminated initials. While the marginal decoration is of conventional acanthus leaves, flowers and fruit, two large initials contain exquisitely painted floral studies of an iris (fol. 33) and carnations (fol. 75v); and strawberries appear in a third smaller study (fol. 97). The tactile beauty of these paintings is the achievement of an artist who responded to natural forms with an enthusiasm founded in the realistic outlook of his time.

PROVENANCE: Raphael de Marcatellis (1437-1501); bought by Hunter at the David Mallet sale, London, 10 March 1766, lot 68.

BIBLIOGRAPHY: Young & Aitken, pp. 148-150; Ker, *William Hunter*, p. 14, Appendix A, V; M. Smeyers, 'Een onbekend Marcatellis-handschrift', *Informatieblad of the Centrum voor de studie van het verluchte handschrift in de Nederlanden*, no. 7, 1986, p. 6; not listed in A. Derolez, *The Library of Raphael de Marcatellis*, Ghent, 1979, but to be described by him in the *Festschrift for Professor Johanne Autenrieth*, Freiburg, 1987.

Initial P with Iris. MS Hunter 206, fol. 33
(*See also Colour Ill. 26*)

Annunciation. MS Hunter 25, fol. 7v. *(See also Colour Ill. 39)*

125. Breviary

Breviarium Romanum.
Flanders, Ghent, illuminated by the Master of the First Prayer Book of Maximilian, 1494.

MS Hunter 25 (S.2.15)

Vellum, 250 × 164 mm.; [iv], iii, 383, ii, [iv] leaves; written space 170 × 94 mm., in double columns of 43 lines; binding by Anthonius van Gavere (d. 1505).

From the mid 1470s a new style of decoration had been introduced into Netherlandish illumination by the Master of Mary of Burgundy, the leading illuminator at the court of Charles the Bold. Standard border motifs of flowers, leaves and insects were treated illusionistically, and became fully-rounded still-life studies casting shadows on a ground which was generally of liquid gold. The Master of the First Prayer Book of Maximilian was one of the foremost exponents of the new style. He was active at the Burgundian court from the late 1470s, and his career lasted for half a century. He was named after a volume illuminated in 1486 for Maximilian, Archduke of Austria and future Emperor (Vienna, Nationalbibliothek, cod. 1907); an early example of his work is the London Hastings Hours (B.L., Add. MS 54782, see T. Kren, 'Flemish Manuscript Illumination 1475-1550', *Renaissance Painting in Manuscripts*, pp. 21-30). The Hunterian Breviary contains eight border panels and one page decorated in all five margins which are by the same hand as the borders of the London manuscript; an iris figures prominently amongst other flowers which include borage, sweet pea, primrose, speedwell, thistle and double daisy.

The Master's chief work in the volume is the movingly serene Annunciation with which the Breviary opens. In contrast to the brightness of the floral borders, the soft tonalities here accord with the contemplative nature of the scene, which depicts the moment of the Virgin's knowledge rather than the moment of her surprise. The space is divided into two halves by the central pillar which separates the Virgin from the angel, but its lines are broken by the curtain which is wrapped around it in the middle. Rather than providing a realistic element of furnishing,

the green hangings help to articulate the composition of the picture in terms of balance and volume. The angel's arms, the divine ray and the architecture all concentrate attention on the meditative figure of the Virgin. The Virgin also occupies a central position in the design of the two open pages seen together. This unified approach to an opening was the chief contribution of the Master of the First Prayer Book of Maximilian to the development of manuscript illumination. It is seen here in a delicate balance of colour and composition, where the stippled lightness of the painting and the mastery of form are subordinated to the effect of the overall design.

The same Master contributed nine small pictures in the text. One in particular demonstrates the continuing influence of panel painting on the iconography of miniatures in manuscripts: the Trinity on fol. 109v is derived from the Trinity panel now in Edinburgh (National Gallery of Scotland) which was painted by Hugo van der Goes in the late 1470s. The link was perhaps through the intermediary of another manuscript such as a Flemish Book of Hours of c. 1490 in London (B.L., Add. MS 35313) in which the subject also appears.

The forms of absolution which end the Proper of the Saints on fols. 229v-230 suggest that the owner of the Breviary, which was intended for Franciscan use, may have been someone's confessor. It is interesting to note that it was completed in the same year (1494) in which Maximilian married his second wife, Maria Bianca, daughter of Galeazzo Maria Sforza, Duke of Milan; it may therefore have been connected with this event. The volume is notable also for preserving its original blind-stamped binding, signed by the binder Anthonius van Gavere of Bruges, who became a member of the Guild of St John in Bruges in 1459/60 and died in 1505.

PROVENANCE: Hunter's source not traced.

BIBLIOGRAPHY: Young & Aitken, pp. 23-25; Wardrop, 'Western Illuminated Manuscripts', pp. 319-322; *Flemish Art 1300-1700*, no. 602; *Trésors*, p. 22, no. 37; *Treasures*, p. 18, no. 51; C. Thompson and L. Campbell, *Hugo van der Goes and the Trinity Panels in Edinburgh*, Edinburgh, 1974, p. 16.

ēe tei filiū: ſʒ ſupꝉegē ꝫ ipo principio teſignaret: nec ſolui legem ſʒ adimplen. Neqʒ eni ꝓ legē ſed � vbo ſciūs eſt mūdus ſicut legimꝰ. Verbo ōi celi firmati ſt. Non ſoluiterṫ ergo lex ſʒ adimplet: vt fiat renouatio hois iā labetis. Un z apłs ait. Erpoliātes vos vetere hoīem: iduite nouū q̃ ſcōm xp̃m creatus ē. R ̃ am nō vocam vos ſeruos ſʒ amicos meos: q̃a oĩa cognouiſtis q̃ opaꝛ ſū in medio vn alla. Accipite ſpm ſcm ꝫ vobis paclitū ille ē quē pꝛ mittet vobis al. Ꝟ. Uos amici mei eſtis ſi feceritis q̃ ego p̃cipio vobis. Acci lc.iij.

T bene ſabbo cepit: vt ipe ſe ōderet creatorē q̃ opa opibꝰ intereret z pſeq̃ref opꝰ q̃ ipe iā ceꝑrat: vt ſi faber tomū renouare viſponat: nō a fūdamētis ſʒ a culmimibꝰ incipit ſoluē vetuſtatē. Itaqʒ ibi ꝑus manū admonꝫ ubi ante teſierat: teinde a mioꝛibꝰ incipit vt ao maioꝛa puemat. Liberare a temone hoies ſʒ in vbo tei poſſūt. Reſurrectiōe moꝛtuis imꝑrare: viuine ſohꝰ ē poteſtatis. Nec quēq̃ mouere tebet q̃ ꝫbu nazareni nomē in hoc libꝛo viabolus viriſſe ꝑmꝰ inducit. Nec eni ab eo xp̃s nomē accepit q̃ te celo angelus ao virginē tetulit. Ao bn.an.

Caritas tei viffuſa eſt in coꝛdibꝰ vꝰis ꝑ ihabitantē ſpm eı in vobis al. Entibus nꝛis q̃s Oꝛo. vīe ſpm ſcm benignius infunde cuius z ſapientia conditi ſumus z ꝓuidentia gubernamur. Ꝑer. in vnitate e iuſtē. Incipit officiū ſanctiſſime trinitatis. Ao veſpe.a.

Edenti ſi ſoluit congratulās triſagiū ſeraphica damous cū patre laudat filiū indifferens principiū recipꝛoci amoꝛis. pͤ Dirit oūs. cū rel. In fine. Laudate oūm omͤs gē. a. Seq̃uiꝰ ꝓ ſuſpiriū q̃ geritur per gaudiū in ſcīs celi choꝛis: leuemꝰ coꝛdis ſtudiū in trinū lucis radiū ſplenfoꝛis z amoꝛis. a. Si noſie vis hec germina nō ſemia a ſʒ lumina ꝓfiteret inoago: lur teus eſt intermina te q̃ res manat gemina tā a moꝛ q̃ vm ago. a Lux nō teaſa radiū viffundēs ꝓ huic mediū mltiplicat ardoꝛē: ſic pꝛ gignit filiū eı ipa ſpirans ēeū ꝓcoꝛdit amoꝛē. a Eterno pꝛi glia erquo ſubliſtūt oĩa ꝓ vbū in amore: cuius ſignauit gꝛa nꝛa ſue coꝛdia imaginis hoꝛe. cap. Ratia oni nꝛi ihu xpi et caritas tei z coicatio ſci ſpūs ſit ſemp cū oĩbꝰ vobis amē. ymnꝰ In maieſtatis. Ꝟ. Binoicaīꝰ p̃em z filiū cū ſcō ſpū. R Laudemꝰ z ſuperal temꝰ cū in ſēcla. Ao mgt a. O ſeraphin iocunditas: o cherubin lympioitas: thronoꝛ robur trinitas: fac vigne te laudemꝰ mēoꝛie ſit vnitas: noti cieqʒ vitas: te vtriuſqʒ bonitas phenniter amemus. Oꝛatio. Omnipotēs ſempitne teus q̃ tediſti famulis tuis ꝫ ꝓfeſſiōe vere fitei etine trinitatis gloꝛiā agnoſcē: z ꝫ potentia maieſtatꝭ aoorare vnitatē: q̃s: vt eiuſtē fitei firmitate: ab oīnibꝰ ſep muniamꝰ aduerſis. Ꝑer. Et

Decorated page with Trinity. MS Hunter 25, fol. 109v

190

126. Book of Hours, in Dutch

Horae. Belgice.
Netherlands, early 16th century.

MS Hunter 186 (T.8.18)

Vellum, 127 × 82 mm.; [iv], ii, 200, i, [v] leaves; written space 71 × 48 mm., 16 long lines.

Despite the small scale of this Dutch Book of Hours, which was intended for private devotions, much care has been given to the decorative penwork as well as to the script itself. The largest of the traditional blue and red initials occupies half of the first page following the Calendar. It is enclosed with finely regulated filigree work in red and purple, which is repeated in the larger initials throughout the volume. Included in the series of texts is Heinrich Seuse's *Getijden van de eeuwige wijsheid*, the popularity of which is indicated by the fact that it survives in over three hundred manuscripts.

PROVENANCE: Trijntjen Pjeters of Delft, 16th century (fol.ii verso); Anna Roemers, 17th century; Hunter's source not traced.

BIBLIOGRAPHY: Young and Aitken, pp. 132-133; P. Stephanus Axters, 'De zalige Heinrich Seuse in nederlandse Handschriften', *Heinrich Seuse. Studien zum 600 Todestag*, ed. E.M. Filthaut, Cologne, 1966, p. 378.

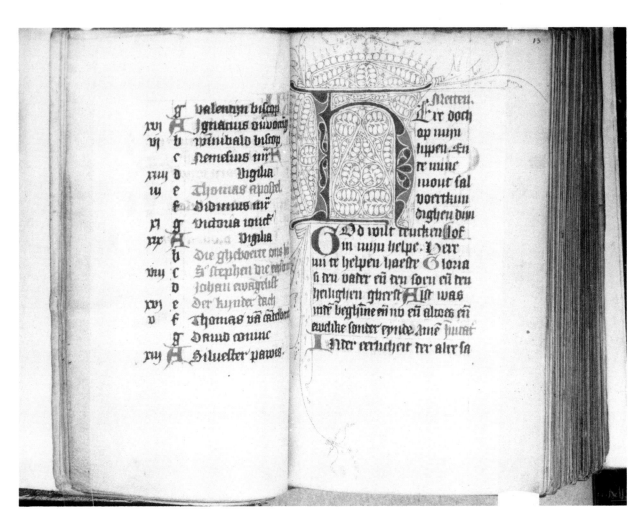

Opening with penwork initial H. MS Hunter 186, fols. 12v-13

Crucifixion. MS Euing 29, fol. 70v

127. Missal

Missale.

Flanders, Geraardsbergen (Grammont), c. 1510.

MS Euing 29

Vellum, 336 × 238 mm.; [vi] , 162, [vi] leaves; written space 238 × 159 mm., in double columns of 23 lines (fols. 71-78 of 18 lines).

Five of the seven full borders accompanying the miniatures in this large and extensively decorated Missal are in the Flemish illusionistic style. Among the flower studies there are iris, pinks, thistle, forget-me-not, strawberry, rose, columbine, vetch, cornflower and lily in addition to acanthus fronds, and there is also a plentiful population of caterpillars, birds, butterflies, snails, beetles and other insects, all placed separately on the gold ground.

Two of these borders frame the pages of a single unified opening at the beginning of the Canon of the Mass. The left-hand page (fol. 70v), contains a full-page Crucifixion with symbols of the Evangelists in the corners of the border; the right-hand page begins with a historiated initial of the Mass of St Gregory to introduce the text. The colours of the figures and backgrounds of the two scenes complement those of the border decoration in the tradition established by the Master of Mary of Burgundy and the Master of the First Prayer Book of Maximilian (see no. 125). The bright colour combinations, the rather flat drawing and the general atmosphere of the painting, however, suggest a painter who is more concerned with surface appeal than with the subtler qualities and compositional unity found in the work of his more eminent predecessors.

The two remaining borders, on fols. 112v and 128v, are of architectural framework in an Italian manner, based on designs by artists such as the Master of the London Pliny (no. 90) and the Master of the Vatican Homer (no. 102). Prominent also in their influence on French book design (cf. nos. 66 and 141), these architectural borders came to be used in the Netherlands from around the turn of the century.

PROVENANCE: Arms of ?De l'Esclatière; bought by William Euing on 28 July 1853 and bequeathed by him to the Library in 1874.

BIBLIOGRAPHY: Ker, *MMBL*, II, pp. 877-878.

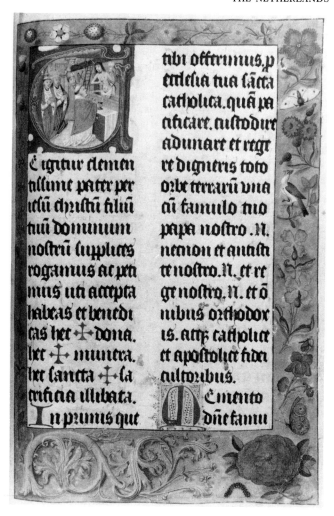

Decorated page with initial T. MS Euing 29, fol. 71

128. Bede, Ecclesiastical History of the English People

Beda, Historia ecclesiastica.
Northern Netherlands, written by Johannes Embriceus of St Paul, Gouda, 1515.

MS Hunter 86 (T.4.3)

Paper, 277 × 203 mm., [ii], 88, i, [i] leaves; written space 206 × 142 mm., in double columns of 36-41 lines.

Both the decorated initial and the penwork border of the first page of Book I (fol. 2), show that flowing penmanship was considered as an acceptably modest form of book decoration for what can be termed a working copy of a standard text. The work is written here on paper which would not have served as a suitable support for the more detailed book painting of the period.

Bede's masterpiece, completed in 731, had a wide appeal all over Europe from the 9th to the early 16th century. Some 120 copies survive of the complete text, and excerpts were frequently made.

PROVENANCE: Bought for Hunter at the Pieter Burmann sale, Leyden, 27 September 1779, lot 1228.

BIBLIOGRAPHY: Young & Aitken, p. 94; M.L.W. Laistner and H.H. King, *A Hand-List of Bede Manuscripts*, Ithaca, N.Y., 1943, p. 96.

Opening to Book I. MS Hunter 86, fol. 2

129. Album of Alphabet Designs, etc.

Netherlands, c. 1529.

Stirling Maxwell Collection, SM 1161

Vellum and paper, 196 × 143 mm.; [ii], 78, [ii] leaves.

The earliest example of lettering in this album is a copy on vellum of two devotional alphabets written in the northern Netherlands in the mid 15th century. The first of these, ascribed to Thomas à Kempis, begins with a half-page initial U in elaborate blue and red fretwork with leaf-scroll infill in pen and wash. The second is a later copy of the Thomas à Kempis text with plain red initials, also on vellum.

The main part of the album, however, is a series of designs on paper for whole alphabets and single letters. Covering 57 leaves, the designs concentrate in turn on different elements, developing ideas for leaf-scroll patterns within the letter form and patterns of fretwork in the letter shape, as well as numbers of combinations (e.g. fols. 45v-46). Since the initial U in the first Thomas à Kempis alphabet is closely followed in the largest of the completed designs (fol. 37) and the tailpiece of the alphabet is also copied, the designer was clearly using the earlier examples as a model. Few pattern books of any kind have

survived and it is particularly interesting in this case to see not only sketches which show designs being worked out but also the original example on which many of them were based.

The appearance of heraldic designs on fols. 38 and 71v with the initials 'E.D.' may give a clue to the identity of the scribe, as these appear to be the first elements of an obliterated ex-libris on fol. 29 in the same hand that supplied a marginal note on fol. 71v. The drawing style of the figurative elements in some of the letter designs fits the date of 1529 which is included in letters on fols. 27v, 33 and 45. Half a century later the volume was evidently owned by Guilielmus Middelborch, whose name appears in an architectural framework with the date 1578. The anonymous English handbook now bound in with the designs, *A very proper treatise, wherein is briefly sett forthe the art of limming*, printed by Richard Totthill in London in 1573, could also have been added to the album by this time.

PROVENANCE: Sir William Stirling Maxwell; bequeathed to the Library by Sir John Stirling Maxwell in 1958.

BIBLIOGRAPHY: For surviving pattern books see R.W. Scheller, *A Survey of Medieval Model Books*, Haarlem, 1963; H. Lehmann-Haupt, *The Göttingen Model Book*, Columbia, Mo., 1971; J. Backhouse, 'An Illuminator's Sketchbook [B.L., Sloane MS 1448 A], *British Library Journal*, 1, 1975, pp. 3-4; ibid., *John Scottowe's Alphabet Books*, London, 1974 (Roxburghe Club).

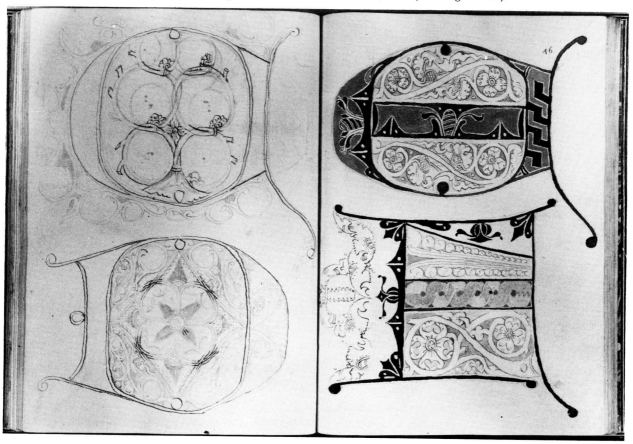

Alphabet designs. Stirling Maxwell Collection, SM 1161, fols. 45v-46
(See also Colour Ill. on back cover)

Syboldus ab Aylva (?). Stirling Maxwell Collection,
SM 658.2, facing p. 19.

130. Adriaen de Jonghe, Emblems

Hadrianus Junius, Emblemata, Aenigmatum
libellus.
Antwerp, printed by Christopher Plantin, 1565.

Stirling Maxwell Collection, SM 658.2

Paper, 162 × 110 mm.; octavo; [xviii], 84, 8,
[xliii] leaves: the text is interleaved throughout.

One of the few types of books in which painting
survived in the later 16th century was the *album
amicorum*. This was a volume of inscriptions,
illustrations or other mementos contributed by
friends of the owner: an emblem book, as here,
was often used as an appropriate accompanying
text.

Junius's *Emblemata*, written by a physician
who was at one time tutor to the crown prince of
Denmark, is a delightful work in its own right,
with 57 woodcuts and delicate filigree borders on
each page. This copy of the first edition was
interleaved for the young Solinus a Sixma, probably from Frisia, who seems from the inscriptions to have been a student at Heidelberg in
1569 and 1570. The earliest dated entry is for
December 1569 and amongst the contributors in
the next few months is Immanuel Tremellius,
the renowned theologian and Hebraist who had
taught at Cambridge and who was professor of
Old Testament studies at Heidelberg.

While many of the entries are coloured coats of
arms, there are also full-length figures of a man
and of a woman playing a lute, and two striking
three-quarter length portraits of very fashionable
young men, one of whom may be Solinus; the
other (facing p. 19) appears to be a fellow
Friesian, Syboldus ab Aylva, who was nineteen
when this portrait was painted in 1571. Both
portraits are finely painted studies of character,
'miniatures' in a more modern sense of the word.

Other contributions are dated from places as
far apart as Cologne, Douai, Frankfurt and Louvain; they continue to 1573. The volume was
then evidently handed down in the family, as it
was used again for further inscriptions by
Aggaeus a Sixma in the mid 1650s.

PROVENANCE: Sir William Stirling Maxwell; bequeathed to
the Library by Sir John Stirling Maxwell in 1958.

BIBLIOGRAPHY: cf. M. Praz, *Studies in Seventeenth-Century
Imagery*, 2nd ed., Rome, 1964, p. 384; J. Landwehr,
Emblem Books in the Low Countries 1554-1949, Utrecht,
1970, no. 276; A. Henkel and A. Schöne, *Emblemata.
Handbuch zur Sinnbildkunst des XVI und XVII Jahrhun-
derts*, Stuttgart, 1967, p. LVIII.

131. Blockbook Apocalypse

Apocalypsis.
Xylographic blockbook, printed in the Netherlands or Western Germany, 1430s-1440s.

Hunterian Collection, Ds 2. 3

Paper, 292 × 215 mm., block frame 264 × 204 mm.; [iii], 42 (of 50), [iii] leaves.

A blockbook is a volume in which each page, generally containing both text and illustrations, is printed from a single wooden block cut in relief. Following the example of devotional religious images printed on one side of single sheets of paper, sometimes with brief texts below the pictures, they were probably first produced in any quantity in Germany and the Netherlands around 1430.

The Netherlandish Apocalypse, which is amongst the earliest of the surviving blockbooks, was first printed in Haarlem or Utrecht. It is ranked amongst the highest artistic achievements of blockbook production. Being a popular work, it was sold on such occasions as fairs; it presents scenes from the life of St John and the Book of Revelation. Few copies survive complete and the Hunterian copy, which corresponds to the second edition listed by W.L. Schreiber, lacks plates 8-11, 20-22 and 24 of his enumeration. Although there is a small number of full-page pictures, the general pattern is of two scenes to each page, allowing four scenes to be seen at each opening, in a series of visions roughly corresponding to the order of their appearance in the Book of Revelation. The strength of the pictures is in the clarity of the linework and narrative, enhanced in this example by the bold watercolour washes.

PROVENANCE: Bought by Hunter at the Anthony Askew sale, London, February 1775, lot 1936.

BIBLIOGRAPHY: R. Donaldson, 'Two Block Books in the Hunterian Library, Glasgow University', *The Bibliothek*, 3, 1961, pp. 103-104; *Trésors*, p. 31, no. 52; *Treasures*, p. 21, no. 60; Baldwin, *William Hunter*, p. 8, no. 15; cf. W.L. Schreiber, *Manuel de l'amateur de la gravure sur bois et sur métal au XVe siècle*, IV, Leipzig, 1902, pp. 160-216; A.M. Hind, *An Introduction to a History of Woodcut*, London, 1935, I, pp. 207-263; H.T. Musper, *Die Urausgaben der holländischen Apokalypse und Biblia pauperum*, Munich, 1961.

Scenes from the Life of St John. Woodcuts. Hunterian Collection, Ds 2. 3, pls. C-D

132. Blockbook Bible

Biblia pauperum.
Xylographic blockbook, printed in the Netherlands, mid 15th century.

Hunterian Collection, Ds 2. 4

Paper, cut to block size 257/267 × 193/195 mm. and mounted; [iii], 23 (of 40), [i] leaves.

The *Biblia pauperum* provided a handbook for the use of poor clerics and friars. In the Netherlands, it was a later product of the same artistic milieu that created the Apocalypse (no. 131), although the date and the sequence of the ten editions of the work so far identified remain a matter of lively debate. The woodcutter's source of inspiration lay doubtless in one of the manuscript versions of the work which had been developed during the preceeding two centuries. Typological scenes depicting allegorical connections between the Old and New Testaments occupy the centre tier of three; these are contained within an architectural framework which is extended above and below by arched windows containing figures of the prophets, flanked by explanatory texts.

While the composition of manuscript illuminations can be felt to underlie the Biblical scenes, their power of expression is related to the woodcutter's need to concentrate on essential outline and use only the clearest forms. Robust and realistic figures, sharply delineated, inhabit well-defined spaces which are remarkable not only for the greater sense of proportion (as compared with the Apocalypse) achieved in the portrayal of people in a landscape or in relation to buildings, but also for the detail of the settings of contemporary life. When Esau sells his birthright to Jacob (block 10), he does so in a domestic interior of the period, complete with fireplace, cooking pots, and hams and sides of bacon hanging from wallhooks. Costumes range from the rustic jerkins, stockings and ankle boots of Oshea and Caleb as they look at the land of Canaan (block 9), to the bourgeois and court dress of the grander characters. Facial expression is also more differentiated than in the Apocalypse and reflects the movement towards naturalism that is characteristic of the later part of the century.

PROVENANCE: Bought by Hunter at the Anthony Askew sale, London, February 1775, lot 1937.

BIBLIOGRAPHY: R. Donaldson, 'Two Block Books in the Hunterian Library, Glasgow University', *The Bibliothek*, 3, 1961, pp. 103-104; cf. W.L. Schreiber, *Manuel de l'amateur de la gravure sur bois et sur métal au XVe siècle*, IV, Leipzig, 1902, pp. 160-216; A.M. Hind, *An Introduction to a History of Woodcut*, London, 1935, I, pp. 207-263; H.T. Musper, *Die Urausgaben der holländischen Apokalypse und Biblia pauperum*, Munich, 1961; J.P. Berjeau, *Biblia pauperum. Reproduced in facsimile from one of the copies in the British Museum*, London, 1859; E. Solterz, *Biblia pauperum, facsimile edition of the forty-leaf blockbook in the Library of Esztergom Cathedral*, Budapest, 1967; R.A. Koch, 'New Criteria for dating the Netherlandish Biblia pauperum blockbook', *Studies in Late Medieval and Renaissance Painting in Honor of Millard Meiss*, New York, 1977, pp. 283-289.

Biblical scenes. Woodcuts. Hunterian Collection, Ds 2. 4, pp. 9-10

VI · Printed Books

133. Roberto Valturio, On Warfare

Roberto Valturio, De re militari.
Italy, Verona, printed by Giovanni di Nicolò, 1472.

Hunterian Collection, Be 1. 10

Paper, 328 × 224 mm.; folio; [vi], 262, [vi] leaves.

This treatise, the handbook of the military leaders of the Renaissance, is the first book printed with illustrations of a scientific or technical character; it is also the first book printed in Verona and the first book illustrated with blocks designed by an Italian artist. The woodcuts were probably made by Matteo de' Pasti, a pupil of Antonio Pisanello (1395-1455/6) and Leone Battista Alberti (1404-1472). Matteo de 'Pasti and Alberti both worked in Rimini at the court of Sigismondo Pandolfo Malatesta, to whom the volume is dedicated. The illustrations, most of which are full-page, show a wide range of weapons from crossbows to cannons and an extensive series of mechanical constructions for large-scale military operations against substantial fortifications. These include battering rams, siege towers, extending ladders and catapults, and there is also a section on marine warfare. Leonardo da Vinci owned a copy of the work when acting as chief engineer to Cesare Borgia, and he copied several of the designs.

A corrected manuscript of the text including drawings close to those of the 1472 edition and accompanied by written directions for their location in the text is in the Rosenwald Collection in the Library of Congress (see E. Rodakiewicz, 'The edition princeps of Roberto Valturio's *De re militari* in relation to the Dresden and Munich manuscripts', *Maso Finiguerra*, 18-19, 1940, pp. 15-82, and Walters Art Gallery, *Illuminated Books of the Middle Ages and Renaissance*, Baltimore, 1949, p. 67, no. 184).

<small>PROVENANCE:</small> 'Rmi. P. Cesaris Quadrij Cruciq.', inscription on fol. 1; François Graverol (1636-1694), lawyer and collector of coins and manuscripts, born in Nîmes.

<small>BIBLIOGRAPHY:</small> Goff, V 88; Sander, no. 7481; *Printing and the Mind of Man* (exh. cat.), ed. N. Barker, C. Batey, J. Dreyfus, London, 1963, p. 33, no. 142.

Fortified ship; siege tower. Woodcuts
Hunterian Collection Be 1. 10, fols. 192v and 168

Woodcut border. Hunterian Collection, Bf 2.7, fol. 4v

134. Petrarch, Lives

Francesco Petrarca, Libro degli uomini famosi, translated into Italian by
Donato degli Albanzani.
Italy, Pojano, printed by Felice Feliciano and Innocente Zileto, 1 October 1476.

Hunterian Collection, Bf 2. 7

Paper, 303 × 217 mm.; folio; [ii], 240, [ii] leaves.

Printers were quick to see the possibilities of providing the framework for coloured designs in imitation of manuscripts by using wood blocks. This edition of Petrarch's *Lives of Famous Men*, mostly from the Bible and Roman history, has two full-page designs which are used repeatedly throughout the volume. The central panel of each block was left blank for portraits of the subjects of the biographies to be added, as they were for instance in a copy of Albanzani's translation made for a member of the Papafava family of Padua around 1400 which is now in Darmstadt (Hessische Landes- und Hochschulbibliothek, MS 101). This volume is the only book to have been printed in Pojano.

PROVENANCE: Bought for Hunter at the Louis-Jean Gaignat sale, Paris, 10 April 1769, lot 3494.

BIBLIOGRAPHY: Goff, P 415; De Bure, II, p. 234, no. 3494; Hoepli, no. 1; Sander, no. 5596; cf. E.H. Wilkins, *Petrarch's Later Years*, Cambridge, Mass., 1959, pp. 283-302.

135. Euclid, Geometry

Euclides, Elementa geometria, translated by Adelhard of Bath and edited by Giovanni Campano; with dedicatory letter by Erhard Ratdolt.
Italy, Venice, printed by Erhard Ratdolt, 25 May 1482.

Hunterian Collection, By 2. 12

Paper, 304 × 216 mm.; folio; [ii], 138, [i] leaves.

Erhard Ratdolt used the same large block and the same initials from his edition of Appian's *History of Rome* (no. 98) for the *editio princeps* of Euclid. Here the block is printed in black and has remained uncoloured. In addition to the decorative initials throughout the volume, there are geometrical diagrams in the margins, also from woodblocks. This is the first printed book to contain geometrical figures.

Seven copies of the work are recorded which have the dedication leaf of the book printed in gold. Ratdolt was one of two printers in the 15th century to have used a technique for gold printing; the other was Zacharias Callierges, a Cretan who also worked in Venice. The copy now in London, printed on vellum (B.L., IB. 20514), was given by Ratdolt to the dedicatee, Giovanni Mocenigo, Doge of Venice from 1478 to 1485; it is noteworthy also in having the first leaf of text decorated by hand with an historiated initial and white-vine designs in three borders, together with the Doge's coat of arms.

PROVENANCE: Bought for Hunter at the Louis-Jean Gaignat sale, Paris, 10 April 1769, lot 1240.

BIBLIOGRAPHY: Goff, E 113; De Bure, I, p. 324, no. 1240; Sander, no. 2605; cf. M.B. Stillwell, *The Awakening Interest in Science during the First Century of Printing 1450-1550*, New York, 1970, p. 50, no. 163; V. Carter, L. Hellinga, T. Parker, 'Printing with Gold in the Fifteenth Century', *British Library Journal*, 9, 1983, pp. 1-13.

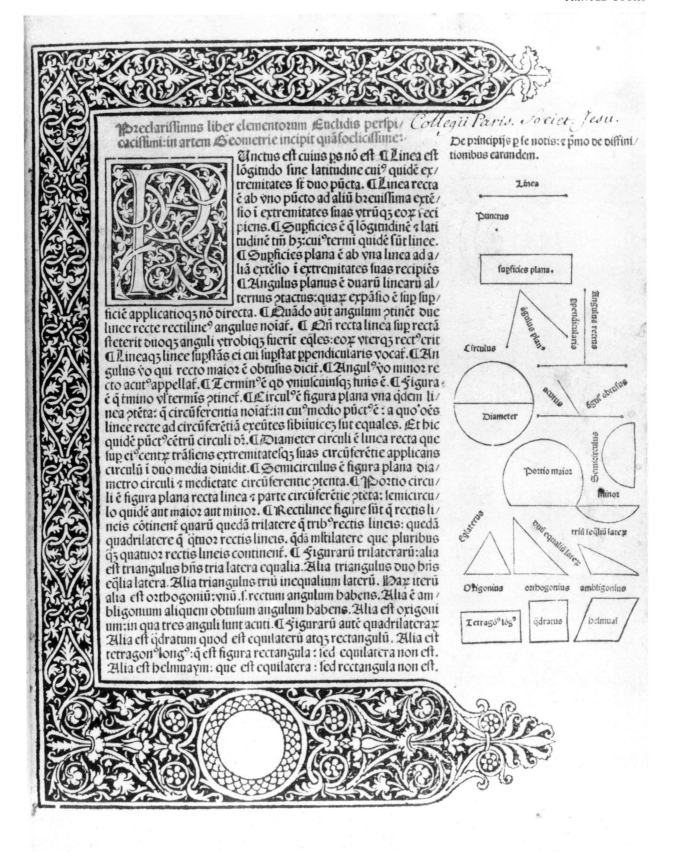

Woodcut decoration. Hunterian Collection, By 2. 12, fol. 2

Saints in Glory. Woodcut. Hunterian Collection,
Bg 1. 1, fol. 1

136. Jacobus de Voragine, Golden Legend

Jacobus de Voragine, The golden legende,
translated into English by William Caxton.
England, Westminster, printed by William
Caxton, after 20 November 1483 (c. 1485).

Hunterian Collection, Bg 1. 1

Paper, 387 × 279 mm.; folio; [ii], 447, [ii]
leaves.

This outsize collection of saints' lives, compiled
between 1250 and 1280 by Jacobus de Voragine,
Archbishop of Genoa, was a very popular devotional work of reference throughout the Middle
Ages and was widely copied and translated (see
no. 114). The translation by William Caxton
(c.1422-1491), who introduced printing to England in 1476, is based on versions of the book in
Latin, French and English, with additions from
other sources, particularly from legends of English saints. A folio volume of almost 900 pages
and 600,000 words, it is Caxton's longest work
and was completed only with the encouragement
of William, Earl of Arundel, who promised to
take a number of copies, paying Caxton an
annuity of a buck in summer and a doe in winter.

The book is lavishly illustrated with seventy
woodcuts, mostly column-width pictures of Old
Testament scenes and of saints. Nineteen are
folio-width, including the arms of Arundel. The
illustration of the Saints in Glory which begins
the work is the largest block Caxton ever used.
Until about 1486, he employed English crafts-
men to cut his blocks. Their lack of sophistication when compared with contemporary work on
the Continent is due to the absence of a native
tradition of block making in England.

This book, with the 1492 edition of Chaucer's
Canterbury Tales (no. 137), shows something of
the development of the design of the printed
book in England in the period when printing was
first becoming established.

PROVENANCE: Bought by Hunter at the James West sale,
London, 29 March 1773, lot 1865.

BIBLIOGRAPHY: Goff, J 148; E.G. Duff, Fifteenth Century
English Books, Oxford, 1917, pp. 113-114, no. 408; New
CBEL, I, 669; Rev. STC 24873; A Manual of the Writings in
Middle English 1050-1500, II, ed. J. B. Severs, New Haven,
1970, pp. 436-439; G.D. Painter, William Caxton, London,
1976, pp. 143-146.

137. Geoffrey Chaucer, Canterbury Tales

England, London, printed by Richard Pynson, c. 1491-1492.

Hunterian Collection, Bv 2. 12

Paper, 276 × 198 mm.; folio; [ii], 324, i, [ii] leaves.

William Caxton printed two editions of the *Canterbury Tales*, in 1477 and 1483. After his death in 1491, this edition was printed from the second of these by Richard Pynson, a native of Normandy who seems to have come to London in the early 1480s after having trained in Rouen. It is likely that Pynson worked under Caxton and that it was Caxton's death that prompted him to set up his own business soon afterwards with a copy of one of his master's books.

The woodcuts used in the Prologue and to introduce each tale are simple and direct compositions that demonstrate Caxton's dependence on the Netherlands for his illustrations. The same blocks are used repeatedly through the work to illustrate different characters, just as with miniatures there could be much repetition of standard drawings.

PROVENANCE: Bought by Hunter at the John Ratcliffe sale, London, 27 March 1776, lot 996.

BIBLIOGRAPHY: Goff, C 433; E.G. Duff, *Fifteenth Century English Books*, Oxford, 1917, p. 25, no. 89; *New CBEL*, I, 569; *Rev. STC* 5084.

Canterbury pilgrims. Woodcuts. Hunterian Collection, Bv 2. 12, 14v-15

138. Marsilio Ficino, Letters

Marsilio Ficino, Epistolae.
Italy, Venice, printed for Hieronymo Blondo by
Matteo Capodecasa of Parma, 11 March 1495.

Hunterian Collection, Bh 1. 24

Paper, 314 × 211 mm.; folio; [i], 204, [i] leaves.

The architectural framework and classical and
floral motifs which figure so prominently in the
work of miniaturists such as the Pico Master
(nos. 104, 105) became the basis for woodblock
designs used by printers to enhance the appearance of their books without recourse to the
individual artist. In this volume the pages with
the preface and prologue have been treated as a
single design: the same borders are used on both
pages, with an element of variety introduced by
exchanging the blocks of the top and the bottom
borders. The figure of God the Father in the
tympanum is an insert which is sometimes absent
from the title-pages of other books using the same
design, and the shield in the lower border is
printed blank for the addition of arms by an
owner.

The central architectural blocks were first used
in an edition of Dante printed by Matteo Capodecasa and Bernardino Benalio in Venice in 1491.
They reappear in works by other printers for
many years, for example in editions of Petrarch
printed in 1508 by Bartolomeo de' Zanni and in
1515 by Agostino de' Zanni. Similar designs
quickly became a standard for the best Italian
and French printers of the period and remained
influential well into the 16th century.

PROVENANCE: Hunter's source not traced.

BIBLIOGRAPHY: Goff, F 154; Sander, no. 2706.

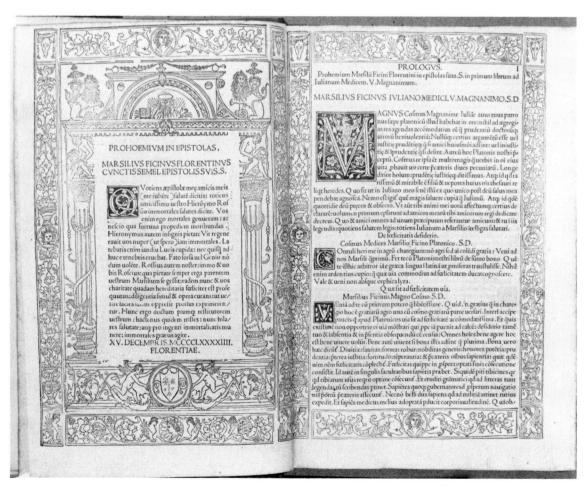

Opening with Preface and Prologue. Woodcuts.
Hunterian Collection, Bh 1. 24, fols. 2A6v-al

ce ligatura alla fistula tubale, Gli altri dui cũ ueterrimi cornitibici con
cordi ciascuno & cum gli instrumenti delle Equitante nymphe.
 Sotto lequale triũphale seiughe era laxide nel meditullo, Neldãegli
rotali radii erano infixi, deliniamento, Balustico, gracilisčenti seposa
negli mucronati labii cum uno pomulo alla circunferentia. Elquale
Polo era di finissimo & ponderoso oro, repudiante el rodicabile erugi-
ne, & lo inceŏdioso Vulcano, della uirtute & pace exitiale ueneno. Sum-
mamente dagli festiganti celebrato, cum moderate, & repentine
riuolutiõe intorno saltanti, cum solenniššimi plausi, cum
gli habiti cincti di fasceole uolitante, Et le sedente sopra gli trahenti centauri. La Sancta cagione,
& diuino mysterio, inuoce cõsone & car-
mini cancionali cum extre
ma exultatione amo-
rosamente lauda
uano.
**
*

EL SEQVENTE triũmpho nõ meno mirauegliosogdel primo. Im
pero che egli hauea le quatro uolubile rote tutte, & gli radii, & il meditul
lo defusco achate, di candide uenule uagamente uaricato. Ne tale certamente gesto e re Pyrrho cum le noue Muse & Apolline in medio pulsan
te dalla natura impresso.
 Laxide & la forma del dicto q̃l el primo, ma le tabelle erão di cyaneo
Saphyro orientale, atomato de scintillule doro, alla magica gratissimo,
& longe acceptissimo a cupidine nella sinistra mano.
 Nella tabella dextra mirai exscalpto una insigne Matrõa che
dui oui hauea parturito, in uno cubile regio colloca
ta, di uno mirabile pallacio, Cum obstetrice stu
pefacte, & multe altre matrone & astante
Nymphe Degli quali usciua de
uno una flammula, & delal-
tro ouo due spectatissi
me stelle.
**
*

Triumphal procession. Woodcuts. Hunterian Collection, Bh 2. 14, fols. k5v-k6

139. Francesco Colonna, The Dream of Polifilo

Francesco Colonna, Hypnerotomachia Poliphili; with additions by Leonardus Crassus, Johann Baptista Scytha and Andreas Maro.
Italy, Venice, printed by Aldo Manuzio, December 1499.

Hunterian Collection, Bh 2. 14

Paper, 303 × 194 mm.; folio; [ii], 235, [i] leaves.

The beauty of the woodcuts in this volume and the virtuoso skill of the printer have led to its being termed the most beautiful book of the Venetian Renaissance, and indeed of the 15th century. The first part of the work is an allegorical description of Polifilo's introduction to the world of the senses and the intellect, in which he has to make the choice between an ascetic life, one of public acclaim or one devoted to love. He chooses love, and the second part recounts his adventures in this realm with his beloved Polia. The narrative takes place in Treviso and is dated 1 May 1467 at the end of the text.

 The identity of the author and a hint of the personal experience that may have gone into the composition is revealed in the sentence formed by the initial letters of each chapter: 'Poliam Frater Franciscus Columna peramavit' ('Brother Francesco Colonna loved Polia deeply'). Colonna (1433/4-1527) was a Dominican monk and poet whose long life was frequently marked by conflict with monastic authority.

 The spendid pictures, which are intended to explain as well as to ornament the text, illustrate the elaborate descriptions of ancient architecture, pagan ritual and triumphal processions in the narrative. They are founded on the lively interest in classical antiquity that characterized the literary scene in Venice in the late 15th century. Their composition has been attributed to, amongst others, Mantegna, Giovanni Bellini and Benedetto Bordone of Padua, but the identity of the artist remains uncertain. The influence of their vigorous conception and execution can nonetheless be traced in Titian and Giorgione and later in works by Bernini and Pietro da Cortona. The book was printed at the expense of Leonardo Crasso, a lawyer at Verona, and dedicated to Guidobaldo, Duke of Urbino. It is the only book printed by Aldo Manuzio to be so extensively illustrated.

PROVENANCE: Hunter's source not traced.

BIBLIOGRAPHY: Goff, C 767; Sander, no. 2056; A.W. Pollard, *Catalogue of Italian Books in the C.W. Dyson Perrins Collection*, London, 1914; A.W. Pollard, *Early Illustrated Books*, London, 1893, pp. 106-107; M.T. Cassella and G. Pozzi, *Francesco Colonna, biografia e opere*, Padua, 1959; F. Colonna, *Hypnerotomachia Poliphili*, ed. G. Pozzi and L.A. Ciapponi, Padua, 1980.

140. Hans von Kircheim, Medical Compendium

Johannes de Ketham, Fasciculus medicinae, including Petrus de Tussignano, Consilium pro peste evitanda, Raimondo de' Luzzi, Anathomia, and Rhasis, De aegritudinibus puerorum.
Italy, Venice, 1500.

Hunterian Collection, Ds 2. 2

Paper, 305 × 213 mm.; folio; [i], 34 leaves.

This collection of medical treatises was in circulation by 1400 and first printed in 1491. It was widely popular, with some fourteen editions appearing over the following three decades in Italy, Spain and the Netherlands. Because of the good service it gave to practising physicians, however, any surviving copy is a rarity. The compiler was a German doctor working in Venice, Hans von Kircheim of Swabia, whose name is obscured in the Latin form in which it appears in the edition.

The stately woodcuts are the work of a superb Venetian artist of the circle of Giovanni Bellini (c.1430-1516), whose illustrations appear in a number of other blocks printed in Venice from 1491 to 1497. The ten plates include a Zodiac man (cf. no. 31), a vein man, a wound man, a pregnant woman and the first printed representation of a dissection scene. This introduces the *Anathomia* of Raimondo de' Luzzi, also known as Mondino, written in 1316. The artist's skill in line and flowing drapery is particularly evident in the moving picture of the visit to a patient stricken with the plague (fol. '71'), where a robed physician holding a pomander against contagion takes the pulse of the victim; he is escorted by two men with torches, one of whom carries a small brazier of aromatic substances as a further precaution. This poignant scene can be compared with the death-bed miniature in the Bartolo *Treatise* of almost a century earlier (no. 73).

PROVENANCE: Hunter's source not traced.

BIBLIOGRAPHY: Goff, K 15; Sander, no. 3746; K. Sudhoff, *The Fasciculus medicinae of Johannes de Ketham, Alemanus*, Milan, 1924; C. Singer, *The Fasciculo di Medicina*, Venice 1493, Florence, 1925; *Printing and the Mind of Man*, (exh. cat.) ed. N. Barker, C. Batey, J. Dreyfus, London, 1963, p. 37, no. 164; G. Wolf-Heidegger and A.M. Cetto, *Die anatomische Sektion*, Basel, 1967, pp. 162-164, nos. 60-63.

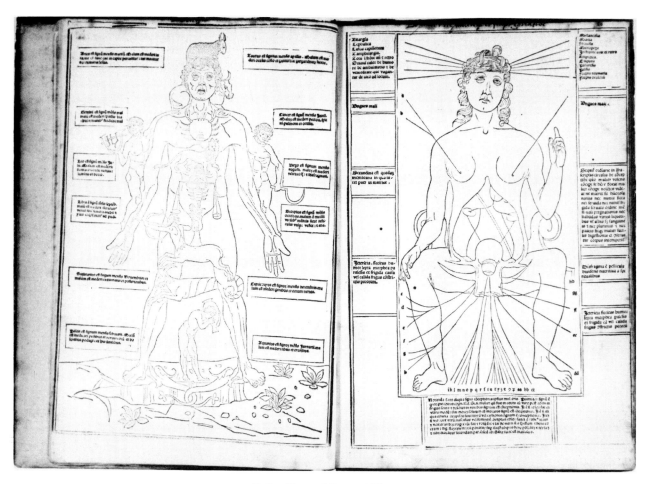

Zodiac Man and Pregnant Woman.
Woodcuts. Hunterian Collection, Ds 2. 2, fols. 60v-61

Patient stricken with the plague. Woodcut. Hunterian Collection, Ds 2.2, fol. 71

141. Book of Hours

Heures a l'usage de Rome.
France, Paris, printed by Nicolas Vivien, 1503.

Euing Collection, BD19 – h. 10

Vellum, 158 × 102 mm; 126, i leaves.

The most extensive development of the manuscript tradition of border illustration is seen in the historiated and decorated woodblock borders of French Books of Hours printed at the end of the 15th and the beginning of the 16th centuries. Since the series of illustrations for the major text divisions allowed little variation of subject matter, printers and publishers used the borders as a means of making their work more individual, adding much new imagery, both sacred and profane. The panels decorating every border of

every page of this edition begin with an extensive series of scenes from the Apocalypse (see no. 59), accompanied by a variety of ornamental blocks with floral and grotesque motifs which are derived from manuscripts produced earlier in France and the Netherlands (see nos. 61-63 and 119). Other sections of the book show a strong Italian influence, with architectural frameworks including classical vases, garlands and putti. Gold initials on blue or red grounds have been added throughout by hand.

PROVENANCE: Bought by William Euing from James Orchard Halliwell-Phillipps in 1866, and bequeathed by him to the Library in 1874 (see MS Euing 49, no. 3325).

BIBLIOGRAPHY: Mortimer, II, pp. 363-367.; cf. J. Harthan, *Books of Hours and their Owners*, London, 1977, pp. 169-171.

Scenes from the Apocalypse. Woodcuts. Euing Collection, BD 19 – h.10, fols. 12v-13

142. Geoffroy Tory, Champ Fleury

France, Paris, printed for Geoffroy Tory and Gilles de Gourmont, 28 April 1529.

Hunterian Collection, H 6.15

Paper, 235 × 166 mm.; folio; 8, 80 leaves.

As an artist, Geoffroy Tory (c. 1480-1533) was a decisive influence on the French Renaissance style of book decoration. His *Champ fleury* is one of the outstanding books of the 16th century. It deals in particular with 'the art and science of due and true proportion of Attic letters, otherwise known as antique letters and commonly Roman letters, proportional according to the human body and countenance'. Visits to Italy had allowed him to study Roman inscriptions and Italian book art at first hand, and he introduced the Italian style into French woodcut decoration, contributing a lightness and delicacy to the existing method of layout and design. Although he was made King's Printer in 1531, this appointment may be related to his zeal for advancing the use of French as the language of literature and scholarship rather than to his activities as a printer, which are far from certain.

PROVENANCE: Leonard Aubry, 1668; Hunter's source not traced.

BIBLIOGRAPHY: Mortimer, pp. 641-643, no. 524; G. Tory, *Champ Fleury* [facsimile reprint, with introduction by J.W. Jolliffe], East Ardsley, 1970.

Letter designs. Woodcuts. Hunterian Collection, H 6.15, fols. D6v-E1

143. Gilles Corrozet, Hecatongraphie

Gilles Corrozet, Hecatongraphie.
France, Paris, printed by Denis Janot, 1543 [i.e. ?1544].

Stirling Maxwell Collection, SM 370

Paper, 164 × 109 mm.; octavo; 104 leaves.

This work is described by its author as 'descriptions de cent figures et hystoires, contenants plusieurs appophthegmes, proverbes, sentences et dictz tant des anciens, que des modernes'. It dates from 1540 and was the second emblem book to be written in French. Stephen Rawles suggests that the typography of this edition, the last of four printed by Janot, makes 1544 a more probable date than 1543 as stated in the title.

Like the 'lettres fleuries' of the initials, which Janot seems to have acquired after Geoffroy Tory's death in 1533 (see no. 142), the hundred woodcuts and borders show the impact of Tory's influence. The majority of the woodcuts were produced for this work; several of them were used only here, and the frames were used only in Janot's emblem books. Like Tory, Janot was appointed King's Printer, in 1543.

PROVENANCE: Charles Nodier; P. Desq; Sir William Stirling Maxwell; bequeathed to the Library by Sir John Stirling Maxwell in 1958.

BIBLIOGRAPHY: H.W. Davies, *Catalogue of a Collection of Early French Books in the Library of C. Fairfax Murray*, London, 1961, pp. 980-982, no. 640; M. Praz, *Studies in Seventeenth-Century Imagery*, 2nd ed., Rome, 1964, pp. 308-309; Mortimer, p. 191, no. 155; A. Henkel and A. Schöne, *Emblemata. Handbuch zur Sinnbildkunst des XVI und XVII Jahrhunderts*, Stuttgart, 1967, p. LIII; S.P.J. Rawles, *Denis Janot, Parisian printer and bookseller (fl. 1529-1544): a bibliographical study* [unpublished doctoral thesis, University of Warwick], 1976, I, pp. 58, 61, 68 and II, Bibliography, no. 195; cf. J. Landwehr, *Romanic Emblem Books*, Utrecht, 1976, pp. 74-75, no. 239.

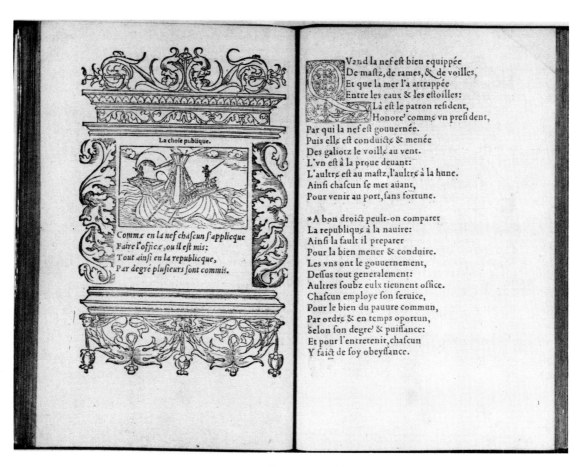

Woodcut decoration. Stirling Maxwell Collection, SM 370, fols. k5v-k6

References and Indexes

BIBLIOGRAPHIC REFERENCES

Young & Aitken	J. Young and P. Henderson Aitken, *A Catalogue of the Manuscripts in the Library of the Hunterian Museum in the University of Glasgow,* Glasgow, 1908
Ker, *MMBL*	N.R. Ker, *Medieval Manuscripts in British Libraries, vols. I – III, Oxford, 1969–; vols. IV and V not yet published*

Other frequently cited sources

Alexander, 'Italian Illuminated Manuscripts'	J.J.G. Alexander, 'Italian Illuminated Manuscripts in British Collections'. *La miniatura Italiana tra Gotico e Rinascimento, I, Atti del Congresso di Storia della Miniatura Italiana, Cortona, 24-26 settembre 1982,* ed. Emanuela Sesti, Florence, 1985, pp. 99-126
Alexander, 'Notes'	J.J. G. Alexander, 'Notes on some Veneto-Paduan Illuminated Books of the Renaissance', *Arte Veneta,* 23, 1969, pp. 9-20
Baldwin, *William Hunter*	J. Baldwin, *William Hunter: Book Collector* [exh. cat.]. Glasgow University Library, 1983
BMC	*Catalogue of Books printed in the XVth Century now in the British Museum,* Pts. I-XII, London, 1908-85
Branner	R. Branner, *Manuscript Painting in Paris during the reign of St Louis.* Berkeley, 1977
Briquet	C.M. Briquet, *Les Filigranes,* 2nd ed., Leipzig, 1923
De Bure	G.F. de Bure, *Supplément à la Bibliographie instructive, ou, Catalogue des livres du cabinet de feu M. Louis-Jean Gaignat,* 2 vols. Paris, 1769
de la Mare, 'Florentine Scribes'	A.C. de la Mare, 'The Florentine Scribes of Cardinal Giovanni of Aragon', *Atti del Convegno Internazionale Il libro e il testo, Urbino, 20-23 settembre 1982,* ed. C. Questa and R. Raffaelli, Urbino, 1984, pp. 245-293
de la Mare, 'New Research'	A.C de la Mare, 'New Research on Humanistic Scribes in Florence', in A. Garzelli, *Miniatura Fiorentina del Rinascimento, 1440-1525,* I, Florence, 1985, pp. 395-600
English Romanesque Art	*English Romanesque Art, 1066-1200,* [exh. cat.], London, 1984
Flemish Art 1300-1700	Royal Academy of Arts, *Flemish Art, 1300-1700* [exh. cat], London, 1953
Goff	F.R. Goff, *Incunabula in American Libraries.* Third census, revised. Millwood, New York, 1973
Hoepli	*Italienische Buchillustration XV. – XIX. Jahrhundert. Ausstellung von Werken aus dem Besitz von Ulrico Hoepli Mailand* [exh. cat.], Zürich, 1928
IGI	T.M. Guarnaschelli and E. Valenziani, *Indice generale degli incunaboli delle biblioteche d'Italia,* Rome, 1943-1981
Ker, *Medieval Libraries*	N.R. Ker, *Medieval Libraries of Great Britain. A list of surviving books,* 2nd ed., London, 1964
Ker, *William Hunter*	N.R. Ker, *William Hunter as a Collector of Medieval Manuscripts,* Glasgow, 1983
MacKinney	L. Mackinney, *Medical Illustrations in Medieval Manuscripts,* London, 1965

REFERENCES

Meyer	P. Meyer, *Documents manuscrits de l'ancienne littérature de la France,* Paris, 1871
La miniature flamande	L.M.J. Delaissé, *La miniature flamande. Le mécénat de Philippe le Bon* [exhib cat.], Brussels, 1959
Mortimer	R. Mortimer, *Harvard College Library. Department of Printing and Graphic Arts. Catalogue of Books and Manuscripts. I: French 16th century books,* Cambridge, Mass., 1964
New CBEL	*New Cambridge Bibliography of English Literature,* 5 vols., Cambridge, 1969-1977
Oldham, *Notes on Bindings*	J.B. Oldham, *Notes on Bindings in the Hunterian and General Libraries in Glasgow University,* 1938 [typescript in Glasgow University Library, MS General 759]
Renaissance Painting in Manuscripts	*Renaissance Painting in Manuscripts,* ed. T.R. Kren [exh. cat. of works from the British Library], New York, 1983
Rev. STC	A.W. Pollard and G.R. Redgrave, *A Short-Title Catalogue of Books printed in England, Scotland and Ireland and of English Books printed abroad 1475-1640,* 2nd ed. revised by W.A. Jackson, F.S. Ferguson and K.F. Pantzer, London, 1976-1986, 2 vols.
Sander	M. Sander, *Le livre à figures italien, depuis 1467 jusqu'à 1530.* New York, 1941
Sandler, *Gothic Manuscripts*	L.F. Sandler, *Gothic Manuscripts 1285-1385* (A Survey of Manuscripts Illuminated in the British Isles, V, gen. ed. J.J.G. Alexander), London, 1986
Scott, *Later Gothic Manuscripts*	K.L. Scott, *Later Gothic Manuscripts* (A Survey of Manuscripts Illuminated in the British Isles, VI, gen. ed. J.J.G. Alexander), forthcoming
Treasures	*Treasures from Scottish Libraries. Catalogue of an Exhibition held in the Library of Trinity College, Dublin,* Edinburgh, 1964
Trésors	*Trésors des bibliothèques d'Ecosse* [exh. cat.], Brussels, 1963
Wardrop, 'Western Illuminated Manuscripts'	J. Wardrop, 'Western Illuminated Manuscripts in the Hunterian Library, Glasgow University', *Apollo,* 14, 1931, pp. 255-260, 319-325

Note

The printed books in the Hunterian Collection are listed in M. Ferguson, *The Printed Books in the Library of the Hunterian Museum in the University of Glasgow,* Glasgow, 1930

Other Reading

Good general studies of manuscript illumination include:

R.G. Calkins, *Illuminated Books of the Middle Ages,* Ithaca, New York, 1983

C. de Hamel, *A History of Illuminated Manuscripts,* Oxford, 1986

O. Pächt, *Book Illumination in the Middle Ages,* London, 1986

LIST OF WORKS EXHIBITED *(in order of pressmarks)*

Manuscripts

Euing 1	Bible	cat. 18
Euing 3	Book of Hours	cat. 118
Euing 4	Book of Hours	cat. 120
Euing 7	Missal	cat. 122
Euing 9	Psalter	cat. 121
Euing 29	Missal	cat. 127
Ferguson 191	Thomas Norton, The Ordinall of Alchemy	cat. 46
General 193	Diodorus Siculus, Historical Library	cat. 84
General 288	Book of Hours, Psalter, etc.	cat. 117
General 326	Pattern Book of Alphabets	cat. 69
General 334	Cicero, Orator, Brutus and Treatise 'On the Orator'	cat. 53
General 335	Abstract and Commentary on Aristotle, Physics and On the Soul	cat. 44
General 336	Statutes of the Realm	cat. 26
General 338	Lanctantius, Treatises	cat. 76
General 339	Raymond of Peñafort, Treatise on Penance, Tancred, Treatise on Matrimony	cat. 23
General 999	Fragment of a Gradual	cat. 25
General 1060	Bible	cat. 106
General 1111	Jacobus de Voragine, Golden Legend	cat. 114
General 1119	Bible, Proverbs to Maccabees	cat. 115
General 1126	Bible	cat. 15
General 1130	The Mirrour of the Blessed Life of Jesus Christ and other works	cat. 33
Hepburn 1	Bible	cat. 17
Hunter 1 (S.1.1)	Giovanni Balbi, Treatise on Latin Grammar, and Glossary	cat. 113
Hunter 4 (S.1.4)	Josephus, Jewish Antiquities and Jewish War	cat. 10
Hunter 5 (S.1.5)	John Lydgate, Fall of Princes	cat. 41
Hunter 6 (S.1.6)	Bartolo de Sassoferrato, Treatise on 'Infortiatum'	cat. 73
Hunter 7 (S.1.7)	John Gower, Confessio Amantis	cat. 35
Hunter 8 (S.1.8)	Bartholomew the Englishman, Treatise on the Properties of Things	cat. 51
Hunter 9 (S.1.9)	Avicenna, Canon of Medicine	cat. 61
Hunter 11 (S.2.1)	Paolo Emili, Antiquities of France	cat. 65
Hunter 12 (S.2.2)	Jean Lemaire de Belges, L'Epistre du Roy	cat. 66
Hunter 25 (S.2.15)	Breviary	cat. 125
Hunter 28 (S.2.18)	Pietro Lando, Ducal Commission to Paolo Delfino	cat. 111
Hunter 29 (S.2.19)	Boccaccio, The Old Crow	cat. 110
Hunter 32 (T.1.1)	Medical Writings	cat. 24
Hunter 36 – 39 (T.1.4 – 7)	Ludolf of Saxony, Life of Christ	cat. 60
Hunter 41 (T.1.9)	Niccolò da Ferrara, Roman History	cat. 79

Hunter 47 (T.2.5)	Quintus Curtius, History of Alexander the Great	cat. 102
Hunter 57 (T.2.15)	Sedulius, Easter Song	cat. 3
Hunter 59 (T.2.17)	John Gower, Vox clamantis etc.	cat. 29
Hunter 60 (T.2.18)	Mirror of Man's Salvation	cat. 116
Hunter 75 (T.3.13)	Pietro de Crescenzi, Treatise on the Advantages of Country Life	cat. 34
Hunter 77 (T.3.15)	The Mirrour of the Blessed Life of Jesus Christ	cat. 42
Hunter 85 (T.4.2)	Writings on the Calendar	cat. 9
Hunter 86 (T.4.3)	Bede, Ecclesiastical History of the English People	cat. 128
Hunter 91 (T.4.8)	Leonardo Bruni, Lives, etc.	cat. 74
Hunter 96 (T.4.13)	Medical Writings	cat. 1
Hunter 98 (T.4.15)	Paolo Emili, French Antiquities	cat. 64
Hunter 110 (T.5.12)	Writings on Alchemy	cat. 28
Hunter 112 (T.5.14)	John of Arderne, Mirror of Phlebotomy and Practice of Surgery	cat. 30
Hunter 186 (T.8.18)	Book of Hours, in Dutch	cat. 126
Hunter 198 (U.1.2)	Matteo Palmieri, Annals	cat. 80
Hunter 201 (U.1.5)	Niccolò Sagundino and Others, On the Death of Valerio Marcello	cat. 107
Hunter 202 (U.1.6)	Jerome, Letters	cat. 72
Hunter 203 (U.1.7)	Chronicles of Saint-Denis	cat. 56
Hunter 205 (U.1.9)	Seneca, Works	cat. 21
Hunter 206 (U.1.10)	Plato, Phaedrus and Phaedo, with Commentaries	cat. 124
Hunter 208 (U.1.12)	Boccaccio, Fall of Princes	cat. 55
Hunter 215 (U.2.6)	Aldgate Cartulary	cat. 32
Hunter 217 (U.2.8)	Cassiodorus, Tripartite History of the Church	cat. 5
Hunter 219 (U.2.10)	Servius, Commentary on Virgil	cat. 83
Hunter 220 (U.2.11)	Treatises on Engines and Weapons	cat. 109
Hunter 229 (U.3.2)	Psalter	cat. 14
Hunter 231 (U.3.4)	Devotional and Philosophical Writings	cat. 27
Hunter 244 (U.4.2)	Anselm, Treatises	cat. 6
Hunter 245 (U.4.3)	Aristotle, Politics and Ethics	cat. 75
Hunter 251 (U.4.9)	John of Arderne, Mirror of Phlebotomy and Practice of Surgery	cat. 31
Hunter 252 (U.4.10)	Les Cent Nouvelles Nouvelles	cat. 58
Hunter 268 (U.5.8);	Book of Hours and Psalter	cat. 37
Hunter 269 (U.5.9)	Guillaume Tardif, Art of Falconry, and Art of Hunting	cat. 62
Hunter 272 (U.5.12)	Boethius, Consolation of Philosophy	cat. 4
Hunter 274 (U.5.14)	Lactantius, Treatises	cat. 38
Hunter 275 (U.5.15)	Bartolomeo Cipolla, Treatise on the Selection of a Military Commander	cat. 82
Hunter 279 (U.5.19)	Boethius, Consolation of Philosophy	cat. 13
Hunter 282 (U.5.22)	Justinus, Epitome of Trogus's History	cat. 85
Hunter 322 (U.7.16)	Seneca, Tragedies	cat. 63
Hunter 338 (U.8.6)	Bible	cat. 16
Hunter 334 (U.8.12)	Festus Rufus or Rufius, Summary of Roman History	cat. 108
Hunter 366 (V.1.3)	Raban Maurus, Treatise on the Universe	cat. 7
Hunter 367 (V.1.4)	Ranulf Higden, Polychronicon	cat. 39
Hunter 369 (V.1.6)	Augustine, Treatises	cat. 19
Hunter 370 (V.1.7)	Livy, History, Books XXI – X	cat. 78
Hunter 371 – 372 (V.1.8 – 9)	Boccaccio, Fall of Princes	cat. 54

Printed Books

Bg 1.6	Guillaume Durand, Manual for the Holy Offices	cat. 91
Bg 1. 9	Giovanni Tortelli, On Orthography	cat. 89
Bg 2. 12	Petrarch, Works	cat. 90
Bg 3. 11	Thomas Aquinas, Summa	cat. 99
Bh 1. 19	Livy, History, Books XXI – XXX	cat. 100
Bh 1. 24	Marsilio Ficino, Letters	cat. 138
Bh 2. 14	Francesco Colonna, The Dream of Polifilo	cat. 139
Bq 2. 11	Valerius Flaccus, Argonauticon	cat. 67
Bv 1. 10	Bible	cat. 94
Bv 2. 12	Geoffrey Chaucer, Canterbury Tales	cat. 137
Bw 1. 12	Gratian, Decretals	cat. 92
Bw 2. 25	Appian, History of Rome	
Bw 3. 24	Avicenna, Canon of Medicine	cat. 105
By 2. 3	Duns Scotus, Commentaries on the Sentences of Peter Lombard	cat. 97
By 2. 12	Euclid, Geometry	cat. 135
Ds 2. 2	Hans von Kircheim, Medical Compendium	cat. 140
Ds 2. 3	Blockbook Apocalypse	cat. 131
Ds 2. 4	Blockbook Bible	cat. 132
Du 2. 9	Thucydides, Peloponnesian War	cat. 68
H 6.15	Geoffrey Tory, Champ Fleury	cat. 142

Stirling Maxwell:

SM 370	Gilles Corrozet, Hecatongraphie	cat. 143
SM 658.2	Adriaen de Jonghe, Emblems	cat. 130
SM 1161	Album of Alphabet Designs, etc.	cat. 129
SMM 2	Petrarch, Canzone	cat. 70

INDEX OF MANUSCRIPTS CITED

An asterisk denotes a printed book

INDEX

(This Index is arranged in six sections: a General Index, and Indexes of Artists represented, of Scribes, of Printers, of Owners, and of Corporate Owners. References are to Catalogue entries.)

I. General Index

II. Index of Artists represented

*(The number in brackets indicates that there is only a
reference to the artist in a catalogue entry.)*

III. Index of Scribes

IV. Index of Printers

V. Index of Owners

*(The list of shelfmarks, pp. 215 – 17, should be
consulted for the provenance of volumes from the
libraries of William Euing, John Ferguson, William
Hunter, Charles Hepburn and Sir William Stirling
Maxwell.)*

VI.   Index of Corporate Owners

LIST OF COLOUR ILLUSTRATIONS

Cover Illustration: Ascension. Psalter, England, c. 1170. MS Hunter 229 (U.3.2), fol. 14 *Cat. no. 14*

Illustration on half-title: Decorated page. Petrarch, Bologna, 1475. Hunterian Collection, Bf 1. 1, fol. 5. *Cat. no. 93*

Frontispiece: Boethius instructing students and in prison at Ticinum. Boethius, ?North-east Italy, 1385. MS Hunter 374 (V.1.II), fol. 4. *Cat. no. 71*

1. Louis de Clèves on horseback. Lemaire, France, c. 1515. MS Hunter 12 (S.2.2.), fol. 1. *Cat. no. 66*

2. St Mark. Gospels, Byzantine, 11th century and later. MS Hunter 475 (V.7.2.), fol. 110v. *Cat. no. 12*

3. Initial A. Josephus, England, 1125-1150. MS Hunter 4 (S.1.4), fol. 136. *Cat. no. 10*

4. Opening from book of medical writings. Southern France, late 8th or early 9th century. MS Hunter 96 (T.4.13), fols. 23v-24. *Cat. no. 1*

5. Pentecost. Psalter, England, c. 1170. MS Hunter 229 (U.3.2), fol. 15v. *Cat. no. 14*

6. Christ in Glory. Psalter, England, c. 1170. MS Hunter 229 (U.3.2), fol. 16. *Cat. no. 14*

7. Initial 'd'. Writings on the Calendar, Durham, 1125-1150. MS Hunter 85 (T.4.2), fol. 35. *Cat. no. 9*

8. Tree of Vices and Tree of Remedies. Raymond of Peñafort, ?France, mid 13th century. MS General 339, fols. 41v-42. *Cat. no. 23*

9. Coronation of the Virgin. Devotional and philosophical writings, London, c. 1325-1335. MS Hunter 231 (U.3.4), p. 83. *Cat. no. 27*

10. Decorated page. Chaucer, England, c. 1440-1450. MS Hunter 409 (V.3.7.), fol. 57v. *Cat. no. 36*

11. Decorated page. Book of Hours, England, mid 15th century. MS Hunter 268 (U.5.8), fol. 7. *Cat. no. 37*

12. Wheel of Fortune. Boccaccio, Paris, 1467. MS Hunter 371 (V.1.8), fol. 1. *Cat. no. 54*

13. Edward III paying homage to Philip IV. Chronicles of Saint-Denis, France, 1450-1475. MS Hunter 203 (U.1.7), fol. 15. *Cat. no. 56*

14. Lunette Scene of Joachim the High Priest. Boccaccio, Paris, 1475-1500. MS Hunter 208 (U.1.12), fol. 206v. *Cat. no. 55*

15. Scenes at an Inn. Cent Nouvelles Nouvelles, France, 1475-1500. MS Hunter 252 (U.4.10), fol. 70. *Cat. no. 58*

16. Falcon and Prey. Tardif, France, c. 1494. MS Hunter 269 (U.5.9), fol. 12. *Cat. no. 62*

17. Last Supper. Seuse, Bourges, 1470. MS Hunter 420 (V.4.4), fol. 94. *Cat. no. 57*

18. St John on Patmos. Apocalypse, Southern France, ?1480s. MS Hunter 398 (V.2.18), fol. 1v. *Cat. no. 59*

19. Vision of Christ appearing to Charles VIII. Ludolph, Paris, 1490s. MS Hunter 39 (T.1.7), fol. 97. *Cat. no. 60*

20. St John and the Seven Churches. Apocalypse, Southern France, ?1480s. MS Hunter 398 (V.2.18), fol. 2. *Cat. no. 59*

21. Decorated page. Emili, France, 1490s. MS Hunter 98 (T.4.15), fol. 1. *Cat. no. 64*

22. Avicenna lecturing. Avicenna, France, 1475-1500. MS Hunter 9 (S.1.9), fol. 1. *Cat. no. 61*

23. Initial A. Lactantius, England, mid 15th century. MS Hunter 274 (U.5.14), fol. 1. *Cat. no. 38*

24. Initial F. Sagundino, North-east Italy, c. 1463 and 1480s. MS Hunter 201 (U.1.5), p. 269. *Cat. no. 107*

25. Initial O with Nativity. North-east Italy, c. 1400-1410. MS Hunter 202 (U.1.6), fol. 8. *Cat. no. 72*

26. Initial P with Iris. Plato, Southern Netherlands, 1483. MS Hunter 206 (U.1.10), fol. 33. *Cat. no. 124*

27. Decorated page with death-bed scene. Bartolo, Bologna, c. 1400. MS Hunter 6 (S.1.6), fol. 1. *Cat. no. 73*

28. Decorated page. Quintus Curtius, Italy, c. 1480. MS Hunter 47 (T.2.5), fol. 1. *Cat. no. 102*

29. Decorated page. Breviary, Venice, 1478. Hunterian Collection, Bf 1. 18, fol. 14. *Cat. no. 101*

30. Decorated page. Avicenna, Venice, 1486. Hunterian Collection, Bw 3. 24, Bk. II, fol. 1. *Cat. no. 105*

31. *(right)* Augustus entering Rome in Triumph. Niccolò da Ferrara, Ferrara, 1450s. MS Hunter 41 (T.1.9), fol. 149. *Cat. no. 79*

32. Initial S with Scipio crossing into Africa. Livy, Milan, c. 1450. MS Hunter 370 (V.1.7), fol. 253. *Cat. no. 78*